Archie – stay out of trouble! (so to speak!) Love

"Our storied pastime should be grateful. . . . Byron's greatest year and the rest of his abbreviated but brilliant career are chronicled in absorbing detail."—*Golf Digest*

HIGH PRAISE FOR GOLF'S GREATEST CHAMPION
BYRON NELSON
AND HIS FASCINATING STORY
HOW I PLAYED THE GAME

"Nelson's earnest, direct voice can be clearly heard in the text. . . . The overall effect is that of an honest man telling the truth. . . . In the manner in which he played, in the gentle, giving manner with which he has conducted himself, and now with his autobiography, Byron Nelson has always done right by golf."
—Jaime Diaz, *The New York Times*

"A round-by-round review of Nelson's stunning career. . . . The [book] has a homey feel to it and is devoid of pretension."
—*Sporting News*

"If a golf biography has been written that's better than this one, well, it doesn't come to mind." —*Golf World*

"Destined to be a classic. . . . If you only have time for one golf book this summer, you would do quite well to choose this one."
—*Golf Collector's Society Bulletin*

Please turn the page for more extraordinary acclaim . . .

"CLASS. THAT'S WHAT EVERYONE THINKS OF WHEN BYRON NELSON IS MENTIONED."

—*Dallas Morning News*

"*HOW I PLAYED THE GAME* is about people and places. . . . It's a venture into how man found peace." —*Oakland Tribune*

"A read-'til-you-drop delight."

—*Woodland Hills* (CA) *Daily News*

"A REVEALING LOOK at professional golf before the money got big and the pants got ugly." —*Booklist*

"A WINNING VOLUME in every sense." —*Publishers Weekly*

"BEAUTIFULLY TOLD. . . . Laced throughout with scores of priceless stories, anecdotes, and opinions. . . . A book for every golfer and fan." —*Braintree Gazette*

"AN ENTERTAINING LOOK at what professional golf used to be. . . . *How I Played the Game* puts today's tour in perspective."

—*Fairway*

ALSO BY BYRON NELSON

Byron Nelson's Winning Golf
(available from Taylor Publishing)

Shape Your Swing the Modern Way

How I Played THE Game

BYRON NELSON

Foreword by Arnold Palmer

A Dell Trade Paperback

A DELL TRADE PAPERBACK
Published by
Dell Publishing
a division of
Bantam Doubleday Dell Publishing Group, Inc.
1540 Broadway
New York, New York 10036

All photos are from the author's collection.

ISBN: 0-440-50637-9

Reprinted by arrangement with Taylor Publishing Company

Printed in the United States of America

Published simultaneously in Canada

June 1994

10 9 8 7 6 5 4 3 2 1
RRH

To Peggy,
the joy of my life
since November 15, 1986
and my favorite golfing partner

ACKNOWLEDGMENTS

Always, ever since I've been in golf, I've been helped by many wonderful people. I believe you'll find I've thanked each of them in turn in this book, but as for the actual writing of it, I first must thank all those friends who insisted that I do it. Without their urging, I never would have thought of it myself. Even with their encouragement, though, I couldn't have begun without all the records, statistics, and so forth supplied over the years by my wonderful friend Bill Inglish of Oklahoma City. Bill knows more about my career than I do, I think. Pat Seelig, an excellent golf writer I've worked with numerous times, read the manuscript at various stages and offered many helpful suggestions. Yet, with all the help of Bill, Pat, and my many other friends, this book still wouldn't have been written without the help of my wife, Peggy. Peggy is a freelance writer who volunteered to be both interviewer and typist for my recollections, and who also spent hours researching old scrapbooks and other records of my career in golf. Finally, to my editor, Jim Donovan, I owe a debt of thanks for his assistance in putting the chapters in the best sequence, checking on the accuracy of my stories, and generally making the book readable. I'm happy so many people expressed an interest in my doing this book—and I'm even happier now that it's done.

CONTENTS

FOREWORD

Back in the late 1970s, when Cliff Roberts was in the process of handing over the chairmanship of Augusta National Golf Club to Bill Lane, they decided to create a private room for those of us who had won the Masters Tournament, a sanctuary where we could relax and have a bite to eat at our leisure during that always-exciting week in April. Appropriate wooden lockers were installed along one short wall of the room. By then, there were some twenty-four living Masters Champions and many more to come, so doubling up of active and inactive players was deemed proper. I have no way of knowing who decided who would share a locker with whom—very likely it was Cliff Roberts, who died before the project was completed—but nothing has ever pleased me more than when I walked into that new Champions Room upstairs in the main clubhouse and saw two plates on one of the lockers, one bearing my name and the other that of Byron Nelson.

It would certainly have been my choice if I had been asked, because Byron Nelson was an idol of mine long before I met that wonderful gentleman and magnificent player. I was in my impressionable teens and wrapped up in golf when Byron was accomplishing things on the pro tour that never have been and never will be even approached.

How many times have people in golf wondered out loud what Byron Nelson might have put into the record books if he hadn't retired from serious competition at such a relatively young age? As a player myself, I absolutely marvel at two of his greatest accomplishments on tour—the eleven consecutive victories he posted from March to August in 1945 and the eighteen tournaments he won that year. I have never won more than three in a row and was quite proud when I won eight times on the Tour in 1960. I can't think of any records that are farther beyond anybody's reach than those two.

I read Byron's first book back in the 1940s and used a lot of his instruction as a blueprint in the development of my own game. Later on, when I was on the Tour and got to know Byron pretty well, I always enjoyed it when we got together and talked about golf. I remember times when he was working as a television commentator that he would come out on the course and walk and talk with me while I was playing practice rounds at the major championships.

We never played together, of course, when Byron was competing on a full-time basis, just once or twice at the Masters, but I well remember the enjoyable day we had when Jack Nicklaus and I joined with Byron and Jug McSpaden—remember those years when the press revelled in calling them the "Gold Dust Twins"?—in an exhibition at Jug's Dub's Dread course in Kansas.

My father was a great influence on me in many ways, not the least of which was my behavior and treatment of others. That all sank in quite well, but I must say that observing and getting to know Byron Nelson reinforced every bit of that. Here has always been a man of the highest personal standards, a man we in golf can hold up as the epitome of a true golf champion.

—ARNOLD PALMER

INTRODUCTION

There has been quite a lot written about me, and I've been fortunate that most of it has been accurate. But there have been a few times when what was written wasn't quite factual enough to suit me, such as the amount of my winnings in 1945, my so-called "nervous stomach," why I left the tour, and a few other things. This is the best opportunity I'll ever have to put my two cents' worth in about how I lived, how I played the game of golf, and to set the record straight for anyone who wants to know.

I hope you'll enjoy reading it.

—BYRON NELSON
Roanoke, Texas
1992

ONE

The Road to Glen Garden

I HAVE ALWAYS BEEN A BLESSED MAN, AND THE FIRST WAY I was blessed on this earth was by having wonderful parents. My father was John Byron Nelson. His family was from Virginia originally, but he was born in Texas in 1889. He was a quiet, gentle man, shorter than me, but his hands were even larger than mine. He was a hard worker, but not particularly ambitious, and my mother always felt he was too kindhearted to be a good businessman.

My mother, Madge Allen Nelson, was born in 1893. Her family came to Texas from Tennessee when she was a small child. She loved Texas, and lived here all her life till her death in 1992 at the age of ninety-eight. She was smart, spirited, ambitious, and full of energy. She taught school some before she married my father, who was five years older than she was. They were married on February 8, 1911, and I was born four days shy of a year later, on February 4, 1912.

I was born at home, out in the country, on our 160-acre cotton farm in Long Branch, in Ellis County outside of Waxahachie, Texas. I was named John Byron Nelson Jr. after my father. My father had inherited the farm when he was just six years old after his father died of tuberculosis. His mother had died of consumption—what we now call TB—when he was just six months old. My father had it too, before he got married, and it ruined one lung, but fortunately it never spread to the other one. My father was raised by two maiden aunts, and he was a fine, hardworking man, so I guess those two aunts did a pretty good job.

Back then, you know, no one ever went to the hospital to have a baby—mostly only if they were about to die. So there was nothing unusual about my being born at home, except for my size.

I'm told I weighed twelve pounds, eight ounces at birth. My mother had just turned eighteen two months before, and she was in labor such a long time that the doctor figured I couldn't have survived it. In fact, he had given up on me and was just trying to save my mother's life at that point. He finally had to use forceps to deliver me, and broke my nose doing so. I still have a few dents in my skull from it. After I was delivered, he just placed me on a table near the bed, thinking I was dead.

After a few minutes, though, my Grandmother Allen, my mother's mother, shouted, "Doctor, this child is alive!" Then my grandmother started working with me, and the doctor did too, and to everyone's surprise I did make it, thanks to an abundance of my mother's milk. It was such an ordeal for my mother, though, it took her quite a long time to recover; in that day and time, there was no medication. I don't know whether my size and the difficult labor had anything to do with it, but she had only two more children, at seven-year intervals. Both my sister Ellen and my brother Charles, though, were of normal size, fortunately.

Our house was very close to the dirt road we lived on, and we stayed there till I was five. The soil in that area was heavy black clay, and having a cotton farm always meant a lot of hard work. I can still remember seeing folks in their horse and buggy going down that road in wet weather, when it would be all the horse could do to pull the load, the road was that slow and sticky.

I guess from the time I could walk, I woke up when my parents did, and my mother had to make breakfast holding me on her hip. I walked when I was about ten months old, which is early, but then, I was about half grown when I was born.

I was always an outdoor child. I hated being in the house, and I never really played much—I "worked." I had a little old wagon, and

I'd take it out and fill it with rocks or dirt and haul it someplace and empty it, then go back for more. That was my idea of play.

Not only did I not like to be inside, but I hated shoes, and went barefoot all the time. I remember when I was about five my mother bought me one pair, for wearing on Sunday. When we came home after church the first time I wore them, though, I took them off as soon as I got in the house. My mother had gone to the kitchen to cook dinner, and there was a fireplace in our living room, and I took those shoes and threw them on the fire.

After a little bit, my mother smelled that leather burning, and came in to see what I'd done. She scolded me and said, "All right, if you don't want to wear shoes, I just won't buy you any more. You can just go barefoot everywhere, winter and summer alike." And that was just fine with me.

I was fair-skinned with blond hair, and because I spent so much time outdoors, I sunburned easily. One time when I'd gotten burned, my mother put a sunbonnet on me, and tied it so I couldn't get it undone. I went out to play in the front yard of our house, which was very close to the road, even though we were out in the country. I tried every which way to get that bonnet off, but I couldn't, and I was getting pretty hot out under that Texas sun. So first I took off my shirt, then I took off my pants, and pretty soon I had everything off but that bonnet.

My mother was back of the house, and every once in a while she'd notice folks driving by and laughing their heads off, so she got curious and came around to see what was going on. There I stood, naked as the day I was born, with that bonnet still on my head. I can't remember whether I got a licking for that, but I probably should have.

It was along about this time that I had the first serious injury of my life. My father had bought a fine team of horses, and while he was busy doing something else, I was feeding an ear of corn to one of the horses. Well, I let my fingers get too close to the horse's mouth, and it bit the tip of my forefinger on my left hand. My father and mother used kerosene, or coal oil, to keep it protected and it healed up pretty soon, but that finger is still shorter than the one on my right hand. And I've always been mighty careful of how I feed horses since then.

When I was six, we moved to San Saba County in southwest Texas, to a 240-acre cotton farm on the San Saba River. The cotton grew well there, and you could see the fields from our house above the river. Only problem was, there were an awful lot of rattlesnakes in that country. One summer, we killed sixty-five of them, just around our house. By this time I'd gotten used to wearing shoes, fortunately.

By the time I was eight, I'd become a pretty good field worker. I'd weed the cotton in the summer, and pick it in the fall. I'd pick it and put it in a canvas sack, and I was so little then that the sack would just drag in the dirt behind me. I can't say I ever liked picking cotton much, because it made your hands bleed and it was powerful hot, hard work. But my parents encouraged me to work hard, because they knew that our field hands would work harder when they saw a child my size working like I did. And their strategy worked.

My father was drafted for World War I, but because he had one punctured eardrum and one collapsed lung from having had TB as a youngster, he was turned down. Then in 1919 my sister, Margaret Ellen, was born. I asked my mother, "Are you going to love her more than you love me?" I guess I kind of liked being the only child.

Because we lived way out in the country, there was never any kind of school within reach till I was eight. In San Saba, the nearest school was fourteen miles away. My mother had been a schoolteacher before she married my father, so she taught me all the basics at home.

But finally they built a schoolhouse three miles away, and I rode a coal-black horse we had across the fields bareback to school. My grandmother used to tell my mother, "You're going to get that child killed." But my mother would tell her, "You couldn't *pull* Byron off that horse!"

I hated school about as much as wearing shoes. I guess it was because I was used to getting all the attention from my mother at home; at least, that's what my brother Charles told me later. But another thing was, the schoolhouse was too warm to suit me. I was always opening the windows and getting in trouble for it. But because I'd get too hot, then go outside in the cold air, I got a lot of bad colds.

They started me off in the first grade, of course. But since I already knew how to read and write, and knew my geography and history, plus my multiplication tables up to 12, I was quickly promoted to the third grade. I still didn't like it, though.

I was always brought up to be honest, and of course everyone back then had to be mighty careful with the material things they did have. I remember one time I was playing over at the house of my friend, J. T. Whitt, and I brought home a nearly empty spool of thread to play with. It was only the spool I wanted, and it just had about eighteen rounds of white thread left on it. But when my mother saw it, she asked if Mrs. Whitt had given it to me. When I said no, she told me I had to take it back, right then. Now, my friend's house was a mile away, and it was already getting on toward dark. I guess I was about five years old at the time, so I was afraid of having to walk all that way and come home in the dark. But my mother wouldn't hear of waiting till the next morning, so off I went. I got there and back as fast as my legs would carry me. And it taught me never to take anything that didn't really belong to me.

The house we lived in when I was very young, like a lot of the houses of country folk back then, was just one-walled. There wasn't any insulation or wallpaper—they were really more like cabins, in a way. And even though it was down in south Texas, it could get pretty cold of a winter. I remember one time it got so cold that when we came in the kitchen one morning, the fire had gone out, and a one-gallon milk can we had sitting in the kitchen had frozen solid during the night.

When I was nine, we moved to San Angelo. Ellen—that's what we called Margaret Ellen—was about two. Our grandfather and grandmother Allen lived there, because their son, our Uncle Benton, had TB, and was staying in the sanitorium. Uncle Benton died, and it turned out later that my sister had a light case of TB herself, probably due to exposure to Uncle Benton, who'd always pick her up and kiss her. Of course, that was before he knew he was sick, and besides, back then people didn't realize how contagious the disease was.

In San Angelo, my father worked for a mohair warehouse that was the largest in the country, and it was right on the Santa Fe railroad line. Santa Fe was one of the largest producers of mohair wool. He loaded and unloaded the wool, but could only work part-time, because jobs were so hard to find then.

I remember the warehouse caught fire one time, and everyone came running to see it and help put out the fire. My mother saw my Daddy up on top of the warehouse, trying to get the fire under control, and she started screaming, "He's going to be burnt up!" Fortunately, they did get the fire put out and my father was all right. But the smell from that mohair burning was awful, and it hung around for days.

We had a wonderful team of horses and a wagon, and part of the time Daddy hauled gravel for a highway that was being built quite a ways away. It was too far for him to come home except weekends, so he found an old wooden crate someone had shipped a piano in and slept in that when he couldn't come home. Our family knew what "poor" really meant.

Next, we moved to Alvarado, south of Fort Worth. Our neighbors, the Majorses, who lived one-quarter of a mile away, had thirteen children living with them. Some of them were Mrs. Majors' sister's kids. Her sister had died some time before we moved there. I played with one of the children quite a lot.

Our place backed up to my Grandfather Allen's. It's from Grandfather Allen that I inherited my woodworking ability, but fortunately I didn't inherit his disposition. Gran didn't like children much, though he and Gram had six of their own. Maybe that's why he didn't like them. Anyway, I was always such an active little child that he would offer me a nickel if I could sit still for five minutes, but I was such a wiggler, I never got that nickel. My mother used to tell him, "Gran, if Byron needs a licking, you tell me and I'll give it to him. But I don't want you to touch him."

One day we were over at their house and the grownups were all sitting inside talking and I went outside looking for something to do. I guess I was about five or six. Gran had a few turkeys he raised, and he'd just fed them, so they were out in the yard pecking at their food. I wanted to see if I could catch one, so I sneaked up behind this old turkey hen and grabbed her by the tailfeathers. She started jumping and flopping around, but I held on, and first thing you know, all her tailfeathers came out in my hands.

I was in trouble, and I knew it. I looked around for a place to hide the evidence, and saw Gram's washtubs sitting on a bench, turned upside down waiting for washday. I hid the feathers under them and went inside, never saying a word. Not too much later, Gran went outside and came back in with this puzzled look on his face and said, "That's the strangest thing—I just went out and checked on the turkeys, and there's one that doesn't have any tailfeathers. She's all right, not sick or anything, but there's not one feather in her tail!" Naturally, I kept real quiet, and no one suspected anything.

Well, it came washday, and Gram went to turn over those washtubs and found all those feathers, and told my mother. Mother came to me and said, "Byron, did you pull the feathers out of Gran's turkey's tail?" I knew I had to come up with something good, so I said, "No, ma'am, I didn't. I just grabbed hold of her and she pulled them out herself!" For some reason, this got my mother to laughing, and I never did get the licking I deserved, fortunately.

We're so used to all our shopping centers and supermarkets now, but I can still clearly recall when we'd go to town in our horse and wagon for supplies once a week. We'd get flour, beans, shortening, and so forth. If you ran out, you did without till the next Saturday. Of course, the Majorses had so many children, they'd run out of something every once in a while, and they'd come to us for oh, some flour, maybe. Mrs. Majors had to get up awful early of a morning to start her cooking, so most of the time the kids would come over before daylight. They'd stand out in the yard and holler "Hello!" until Mother or Daddy answered, then tell us what it was their mother needed.

But they'd always pay us for it, or bring back the amount they'd borrowed next time they went to town. People were like that back then.

It was in Alvarado that my mother developed mastoiditis—an infection in the mastoid bone behind the ear. I was just ten, and I was out plowing the fields with our team of horses and the cultivator. My father came and told me they were going to Fort Worth to see the doctor, and I had to take care of the place while they were gone. When they came back, it turned out Mother had to go back four days later for surgery, and so I was the "man of the house" again, taking care of the house, plowing the cotton fields and all.

A little later, we moved to Fort Worth from our place south of the city. We lived in a town called Stop Six, so-called because it was on the way to Dallas on the interurban bus line, and right near our place was the sixth stop—the interurban was sort of like a streetcar line.

My father got a job as a truck driver and a deliverer for White Swan Foods. I was surprised he even got the job, because he'd had no experience like that. Pretty soon the economy caught up with us and he was laid off. Then he went to work delivering feed for Dyer's Feed Store on 15th Street in Fort Worth. Mr. Dyer was a good boss, but he drank and used bad language, and my father didn't do either one. My father never said a word to Mr. Dyer about it, but pretty soon, Mr. Dyer stopped drinking, and then he stopped swearing, too. Mr. Dyer liked my daddy a lot, just like everyone else who knew him.

That fall, I started school, and pretty soon, I noticed quite a few of my friends would have an extra nickel or dime or quarter to spend. Doesn't seem like much now, I know, but back then, it was very unusual for a child to have any spending money. So I asked them where they got it, and they said, "Caddying at Glen Garden Country Club." I had no idea what caddying was, so I asked more questions, and when they started explaining about golf and what they did to earn that extra money, I decided I'd like to learn more about it. But before I could learn much, I had to learn about something else—rabies.

I have to back up a bit to tell this story. When we had lived at Stop Six, right across the street from us was a family named Wells, with six children. We'd occasionally go back to visit them and I'd play with the Wells children, and one time, they'd just gotten a puppy, so we'd all play with that puppy. The puppy was sniffing us and nipping at us a bit, just playing, and pretty soon we all had a scratch or bite here or there. Well, in a few days, the puppy got sick and started foaming at the mouth. Back then, rabies was rampant because there wasn't any vaccination done like there is now.

When they had the dog examined, he did have rabies, which meant all of us children had to get rabies shots. You don't see much about it now, but back then it meant you had to take one shot a day, in your abdomen, for twenty-one straight days. But if the place you were bitten was above your shoulders, you'd have to have two shots a day.

Mr. and Mrs. Wells decided it was too expensive to get the shots done in Fort Worth, so they took their children and me to Austin, where the state would do the inoculations free. They had gotten permission from my mother and father, naturally, and it was very nice of them to include me.

They rented a house with quite a few bedrooms, which they were lucky to find, because times were really tough then in 1922. Then, every day, we'd all go to get our shots at the insane asylum. You weren't in there with the residents, but that was where we had to go to get the shots. They used quite a large needle, and after a few days, you didn't feel very good, but you had to keep taking the shots so you wouldn't get rabies.

Along about the fifteenth day, I began to feel really bad, and was getting a lot of headaches, which I was not accustomed to. Mrs. Wells gave me some aspirin to keep my head from hurting so much, but she wasn't as alert to signs of sickness as my mother was. She didn't think there was anything else wrong except my reaction to the shots.

When the twenty-one days were up, we headed back to Fort Worth. We got back late in the afternoon, and both my parents were there to greet us. But when my mother put her arms around me—I'll never forget it—she right away held me back from her with her hands on my shoulders, and said to my father, "This child's got typhoid fever."

Of course, in that day and time, typhoid was very prevalent, too, because they didn't have plumbing and water systems like they do now, and I guess down in Austin they just got the water right out of the river. The reason my mother recognized mine was that my father had gotten typhoid right after they were married, and she recognized the odor from when he'd had it. Typhoid basically is an intestinal disease, and creates its own peculiar smell.

So they put me to bed right away and called the doctor, and he agreed with mother's diagnosis: typhoid fever. I weighed 124 pounds when I got it, and over the next few weeks I dropped to 65. They even wrapped me in a sheet one time and weighed me on a cotton scale, and it was true—I'd lost half my weight. I was about eleven at the time, and about 5'8" or so, so you know I was awful thin. I can remember lying in bed and seeing my hipbones sticking straight up so plain.

I also remember that I gave myself a relapse. You weren't allowed to eat anything, just take the small amounts of liquids and things that the doctor authorized, and I didn't realize how serious it was. But there was a bottle of Horlick's malted milk tablets on the windowsill near my bed, and I'd get so hungry, I just kept eating those, and no one ever saw me, so they didn't know what I was doing. It wasn't very much, but it was enough to make me even sicker. My temperature soared to 104, 105, even over 106. They were packing me in ice, and said I'd never live.

By now, the doctors had pretty well given up on me, and it was a Mrs. Keeter, a chiropractor and a member of the Church of Christ we attended, who saved my life. This may sound strange, but she was an expert on giving enemas—I guess they'd call it colon-cleansing now.

She told my mother, "I can help that child. It will take quite a while, but I can cure him." So she treated me once or twice a day, very gently and carefully, and after about ten days, I began to improve. It took me quite a while to regain my strength and get back to my normal weight, but I did. The high fever I ran, however, apparently caused some memory loss, because I have very little recollection of my childhood, other than what my family and friends have told me.

So by the time I got well, I was just barely twelve years old, and had twice been given up on by the doctors—once when I was born, and again when I had typhoid. The fact that I survived both experiences is one of the reasons why I feel I've always been a blessed man.

TWO

From Caddie to Pro

THOUGH I WAS SO SICK WITH THAT TYPHOID, I WAS MORE concerned about something else. My parents were both members of the Church of Christ, and by this time I had been well-taught by them about the Bible and God's laws. My mother, in fact, was a wonderful Bible scholar who worked not only with me but with many other people in her lifetime, teaching God's plan of salvation and all the Bible prophecies and such. I knew I needed to be baptized, and I was worried that I wouldn't have the chance. So as soon as I was recovered enough to go to church, it so happened that we were having a gospel meeting, preached by a man named Brother Hubbard. At that time, people didn't have enough money to pay for a full-time preacher, and Brother Hubbard had a regular job as a railway mail clerk who sorted mail on the train as it went from town to town. He had to develop a peculiar way of walking to balance himself as he did this, and when he preached, he did the same thing. He'd kind of rock back and forth, back and forth as he talked.

During that meeting, I took my opportunity to obey the gospel and was baptized. It made me very happy to know my past sins had been forgiven, and because of my early upbringing and teaching from my parents, I have continued as a member of the Church of Christ and realize more and more that the Bible truly is the inspired word of God. My faith has been a great blessing to me all my life. In fact, I really feel the reputation I've enjoyed all my life, especially after becoming a champion golfer, came very much from that upbringing and my continued faithfulness to the Bible and the church. Even the fact that I never smoked or drank or used bad language, and have tried to treat others as I'd like them to treat me, comes from that.

It took quite a while for me to really recover from the typhoid, but pretty soon I began to think again about my friends at school and the extra money they'd gotten by caddying. I had pretty well determined that I wanted to find out more about being a caddie, because I already knew as much as I ever wanted to know about rabies and typhoid both. When I was well enough, and my parents said it was okay for me to walk over to Glen Garden one day, I started off. Of course, I knew nothing about golf whatsoever. But I'd talked to my mother and father about it, and they said it would be all right for me to do it. As it turned out, it was a pretty important step for me, even though at the time all I was concerned about was that extra change in my pocket.

It may not sound like much, a boy having a nickel or dime spending money, but in the mid-twenties, it was a lot more than most of us had. Families weren't destitute and they had plenty to eat and to wear, but they didn't have extra money to spare.

So when my friends said they caddied at Glen Garden Country Club, well, that gave me an idea that I wanted to caddie also. Of course, I knew nothing about golf whatsoever. But I walked over to the club, which is on the southeast side of Fort Worth, about a mile away from where we lived on Timberline, and I went to the caddiemaster and told him I'd like to become a caddie.

His name was Harold Akey, and he told me, "Well, we have more caddies now than we have players, but if you want to come over on the weekends or on holidays, why, that's fine, 'cause that's when most of the play is." I thanked him and went home, and that weekend, I went over there. It took about six times before I ever got to caddie for anyone, but in the meantime, the ones who weren't getting to caddie were getting caddying lessons from Mr. Akey. We were taught how to look out for the clubs' owner, how to carry the clubs over our shoulders, how to hunt golf balls and keep our eye on the ball, how to stay out of the way, and the other rules that caddies have to abide by.

I knew nothing about caddying at first, but it wasn't difficult to learn. The other caddies, though, didn't like to see any new ones, because that might mean they wouldn't get a job sometimes. So they had what they called a "kangaroo court." It was like a fraternity initiation. They'd form two lines, and we'd have to run between them while each one of them gave us a good hard lick with their belts as we ran by. Sometimes they'd get a barrel and put a new kid in it and roll it down this big hill the clubhouse sat atop of. That was even worse than running the gauntlet, but for some reason, they never did that to me. I don't know why. They did try to run the new boys off, but I didn't run off very well. After I became a regular caddie, I never did pick on the younger boys, because I hadn't liked it when they did it to me and didn't think it was right.

Finally I got a job one Saturday caddying for the Rotarians of Dallas, who had come over to play the Rotarians of Fort Worth. That long ago, there was just one club in each city. The caddie fee was fifty cents, and my golfer was a man named Mr. Shute. Mr. Akey told Mr. Shute that I was a new caddie but that he thought I'd do all right for him.

So we got on the first tee and Mr. Shute said, "You're a new caddie, the caddiemaster told me." I said, "Yes sir, I am. I'll try to do my best." He said, "All right, I'll tell you what. If you don't lose a ball for me, why, I'll give you an extra quarter." Well, he sliced the first ball off the first tee way into the right rough, and I lost sight of it and never did find it. So there went my quarter. But I didn't lose any more and I caddied all right, so he said I was okay, and I got my first fifty cents.

It was late fall when I started caddying, and the club let the caddies play at Christmas time, when they had a party for us. That was the first time I ever played. I borrowed a set of clubs that year, and I shot 118—but that didn't count the times I whiffed the ball completely.

I liked golf right away. I liked any sport where you could swing something like a baseball bat or a stick or anything. And soon I was beginning to practice a little bit. I didn't have any clubs at first, but I remember the first one I bought was an old Standard, a hickory-shafted mashie—what's now a 5-iron. Whenever I could find an old ball, I'd beat it around with that old mashie. Pretty soon I bought a few more clubs with my caddie money, and my game progressed quickly. I learned to play by trial and error, but as I caddied I also watched the people I caddied for and gradually acquired a general idea of how you should develop a swing. I also had one golf book, the great Harry Vardon's, that I studied until I felt confident enough to do a few things on my own.

The next spring, I took up caddying again. A lot of times, I would go to the club just to see if I could get a job. One Saturday, I met a man named Judge J. B. Wade and caddied for him. He knew my parents, and he liked me, so I got to caddie for him every Saturday. He had a regular foursome and one of the fellows that played in it was Mr. Cecil Nottingham, who worked as assistant auditor for the Fort Worth-Denver City Railroad. He helped me get a job with the railroad when I quit school—but more on that later.

One time when I was caddying for Judge Wade, I got myself in trouble. You see, we caddies weren't ever allowed to hit balls while we were working or use the member's clubs without their permission. This one day, though, I'd given Judge Wade his driver, then walked down the side of the fairway. While I was waiting, I just got an impulse and dropped a ball I had in my pocket on the ground, took out one of Judge Wade's clubs, and hit toward where their drives would land.

Don't you know, that clubhead came right off the shaft. There wasn't anything for it but to tell the judge, so I did, and he just said, "We'll have to tell the caddiemaster." I wasn't any too eager to see the end of that round, but I made sure I told the caddiemaster what I'd done before the judge got there. Doing something like this generally meant getting expelled from the caddie yard for a time, but fortunately, Mr. Akey liked me, and just said, "We'll put in a new shaft, and you'll have to pay for it." The new shaft cost $2, which meant three rounds of golf I'd have to caddie to pay for it. But I felt very lucky it wasn't any worse, and I never did that again. However, as I caddied more and more for the judge, he'd every so often have me hit a ball with one of his clubs—usually an iron, and that encouraged me that maybe I had a little talent for the game.

The judge was a large man, about 6'1", big but not fat. He was about a medium golfer, what you'd call a "businessman golfer." He told me I was a "pretty good ballhawk," so I guess I'd improved some from that first time I caddied.

My mother was about to have another baby along about this time, and my parents asked me if I wanted to help name it. I thought a lot of Judge Wade by then, so I asked if it was a boy, could one of his names be "Wade," so that's why he's now Charles Wade Nelson. I really did quite a bit to help raise him—fed him, changed him, took care of him in church, and so forth. He was a naturally good child; he never got mad at me but one time. I don't remember why he was angry, but I remember he was trying to hit me. I was 6'2" by then, so I just put my hand on his head and held him away from me, and he swung at the air until he got tired.

I caddied for some other members, too, including a woman named May Whitney, who was a pretty good golfer and a good friend of the club pro, Ted Longworth. I also caddied for a woman named Hetty Green—not the millionaire from New York, just Hetty Green from Fort Worth, Texas. Mrs. Green was nice to caddie for, and helped me out quite a bit in my amateur career, in a way.

During my amateur years, I sold Mrs. Green nearly all my trophies and prizes, to get enough money to go to my next tournament. Years later—in fact, after I'd left the tour—I contacted her and told her I'd like to buy some of them back. I wasn't interested in the golf bags and such, just the silver trophies for their sentimental value.

Well, she said she wanted to keep them a while longer, and wouldn't sell any of them right then. She said she'd leave them to me in her will. I was kind of disappointed, but they were rightfully hers, so I didn't have a whole lot to say about it. Some time later, I learned that she had died, a widow with no children, but I never was able to discover anything about a will or such, so I never have gotten any of those back.

By the spring of 1927, I'd started working for Ted in the pro shop, putting in new shafts, cleaning the clubs, and so forth. We didn't have chrome in those days, so the irons would rust badly, and we had to use a buffing wheel to shine them up halfway decent. The stuff we used to shine them would come off that buffing wheel as black dust, and it would get on my face and hands till they were practically coal black. I'd always have to make sure I washed up good before I ever went back outside.

I got good enough at working on clubs that Ted asked me to help him make the irons he was going to use to play in the U.S. Open at

Oakmont that year. He'd already qualified, so we got right to work on those clubs. He'd select the hickory shafts out of this barrel of shafts we had, making sure each one was good and straight and strong. Then I'd work down the end of the shaft so it would just fit good and tight in the hosel of the clubhead. I'd drive the shaft in with a maul, and put a metal pin or nail in through a small hole on the side of the hosel to hold it in place. He took those clubs with him to Oakmont and played pretty well, finished about fifteenth or so, I think. I felt real proud of him, and happy I'd been able to help with his clubs.

My first real thrill in golf happened that same summer. It was when they held the PGA Championship in Dallas at Cedar Crest Country Club. Ted took me with him, and I was pretty excited because I wanted to follow Walter Hagen, who was paired against Al Espinosa in the semifinals. I stuck real close to him—in those days they didn't have gallery ropes, so I was right beside him the entire match. It was late in the afternoon on the back nine, and the players were facing into the western sun. On one particular hole, Hagen was squinting to see where to hit his approach shot. He kept putting his hand up over his eyes, and I said, "Would you like to borrow my cap?" He looked at me, looked at my school baseball cap, and said "Yes." Then he took my cap and sat it on his head, just enough to block the sun from his eyes. Of course, he never wore a cap or hat while playing, and he did play to the gallery quite a bit, so I'm certain he was just being kind, but it gave me a good feeling anyway. After he played the shot—the ball landed about eight feet from the hole—he gave my cap back. He sank the putt and tied Espinosa, then won the match in one extra hole. The next day he beat Joe Turnesa to win his fifth PGA Championship. You'd think I would have kept that cap all this time, but I haven't. I've never kept clubs or balls I won tournaments with or anything like that. Just not sentimental that way, I guess.

That Christmas they had the Caddie Championship again, but this time it was just nine holes, not eighteen. By sinking a long putt on the last hole I tied with a small, dark-complected boy named Ben Hogan. Par was 37, and we both shot 40. The members decided since it wasn't dark and the weather was good, we would go another nine holes. The members caddied for us. My caddie was Judge Wade; I don't recall who caddied for Ben. There were even a few folks in the gallery. Since

I didn't yet have a full set of clubs, I borrowed Judge Wade's. I was fortunate and won by one shot, so that was the first time I played against Ben and beat him. I was fourteen then, and Ben would turn fourteen the following August. They gave us each a golf club—mine was a 5-iron, and he got a 2-iron. Well, I already had a five, and he already had a two, so we traded clubs. The club also gave us junior playing privileges, which meant we could practice at the club and play at certain times when the members weren't on the course. That really helped me develop my game a lot faster.

I had met Ben before, of course, but hadn't really gotten to know him. He lived across town and went to a different school, and I didn't see him except at Glen Garden. Though he was short, he had big hands and arms for his size. He was quiet, serious, and mostly kept to himself. The first time I was really aware of him was Christmas the year before, when the members put on a little boxing match for entertainment. Ben liked to box, and so did another caddie we called Joe Boy. They boxed for about fifteen minutes, I guess, but nobody got knocked down or hurt. I was just watching, because I never did like to box or fight. When the members decided it was over, they all gave Ben and Joe Boy a big hand.

I don't recall that Ben and I ever even caddied together. If we did, I hadn't gotten to know him yet, because I sure don't remember it. But that wasn't unusual, because on a weekend there might be at least forty or fifty caddies around, and since we were pretty busy when we were on the course, we didn't get to know everyone. I know for sure that when I was caddying, I was too busy to talk much, and when I wasn't caddying, I was in school, at home doing chores, or working on my game.

I kept at it, practicing whenever I could, especially my short game. I'd practice at home, pitching balls off the rug onto the bed and getting them to just stop dead. I've had several people tell me they've tried this little trick, and it's not as easy as it sounds. Fortunately, I never broke anything in the room when I did it.

There was a practice area at Glen Garden where we could hit balls to one end and then go hit them back. Sometimes, we'd get up a game where the one who hit the shortest shots had to go gather up all the balls and bring them back. I did see Ben out on the practice range quite a lot, even then. Being as short as he was, he had to go get those balls quite often. Well, of course he didn't like that, and he found that if he turned his left hand over on the club and gave himself what we call a strong grip, he could hook the ball and make it roll quite a way on that hard, dry ground. So he didn't have to go chase balls much after that.

I've heard it said a number of times that Ben started out playing left-handed. I don't really know about whether he might have tried playing with a left-handed club sometime, but I never saw him play left-handed, and when we traded our 2- and 5-irons, neither one was left-handed. So I don't know how that story got started, but in all the time I knew Ben, from when we were both about thirteen, I never saw him play that way.

Several of the caddies got to be quite good players. One of them, Ned Baugh, was better than Ben at that time, but he didn't progress as much, because he didn't work on his game as much as Ben or I did. I did run into Ned a little later on, though, at one of my first real amateur tournaments. It was the next spring, when I started to play in local amateur events around town, whatever ones I could get to. The first one I won was in March of 1928, at a course called Katy Lake, south of Fort Worth. There was a full field, it was match play, and in the finals, I was up against Ned, who by this time had another job and was a year or so older than me. I was really nervous, but I just barely beat him. Katy Lake was a short course, but not particularly easy. It's no longer there, but I still have the little silver trophy to prove I won.

Shortly after that Katy Lake victory, I got the worst shellacking I ever had, from another Texan named Ralph Guldahl. Most people don't realize it, but Ralph was from Dallas, where he caddied at Bob-o-link, which is gone now. The same people owned Katy Lake and Bob-o-link, and decided to have a caddie match between the two clubs. We drew straws, and I got picked to play against Ralph, 36 holes at each club, with the first 36 at Bob-o-link, the second at Katy Lake. Ralph was a much more experienced player than I, and after the two rounds at his club, I was 12 down. The next day, we went to Katy Lake, and after the first eighteen, I was down 6 more, so we didn't ever play the last eighteen. Years later, I beat Ralph in three tournaments that I can recall real well, but I never did make up for that awful drubbing he gave me.

We caddies couldn't play or practice on our course during the evenings, but late in the evenings, I would go down to the third green, which was out of sight of the clubhouse. That's where I'd practice pitching and chipping. I'd do it till I couldn't see the hole any more, then I'd spread my handkerchief over the hole and keep at it.

I thought nobody at the club could see me, but I'd forgotten about Mr. Kidd, the club manager. We all called him "Captain Kidd." He lived in a little apartment on the third floor of the clubhouse, and one evening, he saw me down there on the third hole. Naturally, I got called on the carpet the next day, and Mr. Akey told me if I'd promise him I wouldn't do it any more, he wouldn't expel me. The punishment for practicing on the course was one week's expulsion. I felt I had to be honest, so I told him he'd have to expel me, because I couldn't promise never to do it again. I took my punishment—and then I made sure nobody could see me the next time I went down to practice.

Glen Garden's golf course was the only one I'd ever seen at that time, and I never thought there was anything unusual about it. But on the back nine, the holes ran like this: par four, par four, par five, par five, par three, par three, par four, par three, par three. There were two pairs of par threes on the last five holes, which was pretty unusual.

Of those par threes, the seventeenth hole was the only one that was easy. Fourteen and fifteen were both over 200 yards long, and the 15th was a 213-yard blind shot to an uphill green. You couldn't even see the flag from the tee. I realized later that having four par threes on the back nine was unique, but I played there again a few years ago, and it's still exactly the same.

With all that—caddying, playing golf, and school—I still had quite a lot to do at home. We had over a hundred white leghorn chickens, and it was my job to sell the eggs. I sold quite a few to the chef at Glen Garden. We also grew vegetables—black-eyed peas, corn, green peas—and we'd take all our produce and eggs to the neighborhood grocery stores to sell.

I guess it was about this time that I completed my first woodworking project. I used to carry the eggs and vegetables to market in a little wagon, and I remember I built wooden rails for the wagon so it could hold more. I also had some other ways of making an extra few dollars, like selling magazines and other things door to door. One of the magazines was *Liberty,* and one of the products I sold was called Hand-Slick, which took greasy dirt off your hands and worked very well. We had a cow, which I milked, and when my brother Charles developed an allergy not only to my mother's milk but to cow's milk, we bought a goat, and that fixed him right up. So I had a cow and a goat to milk. I sure didn't have to wonder what to do with my spare time.

Of all the things I had to do, I enjoyed school the least. I didn't mind English and some of the other subjects, including regular math, but geometry really confused me. And as I become more and more interested in golf, I became less and less interested in school.

In that day and time, it wasn't as important as it is now for people to have very much formal education. Very few people went on to college, and it was possible to do pretty well for yourself with just a high school diploma, if you were smart enough and willing to work hard.

My history teacher, Miss Nina Terry, used to play golf occasionally. One time I was playing with her, and she told me, "Byron, if you don't at least open your history book, I'm going to have to flunk you." So that got me busy and I managed to pass history all right.

Another teacher I liked very much was Miss Martel, who taught English. A few years ago, my wife Peggy and I were at a dinner at Fort Worth's Colonial Country Club, and we found ourselves seated with Miss Martel. I hadn't seen her for over sixty years, but she still remembered me. She told Peggy that I was "a good student," which I thought was very kind of her, since I had hated school so much.

I finally got to where I not only wasn't doing my homework, I began to play hooky so I could go play golf. Well, of course the school called my parents, and finally, my father told me, "Son, you've got a choice—either go to school or go to work." I'd always liked to work anyway, so I said I'd go to work, and that ended my formal education, when I was about halfway through the tenth grade.

So I had to live up to my word and go to work. I looked everywhere, but since it was 1928, jobs were scarce. I was already working at Glen Garden, not only in the shop, but also mowing the greens. They had a single-reel mower, and you walked while you mowed. I had to start right after daylight, and make sure I guided the mower properly, not overlap too much. I did this the first summer after I left school, and it gave me the opportunity to play a lot of golf. I mowed seventeen greens while another man did the 18th green and the putting clock.

Fortunately, I had gotten to know quite a few of the members by then. Mr. Cecil Nottingham, who worked for the Fort Worth-Denver City railroad, told me that if an opening came up, he'd let me know, and pretty soon after that, he did. I started as a file clerk for Mr. Nottingham in the fall of 1928, and worked there most of 1929 as well. I enjoyed the work, which mostly was sorting waybills and filing them. Since Mr. Nottingham was a golfer, he understood my desire to work on my game, and if I had all my work done for the afternoon, he'd let me go play.

But jobs then were not only hard to come by—they didn't last very long. One day in the middle of the week Mr. Nottingham called me to his desk and told me, "Byron, I hate to tell you this. You've been a good employee, but things are tough and we have so many people. I'm going to have to lay you off." So I was looking for work again.

With or without a job, I kept playing golf whenever I could and working on my game. The following spring, 1930, I played in the Texas Open Pro-Am in San Antonio. In those days, pro-ams meant just one amateur (rather than four) and one pro per team. I was paired with the fine Scottish golfer, Bobby Cruickshank, who was a pro in New England.

The tournament was at Breckenridge Park. I knew the course, and I could putt common bermuda greens real well. We both played well and we finished second, and I kind of expected that Bobby would thank me or compliment my game some way. After all, he'd won fifty or sixty dollars, and I had another silver cup. But all he said was, "Laddie, if ye don't larn to grip the club right, ye'll niver make a good player."

That took the wind out of my sails a bit, but I thought a lot about what he'd said, and asked Ted Longworth, the pro at Glen Garden. I had what they called a typical caddie swing, long and loose, with a strong right hand. Ted made a couple of suggestions, and I paid close attention, because he was a fine player and had been the Missouri state champion. I read some books on the swing and the grip, too, and after I got it figured out, I never had to change it again. In fact, people have often said my grip was one of the best things about my game.

I've never lost a club at the top of my swing as so many players do. Actually, I never changed or had any trouble with it at all until I cut the end of my middle finger off woodworking when I was seventy-six years old.

I was soon playing a lot of local Monday morning pro-ams in Fort Worth with Jack Grout, who came to Glen Garden as assistant to his brother Dick. Dick Grout had recently replaced Ted. Ted had been a big promoter of golf at Glen Garden, encouraging the members to play more and to get involved in various tournaments, which he did himself. But in 1930, Ted left for the pro job at Texarkana Country Club, which had a bigger membership and a fine golf course, with lots of those tall East Texas pine trees.

Jack Grout and I got to be good friends and remained that way the rest of his life. Back then, we played every week or so in the pro-ams. Remember, it was just one pro and one amateur, and there were no handicaps involved. Prize money wasn't much, maybe $25 to the winner, but $25 went a long ways in the Depression. Of course, it was Jack who became Jack Nicklaus's coach for so many years. The Grout brothers also had a sister who was Oklahoma State Ladies' Amateur Champion, so they were a whole family of golfers.

Jack was the best pro around, and I had become one of the best amateurs. We won those pro-ams so many times that the other pros got together and made a rule that a pro could only play with the same amateur once a month. So that gave the other boys a chance.

As for work, I'd had to fill in with first one thing, then another. It was the summer of 1930 before I found another regular job. This time my boss was Mr. Lawson Heatherwick, who published *Southwest Bankers* magazine. I was just a flunky—I helped put copy together, answered the phone, and was the gofer. It tied me down more than the railroad job, but the hours were fairly short, and it was just a monthly publication. While any job was better than none, it had begun to worry me some that I hadn't any background for running a business, or plans for a future of any kind. And between working, playing golf, and still doing my chores at home, I hadn't any time for dating, either. I never had a date in my life, in fact, till I moved to Texarkana when I was twenty years old.

Fortunately, Mr. Heatherwick played a lot of golf and was also willing to let me play, as long as it wasn't the end of the month. I worked about thirty hours a week and my salary was fifteen dollars, though it varied some.

One time he called me from Eastland, where he was playing in a tournament. After checking to see if everything was caught up at the office, he asked, "Why don't you come out here and play?" I hopped on a bus and got there just in time to qualify, playing in the rain. Everyone else had already qualified, so they had to send a scorer with me. As it turned out, I won the tournament, so it was worth the trip.

At that point, I was winning something in nearly every tournament, usually a silver cup or plate or something like that. I'd sell most of the prizes to get enough money to get to the next tournament. I also played in a lot of local invitationals—every city had one back then. I guess I played in twenty or twenty-five tournaments in those two years, plus the pro-ams and such. I was nervous sometimes, but I really enjoyed playing. And of course in between I was working on my game and practicing as much as I could.

In the summer of 1931 I qualified to play in the U.S. Amateur at Beverly Country Club in Chicago, but it looked like I wouldn't get to go. I had enough money for train fare, but not enough to stay at a hotel while I was there. Only two golfers from my area qualified—Edwin McClure and me. His father had a little money, and they were going to stay at the Morrison Hotel in Chicago. They offered to let me stay in their room, so I did. I ended up sleeping on the couch.

I got to Chicago late in the afternoon the day before the tournament began and never had time to play a practice round. The next day I had to play 36 holes. I'd never seen bentgrass greens before, and I had thirteen 3-putt greens. I failed to qualify by one stroke. I remember very little else about that Amateur. The course was fairly hard. The club pro was Charlie Penna, Tony's brother, with whom I became very good friends in later years. The tournament was won by Francis Ouimet, though I didn't get to meet him while I was there, because I had to go back home the next day. I was nineteen, it was the first time I'd ever left Texas, and the only time I ever played in the National Amateur.

The rest of that summer and fall I continued playing in local amateur tournaments. There were so many of them back then, one nearly every weekend. Fort Worth was the clearinghouse for setting them up, so that's how I found out about them. Some of the amateurs I'd played with had turned pro by then, and I quite often would play as well as or better than some of the pros. I won the Rivercrest Invitational in September, and I was also medalist in the qualifying rounds. But for some reason I'd never thought about becoming a professional. That just goes to show you you never know what's around the next corner.

Ted Longworth had been at Texarkana for about two years when he got the members to hold a little Open tournament, with the prize money being $500. It drew a lot of fine players from four states—Missouri, Texas, Arkansas, and Louisiana. In November, Ted wrote me a note from Texarkana (we didn't have a phone yet), saying the club was having a tournament and he'd like me to come play in it. This was to be an Open tournament, with both pros and amateurs playing. The total prize money was $500, Ted said, but of course he thought I'd be playing as an amateur.

A week or so later I got on the bus with my clothes in a little suitcase and my golf clubs at my side. By then, *Southwest Bankers* magazine was defunct, and I was out of work again, living at home and just doing odd jobs here and there to earn enough to keep body and soul together. There were even fewer jobs available then, as you might guess, because it was about the middle of the Depression. On that long ride to Texarkana, I got to thinking about that prize money. I knew you couldn't make much of a living playing professional golf, but there was some pretty good money going at these tournaments, and I felt I was good enough to have a chance at some of it.

It was on that bus that I decided to turn pro. When I got there for the qualifying rounds, I asked the tournament officials what I had to do to turn pro, and they told me, "Pay five dollars and say you're playing for the money." It was as simple as that—no qualifying schools, no mini-tours like they have today. So I did it. I put my five dollars down and announced my intentions, and that was that. It was November 22, 1932.

I finished third and won $75. Boy, I thought that was all the money in the world. I'd never even seen that much money in my hand at one time in my entire life. The tournament was a pretty good one, really. You might be surprised at some of the other pros who were there. Hogan, who'd turned pro two years earlier, was third in the qualifying rounds but didn't finish in the money, which only went to six places. Jimmy Demaret and Dick Metz played, and Ky Laffoon finished second, three strokes back of Ted, who won. So I wasn't in such bad company for my professional debut. I don't have that $75 any more, but I do still have a newspaper clipping about it, sent to me by my good friend, Bill Inglish of *The Daily Oklahoman.*

You have to understand that my parents at the time didn't really approve of me playing so much golf. Golf pros then didn't have as good a reputation as they do now. But when I came home and told them what I'd done, Mother was real proud of me, and though my father didn't say much, they told me, "Whatever you do, do it the best you can, and be a good man." They always supported me, even though they didn't get much of a chance to come see me play.

I'd made my move. I had $75 in my pocket, but still no job. I knew enough, though, to realize my next step was to go on the tour in California that winter, if I could possibly get there. So that was what I set out to do.

THREE

Texarkana and a Girl Named Louise

AFTER I GOT BACK HOME FROM TEXARKANA, I STARTED reading about the tour in California. There were four winter tournaments in the Los Angeles area in the early thirties: the Los Angeles Open, the Long Beach Open, the Pro-Am at Hillcrest, and one at Pasadena's Brookside Golf Course, right next to the Rose Bowl. Of course I didn't have any money to get there, even with my Texarkana winnings. But some friends in Fort Worth decided to back me, and gave me $500—enough to get there, plus some extra. These were a couple of amateurs who'd won some money on me in Calcutta pools, where people would bet on their favorite golfers, and I guess they thought I was a better player than I was. In those days, a one-way train ticket was over $250, so I had to find a cheaper way to get there. Luckily, I found a ride with a man named Lee Davis, and we drove in his car. But I knew I had to win some money if I wanted to take the train back home.

Unfortunately, I didn't do very well. I didn't play all that badly, but most of the tournaments in my time only paid twelve, maybe fifteen places. Today, everyone who makes the cut—usually sixty or so—wins some money. I came close to the money, but didn't win a dime, and pretty soon I'd gone through about all my expense money. When I wired my backers that I needed more cash to continue on the tour, they told me they couldn't send me any more, not even enough for the train, and I'd have to get back home the best way I could. Thank goodness, there was a man I knew from Fort Worth in L.A. on business at the time, a fellow by the name of Charlie Jones. He was headed back to Texas right after the Pasadena tournament, and I got a ride back with him.

That was my first time in California, and I thought it was very pretty country. There were no freeways to speak of, and the traffic wasn't bad at all then. There was more interest in golf, more play at the clubs, and the courses were much harder than those in Texas. They were longer, and had more bunkers, more rough, and a different kind of rough from what I was familiar with.

By the end of January 1933 I was back home, practicing and playing at Glen Garden, helping around the house and garden, milking the cow, and so forth. It was kind of a dead time. I decided to write to Ted Longworth about my experiences in California. Along about the middle part of March I got a letter from him, saying he was leaving Texarkana for Waverly Country Club in Portland, Oregon. He said I might want to apply for the Texarkana job—I wouldn't make any money at it, just enough to eat regular. That was enough for me.

A man named Pharr who owned a general merchandise and hardware store was president of the club at the time, and I had played golf with his wife in an amateur tournament in Fort Worth in early '32. She was a fine player, about middle-aged, and had been both the Texas and Arkansas Women's Amateur champion as well as the club champion at Texarkana. So when I went there, I went to see Mrs. Pharr first before I talked to her husband. She told me she'd help me. I don't know if it helped or not, but I did get the job in the first week of April 1933.

My parents were happy about it in one respect, because they knew by now I had golf in my soul. They were sad to see me leave town, though, and told me to be a good pro, to take care of myself, to be good, and to go to church.

I only took a few things with me—my golf clubs and some clothes. I really didn't have much more than that, anyway. I found a place to live close by, about a par-five distance from the club. It was the home of Mr. and Mrs. J. O. Battle, and they gave me a nice room plus two good meals a day for $7 a week.

That sounds pretty inexpensive, and it was, but it took nearly half my earnings each month. I received no salary, just whatever I got for lessons and anything I made in the shop. I got $2 for a half-hour lesson, but not many people took lessons then—especially not from a young, inexperienced pro like me. We had about sixty sets of members' clubs at $1 per set monthly storage fee, and we sold balls, tees, new clubs, and golf bags. There were no golf shirts or other clothes like they have now. Besides, whatever you wanted to sell in your shop, you had to pay for first, out of your own money, not the club's. Ted left me the inventory, and over the next few months, I paid him what he'd had in it. So I netted about $60 a month. Like he'd told me, enough to live on.

After finding a room, the next order of business was finding a church. In the phone book I saw the Walnut Street Church of Christ, which was about three miles away. I started attending, and they had quite a large group of young people, so I placed my membership there right away. It was a very good influence for me, particularly since this was my first time away from home.

I had no transportation, of course, and even taxis were expensive. I could walk to the club, but had to ride a streetcar to church at first. There was a member of the club named Dyer who owned the local Ford dealership, and he took a liking to me after I'd been there about a month. We got to talking one day and I mentioned that I sure would like to get a car, but there was no way I could buy one on what I was making. He just said, "Come down to my office and we'll talk about it." When I went to see him, he showed me a '32 Ford Roadster, royal blue with cream wheels and top. Since it was already the middle of 1933, he'd had this car over a year. He was willing to let me have it for $500, paying whatever I could each month, with no interest. It didn't take me long to say yes. I worked pretty hard, and after a bit, things got better at the club, so by the time I left for Ridgewood in '35, I had that car pretty well paid for.

It wasn't too long after I got my car, about June of '33, in fact, that I met Louise, my wonderful wife of over fifty years. The way I roped that gal in is a story in itself.

One Sunday at Bible study, there was a new girl—a tiny brunette with pretty brown eyes who came up and introduced herself to me as Louise Shofner. She had been living with relatives in Houston until recently, learning to be a hairdresser—we called them beauty operators in those days. I liked her right away.

The young folks got to talking about the picnic they were having that evening after worship at Spring Lake Park, and they invited me along. Well, I was busy at the club and didn't get to go to evening church, but I went ahead to the park anyway. The food was great and after I'd had my dinner, I went and got a piece of angel food cake with some sort of delicious lemon-flavored butter frosting. After I took the first bite, I said, "Who made this cake?" and found out it was Louise's.

She was dating another boy at the time, so I went and took the seat out of my car—Fords then had seats that came out easily—and invited Louise and her date to sit with me on that car seat, rather than on the grass, while we had dessert. I had seconds, too. She impressed me as quiet and reserved, but friendly. She was about 5'2" and couldn't have weighed more than 100 pounds. The next day, I called and asked if I could have a date with her, but she told me, "No, I'm busy." But I called every day after that with the same question.

The following Sunday when I got to church, Louise was sitting there with her little sister, Irma Drew, who was just a little bitty child, seventeen years younger than Louise. I went up and sat right next to them on Louise's other side. The boy she'd been dating came in, saw me sitting there, got mad and went to sit someplace else.

After church, I asked if I might take Louise and her sister home, and she said yes, so I did, and got her to agree to a date the next Saturday. We went to a picture show—I think it was a musical—then to the drugstore for a sundae, and I remember I had to have her home by 10:30. I was twenty then, and she was nineteen. That was the first real date I ever had in my life, and once I met Louise, I never even thought about dating anyone else.

The next day, Sunday, I sat with Louise and her sister again, and I noticed how she was able to get that little child to behave, to sit up and pay attention to the preacher, even though Irma Drew wasn't but two or three. I drove the two of them home again, and we had to stop at a railroad crossing to let a train go by. While we were waiting, I looked over at Louise and said, "Are you going to make our children behave like you do your sister?" She looked at me a minute, then said, "I guess so." So she never had any more dates with anyone but me. In fact, she used to kid me that on our first date, I had this to say about the boy she had been dating, who worked at a bank: "If I ever catch him on the street, I'll run over him!" So it wasn't too long before everyone understood we were unofficially engaged.

I owe at least some of my success in courting Louise to Mr. Arthur Temple, the president of Temple Lumber Company. I would play in fivesomes with the club members sometimes, and Mr. Temple liked to bet me a dollar that he could beat me. I nearly always shot par or better, so when I played Mr. Temple, I could usually count on having a dollar to spend on a date with Louise. With a dollar, we could go to a movie and then go to the drugstore for what was called a "Stuttgart," kind of an ice cream sundae but with a whole lot of real thick chocolate syrup on top. Boy, that was good. If it weren't for Mr. Temple, most of the time we'd just have to sit on Louise's folks' front porch and talk the whole evening, and I wasn't very good at talking then. So, thank you, Mr. Temple.

Now I had more interest than ever in becoming a good player, because I wanted to impress Louise. My game was falling together well, but I still couldn't put four good rounds together, and I knew I needed to do that to get anywhere.

Texarkana was a good club, and had a great golf course. The original course was cut out of a forest, so there were lots of wonderful pine trees, and that was one of the things that made the place so beautiful. I had a certain spot where I parked my car each day, and I kept a nice soft chamois so I could keep all the dust off it. In fact, I kept it so clean I almost wore the paint off it, and every once in a while I'd wax it, 'cause I had plenty of time.

The course itself had a lot of bunkers, and the sand in them was more like fine gravel. The greens were stiff bermuda grass with a lot of contour to them. The course forced me to learn to hit the ball straight, to get out of deep bunkers, and to play to elevated greens. It was built by Langford and Monroe, who also did the Philadelphia Country Club at Spring Mill, where I won the Open in '39. Through the years, the course gradually got redone and basically ruined until Ron Prichard redid it in 1985. He restored it to its original design, only better, and he did a wonderful job.

The best thing about the Texarkana job was it gave me plenty of time to practice. They had a big practice area. Of course, there weren't any practice balls, you had to furnish your own. And in that day and time, I was not a prominent enough player, so I had to buy my golf balls. No manufacturer was going to give me any like they do with so many of the players today. I guess they did it even then with the prominent players, but I wasn't prominent at all. So I saved my money and bought a few, and eventually I had a good shag bag full of golf balls.

I'd go out to the practice area and—well, back then there were plenty of caddies around, but I couldn't afford a caddie to shag my balls, so I would shag my own. I'd hit 'em down the practice field, then I'd go down and hit 'em all back to where I'd hit 'em from. Then I'd hit them out again, then back. And it wasn't the 8-iron, it was the niblick, or mashie niblick, because we didn't use the numbers back then. I really got to practice a lot there, and it was very good for my game.

I finally did get to where I could afford to pay a caddie to help me practice, and the one I remember best was Miller Barber, who was about thirteen or fourteen at the time. He'd shag balls for me quite a bit, and for years, he's told people that the reason he's bald is because my shots hit him on the head so many times while I was practicing. I wish I could say I really was that accurate. He caddied for me some, too, and sometimes we'd play nine holes together. I'd play him for a dime, and give him four strokes. He told me the other night that he never did beat me, but I never took his dime. See—I wasn't such a bad guy.

I've always been glad Miller became such a good player, though I don't think I had anything to do with it, and I certainly wouldn't want to take credit for his swing. But Miller's a very nice man, loves to play golf, and his wife Karen is a wonderful lady. I feel very fortunate to count them as my friends.

I gave a few lessons at Texarkana, and I'll never forget the first lesson I gave. I think I got a dollar for it. It was a couple named Mr. and Mrs. Josh Morris. He was in the insurance business, and she was a very kindly, soft-spoken lady, and it was Mrs. Morris I was to give my first official lesson to. I told her that I was new at teaching, that I would work with her all she wanted, and I'd try to be as helpful to her as I could.

She was very kind and she thought I did okay. That encouraged me, and I always had a soft spot in my heart for her, and I gave her quite a few lessons. Then some other ladies started coming to me, and I got to where I was giving more and more lessons. Of course, back then people didn't have a lot of money for lessons. And you didn't give just thirty-minute lessons, you just kept on working with them until they got tired and quit, because there weren't all that many lessons to give back then.

Mrs. Morris never did make a very good player, so I guess I didn't really help her with her game. But I did sometimes work with Mrs. Pharr. She would take a lesson once in a while, but I think she did it just to kind of encourage me, because she was a fine player and really didn't need much in the way of lessons. I did teach both of her daughters some, though.

At that time, there was so little play that you could always play fivesomes or even more. I had no problem getting a game, and I usually didn't have too much to do in the afternoons so I could play quite a lot. Wednesday was "doctors' day," of course, but you could get a game Thursday, and then Saturday and Sunday, too.

Playing with these members, I never did gamble, but every once in a while, I would hit a pretty good shot, and these members would brag on me. It got to where I could shoot par or less—par was 73—most all the time after I'd gotten used to the golf course and had practiced a little bit.

By now, I was playing with steel shafts. In fact, I hadn't played with hickory shafts since 1930, because the new steel was so much better. I had a few clubs with hickory shafts in them, but I never did play with them again. I even had a putter with a hickory shaft, which you even see a few of today, modern ones, but by 1933, most everyone was playing with the steel, which had come out in 1931. It caught on very quickly.

There weren't very many club manufacturers back then. The main ones in the golf club business at the time were Spalding, Wilson, and MacGregor. There was another one, Kroydon, and those were the clubs I was playing then. I switched around quite a bit between Kroydon and Wilson.

In the summer of 1933 I had an interesting match with a fellow named "Titanic" Thompson. He was a very nice person, a handsome man, and he could play almost as well right-handed as left. He was a gambler, the kind of fellow who would bet on just about anything. Some friends in Fort Worth contacted me and said they wanted me to play a money match against him where they would be betting on me. I didn't care for betting-type matches, but they really wanted me to come to Fort Worth and do it, so I figured out when I could go home next and told them. We played at Ridglea, but I had nothing to do with the betting, all I did was play. They gave Titanic three strokes, which I wouldn't have done, but since I didn't have any money on it, I didn't have anything to say about it. Anyway, I shot 69 and he shot 71, so he beat me one stroke. You see, I knew Titanic was a better player than most people gave him credit for. He had the ability to do whatever he had to to win, and he always knew the percentages. But he was never quite good enough to play on the tour, and really, he only played where he knew or felt that he had the advantage, like most good gamblers. Several years before that, when I played in the Southwestern Amateur in 1930 at Nichols Hills, Titanic bet he could throw a grapefruit over the Skirven Hotel, and someone was silly enough to take the bet. The hotel was about six stories high, but there was a building right next to it the same height, so Titanic got up on top of that building and sure enough, he threw his grapefruit right over the hotel. So I was wise to Titanic before that match with him ever took place.

I met a fellow named Harvey Penick while I was at Texarkana. He was from Austin, and already was getting a reputation as a good teacher. I'd see him each year at the Texas Open in San Antonio, and he'd be at some of the other tournaments around every once in a while. He and I had quite a few discussions about the swing, and I always found it good to talk with Harvey about golf. He was a quiet, easy, shy sort of a man, a very good man to know and to help anyone understand the golf swing. He's credited me with sending him a lot of students, but I simply passed the word along that he was a good teacher, and quite a few of the younger players were smart enough to go look him up.

All the while I was still thinking quite a bit about the possibility of going to California and playing out there during the winter of '33. Of course, I hadn't said anything to anybody about it, because I hadn't done very well in California the year before.

During this time, I'd met J.K. Wadley, who'd taken an interest in me. He was an oilman and a lumberman at that time—mainly oil. He encouraged me with my golf; he knew quite a lot about the game, and thought I had a good rhythm to my swing. One of the first times we played together, he told me I had one of the best grips he'd ever seen. So I told him about the time I'd played with Bobby Cruickshank, and he really enjoyed that story.

Mr. Wadley hadn't taken up golf until his forties, but he'd become very enthused about it. He wanted to learn all he could about the game, and he already had a substantial amount of income, so one year he hired "Long Jim" Barnes, the 1916 PGA champion, to teach him. The way it came about was Mr. Wadley found out Barnes was going on a barnstorming tour. It was a series of exhibitions all around, wherever he could find someone to pay him to come, though what he got paid, I have no idea. Anyway, Mr. Wadley contacted him and contracted with him for Mr. Wadley to go along and watch the exhibitions, and Barnes would teach him everything he knew about golf.

Mr. Wadley learned a lot about golf this way and studied some more on his own, so he really was helpful to me. He'd say, "This is the way I used to do it," or "This is the way Jim Barnes did it," or "This is the way some of the older players did it." Of course, most of that was different from the way I was trying to do it, but he did encourage me and thought I had a lot of potential. He always liked me because I didn't drink or smoke or swear, and he thought I was a pretty nice young man.

He was going to finance me on the tour that winter in exchange for half my winnings, so I really went to work on my game, practicing and playing every chance I had. By the time fall arrived, I really was beginning to play quite well, though I knew I had a lot to learn yet and a lot of work to do. But in that day and time, you had to go on the tour and play on the tour to learn. Today you play through high school and college and get a lot of competition there, and then you can even go on the mini-tours, so you learn a lot before you actually qualify to go on the main tour. But in that day and time, we got our education and learned about competing on the tour itself.

By then, Louise and I were talking about when we might get married, and without telling me, she had talked to her father some about loaning me money to go to California. When Louise told Mr. Shofner what Mr. Wadley's offer was, her father said he'd loan me a little bit and we wouldn't have to split anything, that if Louise had that much confidence in me, that was good enough for him. I remember Louise telling me her father wanted to see me, and since I didn't know she'd talked to him about my going to California, it scared me a little at first.

But we had a very nice conversation. Mr. Shofner told me, "If Louise has confidence in you, I do, too." He arranged to loan me some money to get to California and get started. Well, I made a little bit, but I had to send back for a little bit more. I'd played in the Los Angeles Open, and then at Brookside Park in Pasadena, then in a pro-am at Hillcrest, and in a tournament in Lakewood, but I was still struggling, and still having to borrow a little bit of money.

I headed back to Phoenix, then to San Antonio for the Texas Open, which was one of the oldest tournaments on the entire PGA tour. After that, there was one more tournament, in Galveston, the only tour event ever played there.

When I got to San Antonio, I figured up how much money I had in my pocket. I knew how much it was costing me per day, and I figured, "Well, I've got enough money to play here and in Galveston, and then I'll go back to Texarkana and go to work." I would have no money left at all to repay Mr. Shofner, and by now I owed him $660. That was a lot of money for me or anybody else then.

At the Texas Open, I was introduced to the gallery on the first tee by a man named L.G. Wilson, who was a golf salesman but no kin to the Wilson company. He was full of hot air, and really built me up, calling me "a promising young player"—I thought he never was going to get through introducing me. The more he talked, the more nervous I got.

This was at Breckenridge Park, where the tournament was still played until just a few years ago. At that time, they had these rubber mats you hit from on every tee, and you didn't dare hit under it or behind it, because you could break your club, or even your hands. So I was being really careful not to hit behind it, and I came over the top of it instead. In fact, if there'd been one less coat of paint on the ball, I'd have missed it entirely. The ball just dribbled off the tee about forty or fifty yards. After that big buildup Wilson had given me, I was really embarrassed.

I did hit a good second shot with my brassie—now they call it the 2-wood. I put it about 125 yards from the green, got it close, and made the putt for a 4. And the thought just popped into my mind, "Well, you silly goose, if you can miss one that bad and make a par, if you ever hit it right, you might make a birdie!"

So sure enough, from then on I played real fine—shot 66 the first round and led the tournament. I got excited and nervous and everything else; it was the first time I'd ever led a tournament in my life. Then I kind of faltered around all the way through the rest of the tournament, even though I didn't play all that badly, and finished second. Wiffy Cox, the pro at Congressional in Washington, D.C. and a fine player, considerably older than me, won it. I was paired with him the final round.

But I won $450, and boy, I thought I was rich. So I figured, well, if I can go to Galveston and play pretty good in Galveston, I can get back home with a little money in my pocket, and pay Mr. Shofner back.

So I went to Galveston and finished second there, too, but there wasn't as much money—I only won a little over $300. Craig Wood won that tournament. Then I jumped in the car and headed for Texarkana. I don't think the wheels hardly hit the ground the whole way from Galveston to Texarkana. It was right around the first of March, 1933.

As soon as I arrived, I walked straight in to Mr. Shofner's grocery store and said, "Mr. Shofner, I owe you six hundred and sixty dollars," and I paid him in cash. Then I said, "How much interest do I owe you?" and he said, "You don't owe me any interest. I'm just glad you finished off your trip real good. I'm proud of you."

So that left me a hundred dollars. I went to Arnold's Jewelry Store (Mr. Arnold was a member at the club, so I knew him pretty well), and bought a hundred-dollar diamond ring, which was a pretty decent little ring in those days. I gave it to Louise and we became officially engaged. Then I was broke again—no money at all!

By now it was the spring of 1934. I kept working on my game, getting a little more recognition, giving quite a few lessons, and things were looking up, so Louise and I decided to get married. Actually, I seem to remember Mr. Shofner saying to Louise, "You and Byron are spending too much time together. I think you should go ahead and get married." We thought it was a fine idea, though of course I had no money saved up.

But that didn't stop us from going ahead with our wedding plans. We decided to get married on June 24, and I guess my first training in learning to be a good husband came a few weeks later, when I was in Mr. Arnold's store again. I noticed a set of blue-and-white dishes in a wooden barrel, and asked Mr. Arnold how much they were. He told me they were on sale, and it seemed like a pretty good deal to me.

So, being young and ignorant in such things, I went ahead and bought the whole set—144 pieces. I was real proud of myself for finding such a bargain, and drove straight to Louise's to tell her. I was in for a surprise. Louise didn't seem to be happy about it at all. Her eyebrows went up, and she said, "I want to see them, *right now.*" You have to understand that in that day and time, you didn't return something you'd bought like you can now. That just wasn't done very often, especially if it was sale merchandise. So if she didn't approve, I was in double trouble.

But back to the store we went, and fortunately, Louise did like the dishes, very much, so I was relieved, and felt I'd learned a good lesson at the same time. In fact, we kept those dishes for thirty-five or forty years, and she finally gave them to her niece, Sandy. In all that time, I think we broke only two of the 144 dishes.

Though my mind was more on my marriage than golf right then, I did have my first hole-in-one at that time. It was on the eleventh hole at the club, and it happened just two days before we were to be married. That golf course will also always be dear to me for another reason. Later that summer I was playing golf with Mrs. Pharr. It was 1934, about the middle of the summer, and the fairways were good and hard, so we were getting a nice amount of roll. The 16th hole then was 560 yards, and I hit a good drive downwind about 300 yards, then took my brassie, now called a 2-wood, and knocked the ball in the hole in two for my one and only double eagle. In fact, the next week I was playing with a foursome of men, knocked my second shot very close and made an eagle. That didn't happen very often to me either, so it was fun and seemed to impress the fellows I was playing with.

Louise and I had no money for a church wedding, so we were married in the living room of Louise's parents' home. No one in my family was able to come, with money being so tight then. But they had all met Louise, and they definitely approved of the match. Louise's sister Delle was maid of honor, and I had "Coach" Warren Woodson to stand up with me. He was a good friend and football coach at Texarkana Junior College at the time, and his wife Muriel played golf. They were club members, and we remained good friends with them both for all our lives.

Our honeymoon, if you can call it that, was a trip to Hot Springs, Arkansas, a nice resort about 120 miles north. But both of us were so nervous from the wedding and all that we got upset stomachs, only stayed one night, and came back home. We found a kitchenette apartment that was roomy enough, but its only drawback was there was no cross-ventilation—no air conditioning either, of course—and in the summer, it was mighty hot. Lots of times we went to her folks and slept outside on the front porch. Louise went back to work as a beauty operator, and did that for several months. She was good at it, and she liked it very much.

That winter, right after Christmas, Louise went with me to California for her first experience on the tour. Jack Grout traveled with us by car, and I remember his golf clubs wouldn't stand up in the back seat and kept falling on one or the other of us. By the time we'd reached L.A., Louise had had enough, and said, "Either the clubs go, or I go." So Jack had to find another way home, but he was very understanding about it. Jack had a wonderfully long, fluid, smooth swing and good rhythm, but he was too nice a guy, not a tough enough competitor, so he never did very well on the tour.

Traveling at night in my little roadster, Louise's feet and legs would get cold. Women didn't wear slacks hardly at all then, and always dressed nice, especially for traveling. But cars had no heaters in that day and time, so we'd heat bricks in the oven before we left home in Texarkana and wrap them in paper. Then she'd put her feet on them and wrap a lap robe around her, which helped a lot. We would stop the next night at her Grandmother Reese's in West Texas, heat the bricks again, and keep going. We were mighty glad when we got a car with a heater, I can tell you.

We stayed at the same place I'd stayed the year before, the Sir Launfels Apartments in Los Angeles. Also staying there were Al and Emery Zimmerman, brothers and pros themselves, and we invited them to dinner one night. After they'd tasted Louise's good cooking, Al said to Louise, "We've got a deal for you, Louise. We'll buy all the groceries if you'll cook for us." Louise liked to cook, and the idea of saving money appealed to her, so she agreed, and we've remained friends with the Zimmermans ever since. Another interesting thing about that apartment building—the owner was a nice lady with a cute daughter named Jean, whom golfer Dick Metz met and later married; they've been together ever since. So it was a pretty good place for us pros.

Fortunately, I did a little better on the tour that winter than I had the year before, although we barely made expenses. The high point of that winter, though, was how I played against Lawson Little in the San Francisco Match Play Open in January. Of course, I was still learning to play then, not prominent at all and not known very well. The tournament was held at the Presidio Golf Club, where Little's father was the commanding officer. At that time, Little had just won both the American and British Amateurs two years in a row, and had twenty-seven consecutive victories in match play.

I think I was paired with Little in the first round because I was the least-known player who had qualified. Since he was a local boy and it was his home club, I guess they figured I was the easiest player for him to play against.

Well, some of the other pros—in fact, I guess just about all of them—were steamed, because they had all had to qualify for one of the thirty-two spots in the tournament, and Lawson Little didn't. Back then, tournaments were often run by local committees, not necessarily by the PGA, so the rules might be different depending on where you were playing. As you might guess, I was pretty nervous about playing him, but the other pros encouraged me, and Leo Diegel told me before our match, "Kid, Little hates to be outdriven, so you just go out on that first tee and shake him up. You can do it."

That's exactly what I did. I was all pumped up anyway, with Leo's encouragement on top of it. Little drove first, and when I stepped up there, I just let one fly and it sailed right over where his ball had stopped. He gave me the old fisheye, but I birdied the hole to his par, and that was kind of key to the match. I was fortunate. I played very well and beat Little, and it got national publicity.

In fact, the headline in the paper the next day—well, the sportswriters didn't know anything about me, but since I'd gotten married the previous June, they wrote, HONEYMOONER BEATS LAWSON LITTLE! Louise was so embarrassed she wouldn't leave the hotel room the next day. You had to read half of the article before my name even appeared. I won all of $50.

I didn't do anything else spectacular that winter, but at least we didn't have to borrow anything from Mr. Shofner, and Louise was a mighty good cook, so we ate regularly and ate well. Still, I've always felt that my performance in San Francisco, plus a few other good rounds I had in '34, were the main reasons I was invited to Augusta to play in the second Masters tournament in 1935.

During the tournament—at that time called the Augusta Invitational—a man named George Jacobus, who was golf professional at Ridgewood Country Club in Ridgewood, New Jersey, and president of the PGA, came to see Ed Dudley, the golf pro at Augusta National. George told Ed, "I'm looking for a new young assistant, a decent sort of a fellow who has a good possibility of becoming a good player." Of course, you were hired then to play some with the members, and to do quite a bit of teaching, too.

Ed Dudley knew me, and had known me for some time. He was originally from Oklahoma, and with me being from Texas, well, I'd met him at a few of those golf tournaments in both states. Ed told George about me and then introduced us. George interviewed me one day and we had a long conversation, and he said he'd like to talk to me again the next day. So he checked back on my record and what the people thought of me at Texarkana where I was head pro. The next day he hired me to come to Ridgewood as his assistant after the Masters tournament.

My salary would be $400 for the summer, plus half of my lesson fees. Doesn't sound like much, I know, but it was considerably more than what I was making at Texarkana, and the season was shorter, which would allow me to play more tournaments in the winter.

I was very excited about going to Ridgewood, because I had known of Mr. Jacobus for some time though I hadn't met him before. Of course I didn't know anything about Ridgewood and hadn't ever played there. In fact, I'd never been east of the Mississippi until the

Masters. But the fact that George was a prominent pro and president of the PGA impressed me very much. He told me Ridgewood was a 27-hole layout designed by A.W. Tillinghast, which would make it an excellent place to practice and work on my game.

This all took place before and after the first round of the Masters that year. I finished ninth with a score of 291 and won $197. I remember I told Dudley then, "I want to win this tournament in about three years." I beat that forecast by one year.

My first impression of Augusta National was one of surprise—there was really no rough to speak of at all. The trees were not very tall then, either—today they're a good forty feet taller. But the flowers were just as beautiful then. I saw the great Bob Jones there, but didn't get to meet him that year. Most people called him Bobby, but those closest to him always called him Bob.

So I went back home to Texarkana and resigned, packed up, and drove to Ridgewood. It was the first time Louise had to leave home, but when I told her the news, she said, "That's fine." Louise was always very encouraging and supportive of me, and often told me I was a hard worker. She came to Ridgewood a little later, because she had to see after all our things and say goodbye to her family. After I left Texarkana, they hired Don Murphy, a fine pro who stayed there forever, practically, and is now pro emeritus.

I also knew Ridgewood would be an excellent stepping stone in my career, with many more opportunities for me. It would be easier to travel to and play in many of the tournaments in the North and Southeast, and would give me more experience playing in all kinds of weather. But if I had known then what awaited me during my time at Ridgewood, I don't know if I could have stood that much excitement.

FOUR

Ridgewood and a New Driver

SINCE GEORGE JACOBUS WANTED ME TO START AT RIDGEWOOD as soon as possible, I drove home to Texarkana right after the Masters, packed as much as my little Ford roadster would hold—which wasn't much—and drove straight to Ridgewood. The trip took two and a half days of hard driving, and I arrived about noon of the third day.

As I drove up to the clubhouse, I was pretty awed. I had never seen a clubhouse so imposing and elegant before, and I was very apprehensive about it all. But back then, to be successful in the golf business in any way, you had to get a club job in the East. You needed that type of experience, for one thing. Of course, making a living came first for me, so playing on the tour was secondary. One thing for sure, I knew I was very fortunate to be working for Mr. Jacobus, who was then and for quite a long time afterwards president of the PGA. At that time, the PGA was really struggling. There was no money to be made running it, and it wasn't anything like what the tour is today. But working for George gave me the chance to learn about all the tournaments ahead of time, and to see what went into running the PGA and its events. In the mid-thirties, like most folks and many other organizations, the PGA was having financial difficulties. They had very little income, hardly enough to operate the tournaments they were involved in. I remember at one point, just to make a little money for the PGA, George negotiated a deal with golf ball manufacturers. They made balls with their name on one side and "PGA" on the other, and the PGA got a small royalty for each ball sold. It wasn't much, but it helped.

When I walked into the clubhouse, George came to greet me and was very happy to see me. He immediately showed me the pro shop and introduced me to the other fellows I'd be working with. Then he told me about the house where I'd be staying, which he had sent me a telegram about before I'd left Texarkana. He even rode out there with me, knowing I was new in town and might have trouble finding my way.

I was anxious to see it, and make sure it would be all right. This was the first time Louise would be moving away from home, and I knew it was going to be hard on her, as she was very close to her family. Not only that, but I'd be away all day and working pretty long hours, so she'd have very little to do other than her hand work—needlepoint and so forth. She wouldn't even have cooking to occupy her time, because we would actually be boarders, with the cost of our food included in our rent. I believe it was between seven and nine dollars per week. That doesn't sound like much now, but remember, I only made $400 plus half my lessons for the whole season, which ran from April 1 to Labor Day. I got $2.50 for each lesson and gave over $50 a week, for a total of about $100. So my monthly income was a little under $400 per month. Whatever we could save had to help pay expenses while I was on tour in the winter.

You might wonder why we didn't find a place of our own, where Louise would have more to do. But even a small apartment back then was more than we could afford, and besides, when I'd go on the tour in late fall, it made more sense for us to go back to Texarkana for the winter, where Louise could be with her family, because I'd be gone for several weeks at a time.

The people who owned the house we lived in were Mr. and Mrs. W. W. Hope, and they were very nice folks. I remember when Louise arrived about two weeks later, Mrs. Hope chuckled because Louise was so small—5'2"—while I was a good foot taller. Mr. and Mrs. Hope were just the opposite, and when she saw Louise, Mrs. Hope said, "I knew you'd be tiny—tall men always marry little women!"

Our room was small but comfortable, with a ¾-sized bed. That's right, not even a double. It was mighty cozy, I can tell you, and we shared a bathroom with another boarder and the Hopes' son. But Mrs. Hope had put a small rocking chair in our room just for Louise. With all the hand work she did, it was great to have that chair.

Mrs. Hope took a liking to Louise, and it made a world of difference. She had her help with the cooking for all the boarders—there were three of us, plus the Hopes' son. That helped Louise quite a bit, because she was terribly homesick. She cried a lot at first, and had very little to do that could help pass the time. Her friendship with Mrs. Hope carried her through the summer, though—in fact, we came back to stay there the following year as well.

Louise didn't come to visit me at the club much. Back then, it was very rare for a pro's wife to come to his club. I don't think Louise came to Ridgewood more than a half-dozen times in the two years I was there. It just wasn't done then, and since she didn't play golf anyway, there was little reason for her to come by.

Getting back to my first day at work, after I unloaded what I'd brought along in the car, George and I returned to the club, which was about a ten-minute drive from the house. I was very much impressed with the pro shop. It was very adequate in size and well-stocked. Also, George had two employees besides me, which was unusual in those days. Most clubs then had just the pro and one man to take care of the clubs. Being just a young kid from Texas, I was very nervous about this new situation, and knew I was most fortunate to be working for George. The others working for him were Ray Jamison, who came to be my assistant and who is still a good friend; and Jules the caddymaster, who also took care of the clubs and the whole back end of the shop. He and I also became good friends.

The next day, Mr. Jacobus and I went over my duties and my teaching methods. George was a good listener, and wanted me to go over my new way of playing golf with him quite thoroughly. I was very pleased to find he agreed with the changes I was making, and that encouraged me considerably. He gave me permission to teach my ideas to my students, who were mostly juniors and younger players, plus a few women and beginners.

I was told that I was always to look neat, which meant wearing a shirt and tie every day. And of course, it was most important to be polite to everyone at all times. Fortunately, thanks to my parents, I didn't have too much trouble with that job requirement. I learned a great deal from George about how to merchandise and promote new clubs, shoes, balls, and clothing—mostly sweaters and argyle socks. It stood me in good stead later in my career as a club pro.

The weather in New Jersey was still pretty cool when I arrived the first week in April. At that time, the Masters tournament was still played the last week in March, rather than the first full week of April as it is now. So it wasn't really spring just yet. In fact, there was a slight snowfall the second or third day after I got there. Still, some people were already playing golf.

I was anxious to play the course myself. Though I hadn't heard of Ridgewood before I met Mr. Jacobus, I learned that Tillinghast was a good architect, and knew the course would be a challenge for me to play and would help sharpen my game.

For the first few days, until I got used to my duties, I only had time to play a few holes by myself in the evenings when my chores were done. There were three nine-hole courses, East, West, and Center, with the East and West being more difficult than the Center course. Though there was water only on the first hole of the Center course, I found Ridgewood to be as difficult to play as Augusta National. The bentgrass greens were slick, much faster than what I was used to in Texas, where we had common bermuda grass then. The whole time I was at Ridgewood, my best score was a 68. But after the '39 Open, which I was fortunate to win, I went back and played an exhibition there and shot a 63. I was happy about that. I also got to see Ladies' Champion Virginia Van Wie and Glenna Collett play while I was there, which was a real treat.

I met Tillinghast shortly after my arrival, because he spent a lot of time at Ridgewood. And I got to know him quite well, though he didn't play a lot and I never played with him. I don't really remember what kind of a game he did play, but he intrigued me. He always wore a loose-fitting tweed jacket and smoked a pipe, and was always very friendly. Of course, I wasn't thinking anything about golf course design then, so I never talked to him about it. But I've now played quite a few of his courses, and his are always among the best, in my opinion.

After a while, I began to meet and play with some of the younger members of the club. I was surprised to see so much play as compared to Texarkana, and especially to see so many women playing. I had to confine practicing to my spare time, which there wasn't much of at first. There were quite a few caddies, though, and we were on very friendly terms right from the start, so some of them would shag balls for me, which was a great help. As for teaching, I did very little until the members got to know me and were willing to take a chance on a young kid with new ideas.

By the time I arrived at Ridgewood, I had developed the style of play which I still use today. I'd take the club straight back from the ball, not pronating as used to be necessary with the old hickory-shafted clubs. After talking with me and watching what I was doing and trying to do with my game, George grew to like my ideas. Eventually, he incorporated some of them into his teaching as well. He was most encouraging to young players, and that's how he helped me the most.

George, who was in his early forties at the time, had a wonderful ability to know his membership. He knew which ones liked to argue, and which ones had to be handled with kid gloves. His shop sold quite a lot of clubs, and also some clothing, which was just starting to be made specifically for golf at that time. But service was the most important thing we offered, by far.

As you might guess, the difference in accents between Texas and New Jersey is pretty noticeable, and I had a little trouble at first understanding people, though I suspect they had more trouble with my Texas twang. But they didn't kid me about it or tell me I ought to change, so I never did.

There were quite a few members I remember well, including Ashe Clarke, Max Kachie, and Ernie Thomas, but the one I played with the most often was Chet O'Brien. Chet was a nice-looking young man, married to a Broadway actress-dancer named Marilyn Miller. I was very impressed with how nicely he dressed—always wore handmade long-sleeved silk shirts and ties, and dressed well all the time. I complimented him several times, and he eventually took me to his tailors, Arco and McNaughton. He had them make me a pair of slacks in a sort of a gabardine called buckskin. Even back then, they were $60 a pair, but I got spoiled real fast, and went back to them often. Later, when I went to Inverness in Toledo, I went to a tailor named Fromme who made all my slacks for a number of years, from that same Arco and McNaughton pattern.

This may make me sound as if I cared too much about clothes, but that was one reason I decided I wanted to be on the Ryder Cup team. The 1935 matches were held at Ridgewood, so I got to be part of all the preparations for the event. Mr. Jacobus was very involved in selecting the team's wardrobes, of course, and when the players arrived and got all dressed in their uniforms, I thought they looked mighty sharp. They had British tan slacks, brown-and-white shoes, brown gabardine blazers, and tweed coats, tan and brown. Their golf bags all matched, too.

It got me to thinking about getting to be a good enough player to make the team. I wanted it as much for the clothes as anything else, but it gave me that much more motivation for working on my game. It was about then I told the caddies one day that I was going to be on the next Ryder Cup team. They laughed and told me, "Quit dreamin', Byron," and that was even more motivation.

I was very excited about meeting the team, because they were the leading U.S. and British players at the time. Paul Runyan, Craig Wood, Walter Hagen, Henry Picard, Olin Dutra, Johnny Revolta, Gene Sarazen, Percy Alliss, Alf Padgham—I did meet them, of course, but I'm sure that few of them were aware of me at all, and no reason why they should be, really. I was just another assistant pro to them. I was even more enthused about seeing them play for the first time. That was great. I watched nearly all the matches, and learned a lot from watching those wonderful golfers play. The United States, by the way, won 9–3.

So I began practicing harder, and one evening I had come back from the practice range with my 3-iron. Some of the caddies were outside the pro shop, and there was a flagpole about a hundred feet away, over toward the first tee of the Center course. The caddies challenged me to see if I could hit that flagpole from the slate terrace in front of the shop, and each of them put down a nickel or a dime—about fifty-five cents total.

Now, hitting a ball off a stone terrace sounds pretty tough, but I'd had plenty of practice with bare lies in Texas. My first shot, I tried to fade the ball, and missed the pole about six feet on the left. But I drew the second shot, and it was right on the money. I hit that flagpole nice as you please. The caddies were standing there with their mouths still open when I picked up my fifty-five cents and went home.

Right after the Ryder Cup matches was the PGA championship. That year it was at Twin Hills in Oklahoma City, and something new had been added—expense accounts. If you qualified for the tournament, you could get ten cents a mile, which was a nice incentive. I had to qualify at a course in New Jersey. The 18th hole was a par 4, and when I got there I had to par to qualify. I put my second shot in the bunker short of the green, bladed it over the green, and made bogey. Most of the reason I missed that bunker shot was I had gotten a special sand iron just for bunker play in the Open at Oakmont just before that, and never learned how to play with it, at Oakmont or anywhere else. But I had foolishly left it in my bag, and it was the only sand iron I had. Just a ridiculous mistake on my part.

I missed qualifying by one shot. I got rid of that so-called "special club" as fast as I could, and never saw it again, nor did I ever see that ten cents a mile that year. The worst part, though, was when I had to tell Louise I hadn't qualified. That made her cry, because it meant we'd have to borrow money from her father to come home. If I remember right, Johnny Revolta beat Tommy Armour in the finals of the PGA that year.

I've never been one to keep old clubs or trophies much. But one thing I do have is a small black notebook that I kept all my tournament records in. It begins in 1935, when I finished second in the Riverside (California) Pro-Am and won $125. It ends after the Masters in 1947, when I finished second again—and won $1500. In that little book I recorded tournament names, dates, my scores, whether I won anything, and what my caddie and entry fees were. In 1944, I expanded on this recordkeeping a bit, and it came in very handy in 1945—but more about that later.

My 1935 record wasn't very good. I was still having trouble putting four good rounds together, and my putting was hit-or-miss an awful lot of the time. Greens were so different then. They were very inconsistent, for one thing. Because local committees were in charge of the tournaments, there wasn't anyone to oversee course conditions everywhere and make sure fairways, roughs, and greens were the same all across the country.

Even in one tournament, the committee might have only half of the fairways watered. Or the greens might be watered one day and not the next, or watered on the front half and not the back. Of course, they used different types of grasses, too. Common bermuda in the south and southwest, and rye, poa annua, bluegrass, or bent in the north and east. They used a particular type of German bent at Oakmont, Inverness, and Merion that I never saw anywhere else. Each type of grass behaved differently. Some had more grain, some were slower, some grew faster—all of which made a big difference depending on what time of day you played.

So with different grasses on the greens and inconsistent watering, when it came to the short game, most of the pros worked on pitching and chipping, and very little on putting. Because it just didn't pay to spend a lot of time on putting. We concentrated more on getting our approach shots as close to the pin as possible.

My biggest triumph in 1935 was winning the New Jersey State Open that August. I won $400 plus another $40 for the Pro-Am. I played in quite a few local pro-ams around and won a few—though sometimes it was hardly worth the trouble. One I have in my black book says that I tied for first and won $10.40. That wasn't good money even then, but it did give me a chance to practice—and it never hurts to win.

My most memorable failure in '35 was my play in the U.S. Open at Oakmont—my first time to play in it. I had a miserable 315, though the course was hard and the winning score was only 299. It was really disappointing. But there's another reason I remember that Open so well, and it's a good one.

When I got home the first night after we got there, I'd just finished my first practice round, and hadn't been driving the ball as well as I thought I should. Not that the rest of my game was flawless—far from it. But my driving was the most inconsistent of all. In the past year, I'd bought four drivers, and probably spent more than I should have, since money was very scarce right then. In fact, we were so poor we were staying in the basement of a parsonage while I played in the Open, so you know we weren't doing too well financially.

Anyway, that evening, I sat with Louise after dinner and thought about my driving, while she did some needlework. Finally I said, "Louise, I need to buy another driver. I'm driving terrible." There wasn't any reaction from Louise for a couple of minutes. Then she put her work down and said, "Byron, we've been married over a year. I haven't bought a new dress or a new pair of shoes or anything for myself in all that time. But you've bought four new drivers, and you're not happy with any of them. One of two things—either you don't know what kind of driver you want, or you don't know how to drive."

Well, that stopped me in my tracks. Because there was no denying what she'd said was right. So the next morning, early, I took one of the drivers I had, a Spalding, to the shop there at Oakmont as soon as they opened, and went to work. Dutch Loeffler, the pro there for many years, was very kind and let me use whatever I needed.

Nearly all the drivers then were made with a completely straight face—same as when they had hickory shafts. That straight face worked all right when you pronated and didn't use your lower body at all, but with the steel shafts, it was very unsatisfactory. Now, I'd had in my mind for quite a while what a driver should really look like. So I began shaving off, very, very gradually, a slight bit off the toe of the club, then the heel, and kept that up till it had a nice little rounded face—what's called a "bulge." When I got it to looking exactly like that picture in my mind, I smoothed it off, put the finish on, and went out to play. And I never had any trouble with my driving after that, even though I didn't score very well in that particular Open.

Eventually, when I went to work for MacGregor, I had Kuzzy Kustenborder, head of their custom-made club department, make a persimmon driver to those specifications, and that was the driver I used from 1940 throughout the rest of my career. It's now in the World Golf Hall of Fame. Today, Roger Cleveland of Cleveland Golf Company makes a driver with my name on it that's an exact copy of the one I used to win nearly all my tournaments. But I guess I might still be looking for the perfect driver if it hadn't been for what Louise said to me back in 1935.

I played in thirty-one tournaments that year, won money in nineteen of them, and my scoring average was a little over 73. My winnings were $3,246.40. Then I had my $400 from Mr. Jacobus, and $1500 from Spalding for selling their equipment in the shop and playing their clubs. Total income: $5,146.40. Net profit: $1200.

In 1936, things started to get a little better. I remember meeting Bob Jones at the Masters that year, though I don't remember anything about the way I played. I think they had built Jones' cottage by then, and I do recall noticing that he was following me some as I played, probably in a practice round. It pleased me to realize he thought I was worth watching, knowing his record and his popularity. I tied for twelfth and won $50, which wasn't as good as what I did in '35, so I wasn't any too happy about it. Just made me more determined to get better, though.

When I got back to Ridgewood, the weather was bad. It rained quite often, which kept most people from coming out to play, so I got to practice a lot, and worked on my game real hard. It paid off, because all of a sudden I stopped having those terrible rounds. Not that I never played badly again, but I quit having two or three bad rounds in a row. To me, a bad round was a 74 or 75, because I felt the key to becoming a really fine player was consistently playing well, shooting par or better all four rounds. And I was getting there.

The third week in May, I won the Metropolitan Open at Quaker Ridge on Long Island, put on by the Metropolitan Golf Writers' Association. At that time, this was considered a very important tournament, though the prize money wasn't big, $1750 total. I felt very fortunate to win it, for which I got $750. The field was great—Craig Wood, Denny Shute, Horton Smith, Paul Runyan—all of the top pros, and I won by three shots. Where were Snead and Hogan? Well, it's surprising to some people, but Sam Snead didn't come on the tour till 1937, and though Ben Hogan had turned pro in 1930, two years before me, he never made it to stay until 1938.

In that Met Open, we had to play thirty-six holes the last day. We had so little money, I couldn't afford to stay at a hotel or anyplace, so I had to commute every day. Got up about four or five and drove two hours, then drove home at night. In fact, I barely had enough for gas and caddie fees, which were about $5 a day then. I also didn't have enough money to eat in the clubhouse, so, wearing my knickers, I sat outside and ate a hot dog and a Coke. We still have that picture, too. And the argyle socks I was wearing in that picture were one of two pair that Louise had knitted for me. They were the same pattern and color, the only good ones I had, and when I'd play in a tournament, I'd have to wash one pair at night and wear the other pair the next day, because it would take them nearly a day to dry.

After winning the Met Open, I had my first real interview. Oh, I'd been asked a few questions the year before when I beat Lawson Little in San Francisco, but this time, it was for real. The newspaperman was George Trevor, and he asked me all sorts of questions. I was unused to this sort of thing, but I was polite as I could be; I answered yes and no and yessir and nosir, but never explained anything. He wrote the next day, "This young man can really play, but he sure doesn't know how to talk." He had also noticed my argyle socks, thought I wore the same pair every day, and wrote that I was superstitious. That wasn't true, of course, but he never asked me about my socks, just about my golf.

It was right after the Met Open that I had my first opportunity to do an endorsement—but it was certainly a mixed blessing. The company that made a cigarette called 20 Grand asked me if I would do an ad for them. I wouldn't have to be smoking or even say that I smoked, simply say that I had read the report saying that the cigarettes were low in tar and so forth.

Well, I had never smoked and didn't believe in it. In fact, I'd been told from childhood that no one in the Nelson family ever smoked or drank, and while my parents never asked me to promise that I wouldn't, it was simply a matter of family pride as well as health with me. I knew that to play well, I had to be in the best possible condition at all times.

To be truthful, I wasn't comfortable with doing the ad at all, but even with the money from the Met Open, we were really struggling financially. So I said I would. They paid me $500 for a six-month contract, and since I'd had quite a lot of publicity already saying I didn't smoke or drink or carouse, I thought it would be all right.

But it wasn't. As soon as that ad appeared, I began getting letters from Sunday-school teachers and all sorts of people, telling me how I had let them down, that the young people really looked up to me and here I was, more or less saying that smoking was all right. It really upset me. I hadn't realized till then that people, especially young people, were already looking to me as a role model. I found it more true than ever what my parents had always told me—that whatever you did would have some influence on someone.

I talked to the 20 Grand people and told them I'd give the money back if they'd stop the ad, but they either couldn't or wouldn't. I promised the good Lord that if he'd forgive me I'd never let anyone else down and try to be a good example, and I've worked very hard at doing that.

As a result, people have given me quite a bit of credit for not smoking or drinking, but quite honestly, I never was tempted to do either one. Alcohol, even in a small amount, always had a bad effect on my system, so drinking didn't appeal to me any more than smoking did. I've probably had no more than a dozen drinks in my life—a glass of wine now and then, and once in a great while a vodka and tonic. But I never liked it and it never agreed with me, so I never enjoyed it.

Louise tried smoking once, though, and it happened about this same time. She and Harold McSpaden's wife Eva had become good friends, and Eva smoked. One day when we were all together, Eva asked Louise if she'd ever smoked. Louise said no, but decided she wanted to try it, and Eva gave her a cigarette. As soon as I saw her put it in her mouth, I said, "No, you don't," but she lighted it anyway, and I reached over and knocked the cigarette from her lips. I didn't touch her or hurt her in any way, but she was upset with me for doing it that way in front of Eva, and I can see why. Still, I made my point, and it would have been her right to do the same thing if I had been the one to light up.

As for drinking, I had one bad experience with it that taught me a good lesson. It was during the Miami Open in 1940, and I was leading going into the fourth round. There was a party that night, and someone talked me into having a glass of champagne. Since I wasn't used to alcohol, I didn't really like the taste, but I drank it and it didn't seem to bother me much, though I could feel it some.

The next morning, I was thirsty when I got up, probably because of the champagne, and I had a glass of water. Right away, I got to feeling what it must be like to be either really drunk or hung over. I felt very bad, and when I got to the course, I hadn't improved much. I was mad at myself for it, and it really affected my game. I shot a 38 on the front, which was just terrible. But I started to feel better on the back, and had a 32, so I managed to win by one stroke over Clayton Heafner. It was a good lesson, and fortunately not a very expensive one.

To get back to my skill at being interviewed, I must have improved some, because when I won the Open in '39, Trevor wrote, "Not only can Nelson play better—he's also learned how to talk." I guess I can thank Mr. Stanley Giles at Reading Country Club for quite a bit of that, and I'll tell you more about him later. However, I must say that when I first talked with Mr. Trevor, I was mesmerized by his appearance. He had one good eye and a pretty sorry-looking patch over the other one, plus he kept a pipe in his mouth all the time, and he wasn't just real careful about keeping his chin dry. I found myself staring at him, I'm afraid, instead of concentrating on answering his questions like I should have. But he was a wonderful golf writer, one who understood the game very well.

When I played in the '36 Open at Baltusrol, Paul Whiteman, the orchestra leader, was walking down the fairway with Louise and me and her sister, Delle, who was visiting us. Now there was of course a family resemblance between Delle and Louise, but to me it wasn't all that strong. Anyway, Paul looked at both of them and said, "How in the world do you tell them apart?" I replied, "I've never had any trouble." I didn't mean anything by it, but something about the way I said it kind of upset Delle a little, and she never did let me forget it. I still had a lot to learn about women, I guess.

My second-best finish in 1936 was at the General Brock Open in July. It was held on the Canadian side of Niagara Falls. I finished second and won $600. There we were, Louise and I, hundreds of miles from home, and the tournament committee decided to pay us in cash from the gate receipts. It was all in ones and fives and tens. We were so nervous about it, we stashed it in a dozen places all around the car that night till we could get home and put it in a bank. None of it was stolen, but we hid it so well that when we got home, we had an awful time trying to find it all. Fortunately, most all the tournaments paid by check, so we didn't have any more stories like that to tell.

Where they held the General Brock Open was such a small town, there was no place for people to stay, and we never had enough money then to stay in a nice hotel. We drove all over the place looking for a room, and finally in desperation Louise said, "Let's try the hotel."

Since it was the General Brock Hotel that was sponsoring the tournament, she thought they might have special rates for the players. Sure enough, she was right—$2 a night. The bad part was that it was awfully hot, and the rooms had little or no cross-ventilation. Everyone was buying fans and ice and trying to keep cool any way they could think of. Air conditioning had only just been invented, so we had to put up with the heat and like it, most of the time.

Besides finishing second and winning all that money, the General Brock Open was when I had my second big thrill in golf—playing with Walter Hagen. I was leading the tournament going into the final round, and I was paired with Hagen himself. Here he was, the golfer who'd once borrowed my cap when I was just a kid, and I was going to actually play golf with him. It was toward the end of his career, and he was more or less just making appearances by that time, but I still was very excited about it.

They didn't have any regulations about making your tee time back then, and Hagen was at least forty-five minutes late, which was a little unnerving. The tournament committee knew he was on his way to the course, but told me I had the right to play with a marker if I wanted to. But I thought it might be my only chance to ever play with Hagen, so I said I'd wait. He finally arrived, and never apologized for being late, but said to me on the first tee, "I see you've been playing pretty well." I said, "Thank you. I'm very pleased to get to play with you today." Hagen himself didn't play very well, but joked and laughed with the gallery as we went along.

But the waiting had done something to me, or else I was just nervous playing with such a great champion, and I shot an awful 42 on the front, gathered myself together, and had a 35 on the back, which meant I ended up second. I didn't have any bad feelings about Hagen or my decision to wait for him, though; it was worth it, and he really was a pleasure to play with. Besides, I should have had enough self-discipline to control myself and play my usual game. He had quite a bit of gallery, so between my fans and his, we had a good group. He never mentioned borrowing my cap all those years ago, and I didn't bring it up, knowing he would have forgotten all about it. It was a great growing experience for me, to learn that a so-called celebrity like Hagen was really just a nice person, as most such folks are.

In the fall of 1936, Louise and I drove back to Texarkana. She stayed with her folks while I went on a tour of the Pacific Northwest. I had to go alone, because we couldn't afford train fare for Louise. I took the train and rode in an upper berth all the way.

I played Vancouver, Victoria, Seattle, and Portland. In the first tournament, I'd been playing my irons beautifully, but not putting particularly well. In the last round, I hit the first five greens in a row, never farther than ten feet from the pin, and never made a single putt. I guess my frustration just got the better of me, because something just flashed over me, and I threw my putter up in some big old evergreen tree back of the green. I thought that putter never was going to come back down, but it finally did. There weren't any people there, so no one was in danger, but I was really ashamed of myself. Then all of a sudden I started making birdies, one right after the other, shot 66, tied with Jimmy Thompson for first money, and won $975. Ken Black, an amateur who was the son of the pro at the club, won the tournament.

During the last two rounds, I had been paired with Horton Smith, who was about ten years older than me, and who took it upon himself to help the younger players learn the ropes on the tour. He never said a word when I threw my putter, but after the round, he said he wanted to take me to dinner that night. We ate at the hotel, and had a real nice meal. Then when we were about finished, Horton said, "Byron, I'd like to talk to you about throwing your putter today. I know you're a nice young man and you know you shouldn't have done that."

I said, "I know, it was terrible. I've never done anything like that before, and I promise I'll never do it again." Well, Horton talked to me a little bit about how being a professional golfer meant being a gentleman all the time, obeying the rules and etiquette of the game and such. Then he kind of smiled at me and said, "But you know, if you hadn't thrown that putter, I don't think you would have shot sixty-six!"

This Pacific Northwest tour drew all the top players—Harry Cooper, Ralph Guldahl, Jimmy Thomson, and Al Zimmerman, as well as Horton. My winnings in those four tournaments, plus what I'd won in the Western and St. Paul Opens, totaled nearly $2500 in just six weeks. After that, I never looked back.

The day after the Seattle tournament, I went out on a yacht for the first time and caught my first salmon. We ate it right on deck, and I still think that was the best-tasting fish I ever had. I've never been much of a fisherman, though, except for a couple of other salmon-fishing trips like that one. I'm not a good sailor, for one thing, but mainly, it's just that fishing's too quiet for me.

At this point, my game was really going well. I liked the flight of my ball and the way it landed softly, with no hook. Even with the smaller British ball, which was harder to control, I could do it. Now, instead of having two or three good rounds out of four, I was playing four good rounds each time. I was achieving the consistency that I needed, and I never changed my grip, my swing, or my game after that.

Following that Pacific Northwest trip, Louise and I stayed in Texarkana with her folks, where we fortunately didn't need to pay room and board. Then we started on the tour in California right after the Christmas holidays. My little black book says that in 1936 I won money in twenty-four out of twenty-seven tournaments, at a time when most tournaments paid only ten or fifteen places, and some of them less than that.

My total winnings for 1936 were $5,798.75. My salary and Spalding bonus and lesson fees added to that brought my annual income total to $7,898.75. I don't know what my net profit was that year, but I hope it was better than the year before. Because we weren't exactly in high cotton.

FIVE

Reading and Some Major Wins

In January of 1937 I tied for ninth in the L.A. Open and won $75. I wasn't quite as happy with that sum as I was back at the Texarkana Open in '32, I can tell you. Next, I tied for seventeenth at Oakland, out of the money, then I finished sixth at Sacramento and won $140. That was kind of the way it went. One week I'd do all right, the next they hardly knew I was there.

At the San Francisco Match Play Tournament, though, I met a fellow who'd just turned pro, a fellow my age from Virginia, name of Sam Snead. I played him in the first round and beat him 2 and 1, but even then, I figured he'd always be someone to contend with. What a smooth swing Sam always had—looked like he'd never worked at it at all.

I look at my scores for that winter tour, and they're kind of interesting. Most of them are in the low 70's, but then in the tournaments where I won some money, there'd be a 66 or a 68. So I was getting a little better and learning to play under different kinds of conditions in different parts of the country.

See, we'd start in California, play four tournaments there, then drive to either Houston or San Antonio (in '37 it was Houston), to

Thomasville, Georgia, then to Florida for four events there. Next, it was Charleston for their Open, and after that the North and South, which was always played at Pinehurst. This time I did better, finishing third and winning $500.

At this point, I'd played in twelve tournaments and had won about $1800—not a very good average, especially considering expenses. I was looking forward to getting back to my job at Ridgewood in April. I wanted to work on my game more and get closer to my goal of being consistent.

However, back in February, Mr. Jacobus had called and told me he'd been contacted by Stanley Giles, president of Reading Country Club in Reading, Pennsylvania. The club was looking for a head golf pro. Besides being club president, Mr. Giles was head of the committee to find a new pro, so he'd called George. He wanted a young man who gave promise of being a good player as well as a good teacher, someone who also knew how to conduct the business of a golf shop. In those days, running a shop well was more important to most clubs than whether or not the pro was winning tournaments.

Of course, all the time I was at Ridgewood, I wasn't just working on my game, because no one could make a living playing golf then. You had to have a club job. So I was also learning how to be a head pro at a good club. I'd had a lot of good experience under George, and I was definitely interested in the Reading job, because the main reason for working for someone else at a fine club was to eventually get a club of your own. I'd done a lot of teaching and my game was getting better. In short, I felt I was ready.

So, with a good reference from Mr. Jacobus, I drove to Reading from Pinehurst, which was about a three-hour drive, and had an interview with Mr. Giles. I could see he really knew what he wanted in a golf pro. Somehow, I convinced him I could fill the requirements he had, so we signed a contract. It was about two weeks before the Masters in '37, and I was guaranteed $3750 per year, plus whatever I could make from the shop and my lessons. That was considerably more than I was making at Ridgewood. It certainly looked as if we wouldn't have to borrow any more money from Louise's folks.

Naturally I was all excited about having a club of my own, so when I went to Augusta to play in my third Masters, I was high as a kite. That may be part of the reason why I played as well as I did. But

I also had a practical reason for wanting to play well. I didn't have any money to buy things for my shop at Reading. Ralph Trout was going to be my assistant there, and he would have my shop open by the time I got back from Augusta, so I needed to be able to stock it with new merchandise as quickly as I could.

With all the adrenalin flowing about my new job and playing the Masters for the third time, I managed to win it, with a great opening round of 66 and a great last round on Sunday. That 66 stood as the best opening-round score by a Masters champion for thirty-nine years, until Raymond Floyd topped me in 1976 with his 65.

Though the Masters was already considered a major tournament in the golf world in '37, none of us had any idea it would get to be as popular as it is today. To think of all these people today trying every way to get tickets, when back then they maybe charged $3 and hardly had enough gallery to count—well, it sure is quite a change. And in most ways I think it's good.

Getting back to that 66, though, it was the best I'd ever played any golf course in my life, tee to green. I hit every par 5 in two, every par 4 in two, and every par 3 in one, for 32 strokes. Add 34 putts to that—pretty average putting, really—and you have an easy 66. I was paired with Paul Runyan that round. He called himself Pauly, and I remember he'd talk to himself quite a bit. "Hit it, Pauly," or "Pauly, you sure messed up on that one." But I wasn't really paying a whole lot of attention to him. I was concentrating real well that day.

We were staying at the Bon-Air Hotel then, a large hotel with a big foyer. The dining room was just off the foyer, and when I came down for breakfast that first morning, there was a lady in the foyer demonstrating a Hammond organ. She was playing soft, quiet music, mostly waltzes like "The Blue Danube." I listened to her play for about thirty minutes while I ate, and never really thought much about it. But my rhythm was so good that day, I later thought listening to that waltz tempo might have had something to do with it. Funny, because I don't really like organ music.

In the second round, I shot even par 72, and in the third, 75. I'd now lost the lead. In the fourth round, I was still faltering—shot a 38 on the front nine, leaving me three strokes behind Ralph Guldahl. Walking down to the tenth hole, someone in the gallery told me Guldahl had already birdied the tenth. That meant I had to birdie it too, or

I'd be 4 back with eight holes to go. I put my second shot on the green about fifteen feet from the hole and made it. I was paired with Wiffy Cox, the pro at Congressional in Washington, D.C. When I sank that putt, he said, "Kid, I think that's the one we needed."

I parred 11, and next was the wonderful, difficult 12th hole, one of the most famous par threes in the country. Rae's Creek runs diagonally across the front of the green—on television, it looks like it's straight across, but it's not. If the pin's on the right, it plays one club longer. And with that Amen Corner wind, it's always a tricky shot, no matter where the pin is.

Standing on the tee, I saw Guldahl drop a ball short of the creek, which meant he'd gone in the water from the tee. If he got on and 2-putted, he'd have a 5. Watching his misfortunes, I suddenly felt like a light bulb went off in my head, like the fellow you see in the cartoons when he gets a brilliant idea. I realized then that if I could get lucky and make a 2, I'd catch up with Guldahl right there. Fortunately, I put my tee shot six feet from the hole with a 6-iron into the wind, and holed it. So now I was caught up, with six holes to go.

The 13th hole is a very famous par 5. I hit a good drive down the center of the fairway, just slightly on the upslope. I saw Ralph fooling around on the front of the green, and learned he'd made a 6. There was water in a ditch that runs just in front of the green, and there were a lot of rocks in it. Once in a while, if your ball landed in the right place, you could play out of it, but that day, Ralph didn't have any luck.

The green then had a real high left side, up on a ridge, making the left side much higher than the right. It's been changed since then. The pin that day was on that high left side. Waiting to play my shot, I knew I'd have to play a 3-wood to reach the green. If I played safe and got on in three, I'd probably make a 5, or could even make a 4. That would put me in the lead by one shot, but I knew that wasn't enough. So I said to myself, "The Lord hates a coward," and I simply tried to make sure my ball didn't go off to the right and into the water. I pulled it slightly, and it stopped just off the green, about twenty feet from the hole. I chipped in for a 3, which made me feel pretty good, because I was now three strokes ahead of Ralph.

I parred fourteen, then got on fifteen in 2 and three-putted for par. Guldahl had made a 4 at fifteen, and we both parred in after that, so I won by two shots, with a 32 on the back nine. That 32 did more for my career at that time than anything, because I realized my game could stand up under pressure, and I could make good decisions in difficult circumstances.

There was no green jacket then, but I got a great thrill out of winning, especially after leading, losing the lead, and finishing strong. The other thing that pleased me was having Bob Jones present me with the gold medal. He was the "King of Golf" then, so that was a real thrill. As I recall, Clifford Roberts and Jones made a few remarks each, and then presented medals to the first- and second-place players. And that was it.

I still have that medal, and when my playing career was over, I looked back and realized that was the most important victory of my career. It was the turning point, the moment when I realized I could be a tough competitor. Whenever someone asks me which was the most important win of all for me, I never hesitate. It was the 1937 Masters, the one that really gave me confidence in myself.

You know, in the early days of the Masters, it was the most enjoyable tournament to go to in the whole country, from the players' point of view. The tournament was small enough, and with the smaller number of players, you got to enjoy a lot of wonderful Southern hospitality. Every year, several members would host an early evening party, with country ham and all the trimmings. Everyone felt free and easy, and we all had a wonderful time. There was a black quartet that sang each year. They'd go to wherever the party was, and that was the entertainment. They were mighty good. But as the tournament grew, it got too big for folks to have parties for all the players. It wasn't done at all after the war.

Because the tournament was so small then, there were only a couple of hotels in Augusta. It was a small town and didn't have much going on the rest of the year. So even then it was difficult to find a place to stay. It wasn't too long before people began renting out their homes to pros and others who might want to entertain friends, customers, and so forth during Masters week.

Louise was there all week. She wasn't at the medal ceremony afterwards—wives were never included in such things then. But she was at the course, and up around the clubhouse. Wives then didn't follow their husbands much. Most of them didn't play golf at all, and the women dressed up more then than they do now, so it was difficult to walk such a hilly course.

Many people have wondered how I got the nickname "Lord Byron." Well, O.B. Keeler was a sportswriter for the *Atlanta Journal* and also for the Associated Press. He had one stiff knee but still went out and watched the play so he would know what questions he wanted to ask—he didn't just wait in the clubhouse for players to come in and talk to them afterwards. After I won in '37, he interviewed me in the upstairs locker room that the pros used during the tournament. Things had kind of quieted down by then, and he said, "Byron, I watched you play the back nine today, and it reminded me of a piece of poetry that was written by Lord Byron when Napoleon was defeated at the battle of Waterloo." We did the rest of the interview then, and the next day, the headline in his article for the Associated Press read, "Lord Byron Wins Masters," and the nickname stuck. Oddly enough, I was sort of named for Lord Byron, who unfortunately was not an admirable man and drank himself to death at a very young age. But my grandmother Nelson had liked Lord Byron's poetry, and she named my father John Byron. I was named John Byron, Jr. when I was born, but dropped the John and Jr. when I was twenty, and I've had good luck ever since then.

It wasn't too hard going off to Reading after that great week in Augusta. All we'd had in Ridgewood were our clothes, no furniture or anything, so all our personal belongings were in our car. Since I'd left Ridgewood in the fall of '36 and played the winter tour in California, then the spring in Florida and the Carolinas, we hadn't been back to New Jersey. But when George Jacobus heard the news, he called to congratulate me. It sure was good to hear from him and realize I'd come quite a ways from when I first arrived in New Jersey just two years before.

My first impression of Reading was quite a bit different, since by now I'd been to New Jersey and New York. It was a bigger city than Texarkana, of course, but not anything like Ridgewood. Reading sits in the foothills of the Blue Mountains, southeast of the Appalachians, and that means coal mining country. The roads were narrow and hilly, so the traffic was pretty slow. The weather was different, too—lots of lightning storms, which took some getting used to. Besides the coal industry, there were several large textile mills in Reading, including Berkshire Mills.

The people were more reserved than at Ridgewood, mostly Pennsylvania Dutch. But once they decided to take you in, they were very warm and hospitable. They loved desserts, and I remember we'd go to play bridge of an evening at someone's home, and afterward they'd have what amounted to a full, heavy meal, complete with several desserts. I'd really have to watch it not to gain weight.

I have to admit, at first we weren't very impressed with Reading, but once we got to know the people and their ways, we had a very good time. In fact, when we left for Inverness in '39, it was the first time Louise had cried over such a thing since she'd left Texarkana. Mrs. Giles, the wife of the club president, was especially nice to Louise and me. She'd have us over to dinner and they'd play bridge with us several nights a week, and my, she was a good cook. She was quiet, easy, didn't play golf but did all the usual housewifely things and did them very well. Mrs. Giles died in the summer of '92, at the age of ninety-nine, and I was fortunate to have had a good visit with her two years earlier.

The Reading clubhouse itself was done in English Tudor style, and was quite impressive. The course was fine—not as good as the Tillinghast design at Ridgewood, but very adequate. It had small greens, and while not really hilly, was quite rolling. I found out quickly that I wouldn't have as much time to play and practice, because my responsibilities were quite a bit different from Ridgewood, since I was the only pro and did all the teaching. One big difference was that Reading had no practice range or practice bunkers. I used to use the bunker on the ninth green, next to the clubhouse, for my sand practice. Mr. Giles was kind enough to give me permission to do that. But he was the only one I ever had to get permission from—I never had to go to a committee or anything like that.

They had to replace the sand in that bunker at least four times while I was there because I practiced so much. I got to where I could hit the ball out and deliberately spin it back in. And Mr. Giles used to get me to demonstrate that shot to his friends.

A few days after we arrived, Mr. Giles called me and said, "I've got a Rotary Club luncheon this afternoon, and I want you to go with me and give a talk."

"Give a talk?" I said, scared to death. "Mr. Giles, I don't know anything about giving a talk. I've never done anything like that in my life." I started crawfishing any way I could, trying to get out of it. But he said, "All you have to do is tell them how you won the Masters." I replied, "I shot the lowest score." He laughed and said, "Here's how we'll do it. You'll get up and tell them everything you can think of about how you won—the shots you hit on the last nine, and all that. Then when you run out of things to say, I'll be sitting right next to you, and I'll ask you questions and keep it going." So that was what we did, and it worked out fine.

Since that day, I've given more "talks" than I could count, and now people tell me what a good job I do. But if it hadn't been for Mr. Giles, I don't know that I'd ever have gotten started.

Another story about Mr. Giles concerns his golf, not mine. He was the most consistent 83–85 shooter I ever saw. He just never varied hardly at all above 85 or below 83. He had a good short game, and he was pretty good with his irons, but never could hit a wood very well—especially off the tee. He'd hit this little old pecky slice about 150 yards down the fairway every time. Just never could play his woods very well at all.

Well, he'd watched me play for quite a few months at Reading, and one day he told me, "Byron, if I could drive like you, I'd eat your lunch." I just looked at him and smiled a little and said, "You think so, Mr. Giles?" He said, "I sure could. If I had your drives, I'd just beat you all to pieces!"

I thought about it for a few days, then I called him. "Mr. Giles, I've been thinking about what you said the other day, and I've got a game worked out for us. We'll each hit our drives, then we'll switch balls, and play to the hole." You could feel him smiling into the phone. He said, "I can't get there quick enough!"

So he got a couple of his buddies and we played. But he didn't know he was playing right into my hands, because my long irons were about the best part of my game right then. I have to admit that playing his drives, I was on parts of the golf course I'd never seen before, and my score went up a few strokes. But his score didn't come down quite enough, so I beat him.

He couldn't believe it. We played that way two more times, and he never got below 77, while I never went above 75. After the third match, he'd had enough, and he told me, "If I'd been a betting man, I'd have bet a thousand dollars that I could beat you using your drives!"

And $1000 then was a lot of money, so I was glad he didn't bet it. He was a good sport about it, though.

The biggest surprise about Reading was the number of row houses. Being from the wide-open spaces out West, I was used to freestanding homes, so it was a little difficult, getting used to living that close to our neighbors. We rented a corner row house from a family named Corbitt. John Corbitt was the local Studebaker dealer, and he and his family moved out, come June, to their summer home on the Schuylkill River, where it was much cooler.

Since we'd arrived the first of April, we lived in the Berkshire Hotel until May 1. While we were living in the hotel, waiting for the Corbitts to move to their summer home, Mrs. Giles practically adopted us, realizing it was difficult for both of us, and especially for Louise. Then, after we moved into the Corbitts' home, Mr. Giles kept us in fresh cut flowers the entire time we were there. One of the best things about living in the Corbitts' home was that years before, they had befriended a young Polish Catholic girl, Josephine Brynalrski, who lived there and did the cooking and housekeeping. Her room was on the third floor, and Louise and Josephine became very good friends during our time in Reading. Josephine also had a job as a waitress in a fine restaurant in Reading, so her cooking was very good, too.

The Corbitts would move back to town in mid-September, but we didn't leave for Texarkana till a little bit later. So back we'd go to the Berkshire Hotel for a few more weeks. On the first floor of the hotel were the offices of the Reading Auto Club, of which Mr. Giles was president, in addition to his floral business. So I got to see quite a bit of him during our hotel stays.

At Reading I got to teach players at all levels. One family, the Lutzes, was especially interesting. Mr. Lutz owned one of the leading mortuaries in Reading and had three young children—a son, Buddy, ten years old and two daughters, twelve and fifteen. Mr. Lutz was a pretty fair businessman golfer who loved to play and wanted his children to play too. He came to me one day and said, "If you can teach them to play, Byron, I'll buy each of them a set of clubs plus pay for all their lessons." That was certainly a good incentive for me to work hard with those children.

Now Buddy was a total beginner, but he caught on quickly, and his twelve-year-old sister was coming along pretty well, too. I started her with just a 7-iron and graduated on up, and she was getting the ball airborne all right. But the older girl, I never could get her to progress at all. This went on for quite a while, as the children were taking a lot of lessons because it was summer and they were all out of school. Well, Mr. Lutz came out one day and asked, "How are my children doing, Byron?" I told him, "Mr. Lutz, Buddy and your younger girl are doing quite well, but I haven't made any progress at all with your older daughter, and I feel ashamed." He smiled at me and said, "Do you want me to tell you what the problem is?" I said, "I sure do, because maybe I can correct it." He answered, "No, I don't think you can because it's your blue eyes—that's all she ever talks about!" I was amazed, because I'd had no idea anything like that was going on in that young girl's mind while I was trying to teach her how to play golf. So that was the end of that, but I did sell two sets of clubs, anyway, and in all the teaching I've done, that was the only time anything like that ever happened.

Obviously, when it came to women, I still had a lot to learn, and my next lesson in this area came from Ann Metzger, a lady in her mid-forties who was married to a dentist at the club, Dr. Paul Metzger. I had been working with Mrs. Metzger a little while and making some progress, but not getting her to do the things I really wanted her to do. I felt bad about it because she was nice and her husband was a pretty good player. Mrs. Metzger was a rather buxom lady, and one day she saw Louise and told her, "Louise, I've been taking a lot of lessons from your husband, and we're not getting very far. I wish you'd explain to him how we women are made, because I get in my own way and that's why I can't swing the way he wants me to!" So Louise gave me the message, and the next time I saw Mrs. Metzger I said, "I'm going to change my procedure today. From now on I want you to stick your back end out further, bend over a little more, and take your arms out a little further away from your body." She looked at me and said, "Louise must have talked to you," and I said, "Yes, she did." Fortunately, I was able to help her a lot after we'd gotten around the anatomy question, so to speak.

As the only pro, I was more restricted on how many tournaments I could play in, as well as not having as much time to practice and play at the club. I only had one boy in the shop to clean clubs on weekends. Fortunately, I didn't need to do much teaching on weekends, because that's when most of the men played. Also, we had "doctors' day" on Wednesdays. I remember Dr. Mike Penta, who was such an avid golfer that he took lessons from me twice a week—at sunrise. And there was Dr. Metzger and his wife, Ann. They were both good golfers. She followed me in all the local tournaments I played in, and walked down the fairway with the other folks in the gallery. When I'd get a little tense, she'd get up alongside me and just say, "Smile." That's all. And of course, when you smile, it relaxes the muscles in your face, and somehow it would help me relax with my game and play better, too.

My second win that first year at Reading was the International Match Play Championship in Boston at Belmont Springs that fall. Actually, though the Masters was considered more important and the Belmont Match Play doesn't exist anymore, I won quite a bit more money for that—$3000, according to my records. After qualifying with 141, I played John Levinson; he was a left-hander, but quite good. That match had kind of a strange ending. I was one down going to eighteen, and I hit a long drive down onto a gravel road that crossed the fairway. A spectator picked up my ball and threw it backwards several yards onto the fairway. The rule was that you could get relief from the gravel and drop back, but the official naturally and correctly ruled that I had to drop it myself, which I did. I ended up making par, while Levinson bogeyed. I then eagled the first extra hole to win the match 1 up. That seemed to help my game all of a sudden come together, and I went on to beat Frank Walsh 1 up, Lloyd Mangrum 2 up, Charlie Lacey 5 and 4, Harry Cooper 5 and 4, and Henry Picard 5 and 4 in the final. I remember it was one of the few times Dad Shofner ever got to come and see me play, and he became interested in watching Ralph Guldahl, who was known for being a slow player. Mr. Shofner told me later that it took Ralph five full minutes to play a shot. Anyway, I was very happy to win with Dad Shofner there, because by now, he knew for sure he hadn't made a mistake loaning me that money in Texarkana.

The funny thing about the whole tournament was that I hadn't planned on playing in it at all. Harold McSpaden, who was the pro at Winchester in Boston, had called and begged me to come; he even let Louise and me stay with him and Eva. I hadn't been playing very well and was awfully busy at the club, but I decided to go anyway. Like I've said before, you just never know . . . .

Also, I was medalist in the PGA Championship qualifying at Pittsburgh Field Club, which back then was played at the end of May. I was determined to qualify, because I'd missed by one stroke the year before. Then I kept going—beat Leo Diegel, Craig Wood, and Johnny Farrell before losing in the quarterfinals to Ky Laffoon, all of which netted me $200. The course had very high, very dense rough. I drove the ball straight most of the time, but when I got in that rough, I used a small-headed wood called a cleek, with extra lead in the head, to play out. I'd bought it specifically because of the rough there, and most of the other players had one like it.

It was a 36-hole qualifier—eighteen in the morning, eighteen in the afternoon. The course was interesting. You drove off the first tee into a valley, then played the entire course in that valley till the 18th. The fairway going up to the 18th green was so steep, there was a rope tow for the players to use, and by the time we'd played thirty-six holes, we weren't too embarrassed to use it, either. The photo that was taken of me for being the medalist in that qualifier is a good one, if I do say so, and it's when we still were wearing shirts and ties to play. I often wonder what it would be like for the boys today, playing in those kinds of clothes and conditions.

To back up a bit, it wasn't too long after the Masters that I learned I had been chosen for the Ryder Cup team. Boy howdy, was I excited. I'd never even been outside the United States before. I didn't think it was possible that the dream I'd had just two years before at Ridgewood could be coming true already. The PGA of America picked the team then, and they didn't keep any long-term, detailed records like they do now. They didn't pick anyone who wasn't playing well, naturally. But of course, if you won a major, that did have some effect on their decision, and so I was selected.

There were a few on our team who'd never played in a Ryder Cup before—myself, Snead, Ed Dudley. So we were inexperienced to some degree, and we also knew that the Americans had never beaten the British on their own soil before. But Walter Hagen would be our captain—that really was a thrill.

First, though, I had to see what I could do in the National Championship—what everyone now calls the U.S. Open. I did much better than in '35 and '36—finished tied for seventeenth, according to my black book, and won $50. The tournament was at Oakland Hills in

Birmingham, Michigan, a very tough course. Naturally, I wasn't thrilled with my performance, but I already had my mind on the trip to England.

Toward the end of June, Louise and I rode to New York with Mr. and Mrs. Giles, and met all the other fellows and their wives there. The PGA threw a big party for us before we left on the USS *Manhattan* the next day, June 24. I was kind of worried about the crossing, because I was a poor sailor. I'd only been out on a small boat on a lake once or twice in my life and it disagreed with me. Even swinging on a porch swing could make me queasy. So I wasn't looking forward to this part of the trip.

But as it happened, the ocean was smooth as a millpond the entire six days out. The captain himself, a veteran of twenty years' sailing, said he'd never seen it that calm. That made me feel quite a bit better, having that ocean trip go so well. The trip back was another story.

When we arrived in England, we were met by the British contingent—the Royal and Ancient representatives. Our accommodations were comfortable but not luxurious, adequate for the team and their wives, six of whom went along.

There's nothing as exciting in golf as playing for your country. In the first matches, we played a Scotch foursome, alternating shots. One player would drive on the odd holes, the other on the evens. Hagen had paired Ed Dudley and me against Henry Cotton and Alf Padgham, the reigning British Open champion. Hagen came to me before the match and said, "Byron, you've got a lot of steam, a lot of get-up-and-go. And Dudley needs someone to push him. So I'm going to put you two together. You can get him fired up."

We were unknowns in England, so the headline in the paper the next morning said, HAGEN FEEDS LAMBS TO THE BUTCHER. Well, we did get steamed up over that. I drove against Cotton all day, and on the par threes, I put my ball inside his every time, and we ended up winning the match. The next day, the headline read THE LAMBS BIT THE BUTCHER. It was a great thrill to win, especially against a player like Cotton.

The weather for the matches was fine except for the last day, when it turned terrible. Cold, windy, drizzly. And pros weren't as welcome at these clubs as they are now. We were just barely allowed in the locker room, and our wives weren't allowed in the clubhouse at all.

There they were, standing outside, freezing, all six of them huddled together, trying to stay out of the wind, when the mayor's wife saw them. She had enough compassion to invite them all into the clubhouse, and because she was the mayor's wife, no one could say no to her. Then she served them some 200-year-old port, and they warmed up quickly after that. They said later they'd never tasted anything as good as that port in all their lives.

Fortunately, despite the bad weather, we held on to win, 8 to 4. It was the first time we'd ever defeated the British on their home ground. It made all of us feel proud, especially since we weren't used to playing the type of golf courses they had at Southport and Ainsdale.

The next week, we went north to Scotland for the British Open at Carnoustie. The gallery walked with us there, just like in the U.S., and in the first practice round, I was walking along with my driver under my arm, when a fellow accidentally tripped me. I landed crooked because of having the driver tucked under my arm, and hurt my back pretty bad. In fact, I didn't think I'd be able to play at all. But the local people found me someone like a modern chiropractor, and he worked on me quite a while, using some strong liniment, and I was okay in a couple of days.

Carnoustie was a very different course from what I'd seen before. In the driving areas, even if you were a long hitter, you'd have to go right or left to avoid the bunkers in the middle of nearly every fairway. The bunkers had high lips, too, but at least they were clearly visible from the tee. And there was this small creek, called a "burn," that wandered through the course.

Carnoustie used to be one of the seven courses in the rotation for the British Open, but some years ago they had to take it out, because there simply wasn't room for all the people and the cars and so forth, golf had gotten so big. I understand they're trying to do something about that now, because it's a fine course and it would be good to see the Open played there again.

It was normal Scottish weather, cold, windy, and damp. In the third round, it turned worse, but I shot a 71 and came from way back to third place, with Cotton in the lead. The final round I shot 74, finished fifth, and won $125. Our boat tickets came to $1020, plus I'd lost a month out of the summer in the shop with both the Ryder Cup and the British, so you can see why we didn't play in the British Open much back then. The PGA did cover some of our expenses, but I lost $700–$800 out of my own pocket. For the same reasons, the British players weren't able to play in our Open much, either.

Those British galleries—they were much different from Americans. They really knew their golf, and they'd applaud only for a really marvelous shot. If you hit an iron or chipped up eight or ten feet from the hole, they wouldn't make a sound. But a difficult pitch or a long iron to within a few feet or inches, they'd really appreciate that.

All in all, we had a very good time, and we were elated when we climbed back on that boat. It was a good thing, too, because the crossing coming home was bad. Most of the passengers stayed in bed nearly half the trip, it was so rough. And if we hadn't won, it would hardly have been worth it.

The food on our trip was also very different from what I was used to, and I'm afraid I can't say it was very good. There was a lot of mutton and a lot of thick porridge. About the only things I liked were the tea and cookies.

There was an even bigger party for us when we returned to New York, and though it had been a great experience to play in the Ryder Cup and the British Open, we were sure glad to get back to our home in Reading and return to a more normal life. I played very few other tournaments that summer, because I'd lost so much time out of my shop with the Ryder Cup trip.

An interesting sidelight to my time in Reading was the change in how club members saw the club professional. Louise and I played bridge and went to parties at the homes of several of the members. This was kind of a transition time for club pros, because up till then they were considered more in the lower working class. But we had quite a busy social life in Reading, and made many good friends during our stay. Of course, it didn't hurt that I'd won the Masters before I arrived and the Open a few months before I left.

One of my more interesting experiences as a teacher at Reading was with a young lady named Betty Pfeil. Her mother made an appointment for me to give Betty a lesson, and before I ever met Betty or her mother, several people had told me that Betty had the makings of a good player if someone could teach her not to overswing.

Well, Betty and Mrs. Pfeil came out for the lesson, and I watched Betty swing for a good forty-five minutes, talked to her a little about this or that part of her game, but never mentioned anything about overswinging. When I was done, her mother asked me why, and I said, "Mrs. Pfeil, Betty doesn't overswing. She's extremely supple, and she doesn't lose the club at the top or move her head, so she's not overswinging." That seemed to give Betty more confidence in her game, and she went on to be quite a good player. Won the Pennsylvania State Amateur several times, I believe.

Another fine woman player I became acquainted with while I was at Reading was Glenna Collett. She lived in Philadelphia, and though she was several years older than I, she liked to watch me play, so she'd come see me in quite a few local tournaments. I got to see her play quite often, too, and she was the finest woman golfer I'd ever seen at that time. Now, she couldn't have beaten Babe Zaharias or Mickey Wright or the good modern women pros, but she was a fine player, with a beautiful swing—and no one can argue with her record. In Glenna's day, it was still "ladies' golf," not women's golf as it became later and is today, and the ladies then didn't have the strength or the distance they developed later on.

In the fall of '37, I was invited along with Denny Shute and Henry Picard, who had played with me on the Ryder Cup team, to go to Argentina to do a series of exhibitions and play in the Argentine Open. Louise and I went back to Texarkana before the trip, and I worked steadily on my game. There was no one around to bother me and I wasn't working there, so I had the practice area all to myself most of the time. I shagged balls for myself, and just kept refining my swing and working on my short game. Don Murphy, the pro who had come in after me, would come out sometimes and we'd talk about the golf swing. He taught pretty much what I was doing. He continued there till he retired a few years ago, and now is pro emeritus. A good man.

We were in Texarkana for about a month before we flew to Argentina. Folks today would find this hard to believe, but it took, by actual count, seven days to fly there. We flew a combination of DC-3's and PBY's—planes that would land and take off on water. We'd start early each day and stop about the middle of the afternoon, because none of the airports or water landing areas had any lights or radar.

With those PBY's, when we'd take off, they'd have a speedboat go out ahead of us and create a wake for us to take off on. And you'd land between these floating logs they'd anchored on the water. It wasn't the most enjoyable thing, believe me. In fact, looking back on that trip, I'd say aviation has improved since then even more than golf!

The worst part of the trip down was going through the mountains. That was something, flying through the Andes in a cabin that wasn't pressurized, at 23,000 feet or more. The plane was dipping and shifting in the wind currents like a blue darter looking for a bug, and we had to take oxygen through these tubes you held in your mouth. Denny Shute got terribly sick, but it didn't seem to bother me much at the time. Years later, when I began to fly for ABC and found I would just about get the shakes every time, I realized that experience in '37 really had affected me. I finally had to go see a hypnotist—Dr. Charles Wysong, brother to Dr. Dudley Wysong, whose son now plays some on the Senior Tour. His office was in McKinney, Texas, and he cured me in about a half-dozen sessions. I've never had any more trouble with it.

Anyway, the airline had made advance hotel reservations for us, which helped. The mosquitoes were so bad that the beds had mosquito netting all around them, or we never would have gotten much sleep. A Mr. Armstrong of Armour Meat Packing Company had arranged the whole trip; he also made sure our meals were set up ahead of time. I believe he was the head man for Armour in Buenos Aires. We had very good food in Argentina, and as you might expect, wonderful steaks much of the time.

It took us a week to get there. We were there a month, and spent another week getting back. We were paid our expenses plus $1500—and nothing for the two weeks of travel time. We played in a couple of small tournaments, the Argentine Open and another match play event. I didn't negotiate the greens very well—they were stiff and wiry—so I didn't score well at all.

One interesting thing happened during one of those exhibitions—a plague of locusts. The air was so thick with them that every time you swung a club, you'd kill six or seven of them and have to wipe off the club before you could hit again. Kind of upset your stomach, really. You could hardly see for all the locusts in the air, plus you'd crunch dozens of them under your feet when you walked. We played three holes before they finally called a halt, and we had to wait about three days till the wind switched directions and the bugs flew off somewhere else and let us play. We have a photo of it, and it's amazing—people can't believe we even tried to play under those conditions.

One other note: I got the first case of hives in my life down there. Thought it was the stress of traveling or something, but a doctor determined that it was the avocados with hot sauce I was eating every day. He told me to quit eating them, and the hives cleared up. But I've never had any trouble with avocados since then, so maybe it was the hot sauce—who knows?

We played about four exhibitions a week, plus those other tournaments, then flew to Rio de Janeiro, heading home. We stopped to give an exhibition in Rio, but I was tired and homesick, so I came on home. It was a great homecoming. Louise was always glad to see me come back when I went off to play in tournaments, but this time, with me being so far away for six weeks and her worrying about me flying and all, she was happier to see me than I ever expected.

The whole effect of the trip was so negative, really, that a few years later I turned down an offer to go to South Africa and play with Bobby Locke. Sam Snead went instead and got beat fourteen out of sixteen matches, but he was paid $10,000 and they gave him a real nice diamond. Louise didn't want me to go, of course, but she said later that she wouldn't have minded having that diamond.

You could say that 1937 was a whirlwind year for me, with my first Masters win, my first Ryder Cup, first British Open, my win in the International Match Play Championships, and the trip to Argentina that fall. So it's no wonder that I only played in a couple more tournaments by the end of the summer, not doing particularly well in either one. The first was in Miami, and from there, McSpaden and I went on to play in Nassau. It's interesting to note that our trip there and back was paid for. That was long before the PGA developed the idea of not accepting expenses or appearance money, which I think is a good idea and has been good for the integrity of the game all the way around.

Before we left for Texarkana that fall, Mr. Giles drew up my contract for renewal. He didn't say anything about a raise, so I told him very politely that I felt I had earned one, that I'd done a good job in the shop and had played well for the club. He agreed, and without another word, he raised my guarantee from $3750 to $5000. That wasn't salary, you understand. It was simply that if I didn't clear $5000 from my shop, club care costs, lessons, clothing, clubs, balls, etc., then the club would make up the difference. Fortunately, I had no trouble meeting and even surpassing that guarantee each year, due to increased play and more lessons. I was fortunate in that there was very little cash involved, as nearly everything was charged to each member's account. Also, the club paid Ralph Trout, my assistant, so I didn't need to worry about that. In 1939, I didn't get another increase; it stayed $5000, but once again, I wasn't worried about making it. Naturally, if you didn't make your guarantee, the club wouldn't be very happy with your performance if they had to pay out a lot of money. It was more of a protection in case you had a lot of bad weather or some such thing. Still, that raise surely was some good news to take home to Louise that night.

My winnings in '37 were $6,509.50, and my caddy and entrance fees were a little over ten percent of that, $712. I did get a $500 bonus from Spalding for winning the Masters, but not anything else that I remember. I ranked seventh on the money list, which was by far the best I'd done yet.

In 1938, I played in twenty-five tournaments and won two of them. Finished well in several more, but I wasn't burning up the course anywhere. I did play in the second Crosby Pro-Am, at Rancho Santa Fe in California. My partner was Johnny Weissmuller, the movie "Tarzan" and Olympic swimmer. Originally, you know, the amateurs played without any handicaps at all. We didn't do very well, as I recall, but Weissmuller sure was fun to play with.

Another amateur who played in that tournament was Eddie Lowery, who had McSpaden as his partner. Eddie had been Francis Ouimet's caddie in the U.S. Open in 1913. He told me once that he'd had to play hooky from school to do it. He would hide out until just before the round started, because they had truant officers in those days, and they were tough. But they didn't bother him after he got on the course. I'd met Eddie before, but spent quite a bit of time with him that week, and it became the start of a wonderful, lifelong friendship. Eddie was also the one who started me working with Kenny Venturi and Harvie Ward.

One of the most interesting stories that year was the weather during the San Francisco Match Play Tournament. The wind was blowing so bad that there were hurricane flags up out on the bay, but we played anyway. I led after the first qualifying round with a 77, if you can imagine that. I don't believe they'd play in weather like that now, and I'm glad. It really was scary, and dangerous.

In '38, I won a little money in most of the tournaments I played, had a good mini-streak of two out of three wins in Florida that spring, and then finished fifth at Augusta. Maybe I didn't win the Masters because they weren't demonstrating the Hammond organ this time. It wasn't a bad year at all, but it would have been hard to equal '37 anyway, and I didn't expect to.

Ben Hogan had turned pro two years before I did, but he was a late bloomer. He had trouble with hooking the ball too much, and it took him quite a long time to get that under control. So it took him a long while to make it on the tour to stay. He'd come out for a while, run out of money and go back to Fort Worth, come out again, go back to Texas, and so on. He grew quite discouraged at times, but I could see that he had not only talent, but a kind of dedication and stubborn persistence that no one else did. I encouraged him to keep at it and keep working on his game, and he did all right, finally. Ben practically invented practice, because back then, most clubs didn't even have a practice area, but Ben would spend hours working on his game wherever he could find a place to practice, and it's a great part of the reason he was so successful.

But it did take a while before he was on the tour to stay. In the early days of the Masters, they had a Calcutta pool, and in 1938, I was there at the party because I was the defending champion and Mr. Roberts asked that I make an appearance. So Ben Hogan's name came up, and no one bid on him at all. They were about to put his name in a pot with a couple of other players when I decided to buy him, and I gave $100. The next day, Ben saw me and said, "I hear you bought me in the Calcutta pool last night for $100." I said, "Yes, Ben, I did." He said, "Could I buy half-interest?" So I agreed and he scrounged around and came up with fifty dollars. But he didn't play very well at all and finished out of the money, so at least I only lost $50.

In the '38 Masters, I was the defending champion, of course, and in the first round, by tradition, I was paired with Bob Jones. It was the second big thrill I had in golf, as far as playing with the legends was concerned. At that time, Jones always played the first round of the Masters with the defending champion, and the last with the tournament leader. He was very nice to play with, talked just the right amount, and encouraged me. He shot a 76 that day, and I had a 73, but it was quite a while after he'd quit playing publicly, and he was really serving as the host of the tournament more than as a player.

When he became too ill to play a few years later, he gave me a great honor by asking me to play the final round in his place, which I did from 1946 until 1956, when Kenny Venturi was the leader. Then the committee decided that since I had worked closely with Kenny, it would be unfair to the other players to have me paired with him, and they put Snead with him instead. After that, they changed to putting the leader with whoever was closest to him, like they do now.

On that spring tour I recall something else pretty unusual happening in a tournament at St. Petersburg, Florida—I whiffed one. That's right, flat missed the ball. It was in the last round, on a par five, and I drove over to the left side of the fairway, right in front of a nice, five-foot-tall palm tree. When I took a practice swing, my club just barely touched the leaves, so I figured I was okay. But when I took my 4-iron back and started down, the club hit a leaf just hard enough to kind of grab on to it, and I swung right over the top of the ball—never even moved it. No choice but to knock it out in three, and I hit my approach close enough to make my putt for a fairly unusual five.

One interesting thing about the North and South Open, which was always held at Pinehurst. For the money we were making, it was a very expensive place to play, since about the only hotel was the Carolina Inn, where you had to dress for dinner every night—black tie, the works. We never actually stayed there until '39, and they put all the golfers on the ground floor. Naturally, as we came in after our rounds, we'd be talking about how we'd played, and first one and then another fellow would come out of his room, and pretty soon we'd all be standing out in the hall, talking about golf. It was really fun. Louise and I felt we were living high on the hog in those early days at Pinehurst.

But in '38, I really was even busier at the club than I had been the year before, so I couldn't play in as many tournaments as I had at Ridgewood, particularly if they were very far away. One I did play in was the Cleveland Open, when a fellow named Babe Ruth played. After watching him, I thought it was good he played baseball and not golf, because I don't think he'd ever have made a good golfer. But the gallery loved seeing him.

The U.S. Open in '38 was at Cherry Hills. I finished fifth and won $412.50, but my clearest memory of that tournament was the rough. It was very inconsistent, and one time, I know it took me two shots to get out of it. Tough course. For the last thirty-six holes I was paired with Dick Metz, who was leading the tournament at the time. But he started leaving every approach shot short of the green, and leaving every putt short, too. I liked Dick very much, and felt sorry for him, but there wasn't anything I could do to help him. He had a terrible score and finished way out of contention.

The PGA was at Shawnee Country Club in Shawnee on the Delaware, Pennsylvania. Fred Waring, the wonderful bandleader, owned the course. He was also involved in the Waring Company, and as a result, all of the players were given a Waring blender. Quite a newfangled gadget at the time. Unfortunately, it was one of those times when I got hot too early. I beat Harry Bassler, a pro from California, 11 and 10 in my third match, but lost steam after that and got beat in the quarterfinals by Jimmy Hines, 2 and 1.

Runyan and Snead made it to the finals that year, and Runyan used a 4-wood to Snead's 6-iron and put his ball inside Sam's every time, nearly. He was already being called "Little Poison" then, and beat Snead 8 and 7. We didn't have match play tournaments very often—usually in the PGA Championship and a few other events. Even then, tournament organizers were realizing it was hard to predict whether the so-called big names would make it to the finals, and that really affected their ability to sell tickets and make money, or even break even. My own match play record was good, but it should have been better. I had quite a few early matches with what I would call less experienced players, but felt I had to play hard in those matches to keep myself fired up, and I'd peak too early. In the PGA at Pomonok in '39, for instance, I beat Dutch Harrison 10 and 9 in the semifinals, but I must have used up all my good shots, because I lost to Picard in the final on the 37th hole. Still, I was tenth on the money list that year, and got some sort of a bonus from Spalding, plus balls and equipment. Not a great year, but certainly nothing to be ashamed of.

1938 was also the year I got started in the golf shoe business. While McSpaden and I were at Pinehurst playing in the North and South, we got to talking with Miles Baker, a salesman for Field and Flint, who made wonderful men's street shoes. Miles was from Kansas City and a good friend of Jug McSpaden, and he liked golf. Lots of times he would arrange his schedule so he could be where the tour was. We saw him at quite a few of the tournaments. Anyway, this evening we were complaining to Miles about the sorry state of golf shoes. The soles were so thin you could feel the spikes almost right through the leather. And of course, when it rained or we had to play on a wet course, the shoes wouldn't hold up at all.

So we were telling Miles all this, and we said, "You make such excellent street shoes—'Dr. Locke' and 'Foot-Joy.' Why couldn't you make good golf shoes, too?" Miles asked us what we wanted, so we told him. We felt the sole needed to be thicker, and the shoes needed to be broader across the ball of the foot. A little while later, he had us come up to Boston to the factory there, and they made special lasts for us. Then they made up one pair for each of us to try—mine were British tan and brown with wingtips, and McSpaden's were white buck.

When we came out to the golf course in those new shoes, the players had a fit. "Where'd you get those shoes?" everybody was asking. So all of a sudden Field and Flint was in the golf shoe business, and McSpaden and I each received a 25-cent royalty per pair for quite a few years.

I shot my highest score ever, 434, in a tournament that year of '38, but I tied for third and won $950. For some reason I don't recall, we played 108 holes at Westchester, for a purse of $10,000. Guess they wanted to make sure the fans got their money's worth.

Toward the end of September in 1938, McSpaden and I went to do an exhibition in Butte, Montana, on our way to the Pacific Northwest. Louise came too, and we were to fly into Butte, but in those days you didn't fly very quickly. We took off right after playing in Tulsa and made a lot of stops; by the time we reached Butte it was about midnight. What was worse, though, was there was a snowstorm and we couldn't land, so we flew on and landed at Missoula. Then we caught a milk train from Missoula back to Butte that stopped at just about every little station to load five-gallon milk cans into the baggage car. It was terribly cold, but fortunately, there was one car that had a little old pot-bellied coal stove, and that's how we kept from freezing. The seats were just straight down and up with no padding, so they weren't very comfortable. We got to Butte about two and a half hours later and went straight to bed. When we woke up there was snow on the ground, but the man in charge said we still were going to play. At the golf course, thank goodness, there were just patches of snow, so we put on a clinic and then went out to play. Believe it or not, quite a few people had come out for this, but not being used to the cold weather, we were about to freeze. I finally noticed one man in the gallery who had on a beautiful, warm-looking down jacket. I said, "That sure looks good—I'd like to have that on me about now!" He said, "Well, I can't give you this one, but I'll send you one—what size do you wear?" Sure enough, he did send me one just like his, and though I don't get to wear it much here in Texas because we have such mild winters, it does come in handy once in a while.

That fall, we returned to Texarkana and Louise's folks' place. We'd been married over four years now, and we were beginning to wonder why we hadn't had any children. So Louise went to her doctor and was tested, and the doctor said there wasn't any reason he could find why she couldn't get pregnant. My turn was next, and that was when they discovered the high fever I'd had with the typhoid had made me sterile. Louise was very disappointed, naturally, and I was, too, but she took it very well, didn't brood about it, though it made her sad for quite a while. Some time later, she wanted to adopt a child, but I wasn't in favor of it. We had to travel so much, and it wasn't like it is on the tour now, with nurseries and special arrangements for babies. You almost never saw a tour player's children at any tournament, unless it was being played in his city. It was just too much trouble, driving from city to city as we did then, to have children along and try to bring them up that way.

The other problem was I'd seen so many adopted children who just didn't turn out right, for one reason or another. I was very reluctant to take that sort of a chance, and after a while, Louise gave up the idea and turned her energies instead to her nieces and nephews. I guess that in all our fifty years of marriage, that was the one regret she had. This may sound strange, but I never particularly regretted not having any children, except for Louise's sake, because I always wanted to please her and make her happy. She was a wonderful wife in every way, and I know she would have been a wonderful mother, too. As it turned out, when we moved back to Texas and settled in Roanoke in '46, we spent so much time with Louise's nieces and nephews that we almost felt we'd helped raise quite a few of them. That helped Louise tremendously, and I enjoyed it, too.

In 1938, though, we spent the fall in Texarkana, with me practicing quite a bit and Louise enjoying being with her family. We lived at her parents' home, since they had a spare bedroom. It was good to be free of the responsibility of running a club for a while, because it gave me more time to concentrate on my game. Really, those times in Texarkana were about the only vacations we had while I was on the tour.

I didn't do anything spectacular in California those first weeks on tour in '39. Probably the most interesting thing I did was play in a pro-am at Hillcrest in Los Angeles with Chico Marx. He was very animated and funny, though he didn't say much. When he signed the scorecard, he wrote, "I enjoyed it—bet you didn't." But I did tie for seventh in L.A., finished eighth in Oakland, and lost the first round in the San Francisco Match Play tournament. Then I tied for second in the Crosby Pro-Am, and was third in the Texas Open at San Antonio. In that Texas Open McSpaden and I played a practice round against Runyan and Ben Hogan, and McSpaden shot a 59. I helped four shots, making our best ball 55. Not everyone knows that the Texas Open is one of the oldest on the tour. Only the Western, the PGA, and the U.S. Open have been going on longer.

The next tournament in '39 was the Phoenix Open, and that was when I finally woke up. I won by twelve strokes. Mind you, that was a 54-hole tournament, so I had to be playing good to be leading that much after three rounds. I shot 64 in the Pro-Am, then 68-65-65. All that work for $700. Believe it or not, it snowed so much in Phoenix Friday and Saturday that we couldn't play either day, and had to play thirty-six on Sunday just to have a tournament at all. The two 65's I shot that Sunday were the record for one day for quite a few years.

I let up a little bit after Phoenix, and didn't play particularly well for the next couple of months. One thing of interest, though, was the Thomasville tournament in Georgia. The course was Glen Arven, and it had the oddest finishing hole I ever saw. It was a par 5, and horseshoe or U-shaped, so the green was no more than a hundred yards from the tee. The area within the "U" was considered out of bounds, and that wasn't so unusual, but they had a local rule that said you couldn't even cut across that out of bounds area. If you hit your drive to the right spot to try and go over the "U," they could rule your ball O.B., even if it landed on the green. Kept us all honest, I guess.

It's also interesting to realize that there was often quite a bit of difference in the purses among various tournaments, much more so than there is now. Most had a purse of $5000, and occasionally one would offer $10,000, but there were still quite a few of $3000 or less. And even the $10,000-purse events didn't pay everyone who made the cut—mostly only the top twenty places or so. We still played in every one we could get to, though. Obviously, we weren't playing just for the money sometimes, more for the fun of it and the chance to keep working on our games.

Back then, you learned to play winning golf by playing on the tour. None of us had college degrees or any other kind of jobs other than club jobs, and we hadn't had all the training that the young men and women have today on their tours. We had what I guess you might call on-the-job training. It was tough at times, but life was good, too.

In St. Petersburg that spring, I played with Frank Walsh, whose brother became president of the PGA some years later. Frank was a pretty good player himself, but had some odd ideas. For one, he always believed that good players carried their clubs in their left hand. Jimmy Demaret was the only one I knew of who did, and he was a pretty good hacker, but I never really noticed anyone else doing that consistently. Guess I had my mind more on my own game.

My next big target that year was the North and South Tournament at Pinehurst #2. I hadn't yet played as well there as I felt I should have, and I was hoping to do better this time. I played very steady, nothing really very unusual, shot 280 and won by two strokes. They say when you're playing well, you get a lot of breaks—or another way of putting it, the harder you work, the luckier you get. But on the seventeenth hole in the last round, I really did have a bit of luck—both good and bad.

The bad part was my tee shot buried in the face of the right-hand bunker on a fairly steep upslope with the pin cut on the right side. The good part was I holed out for a 2, and that birdie ended up being half of my two-stroke winning margin.

The reason I say I was fortunate was that I didn't putt very well through the entire tournament. In fact, after it was over, R.A. Stranahan, the president of Champion Spark Plug in Toledo, Ohio, and the father of Frank Stranahan, who later became a fine golfer, came to me in the locker room and said, "You made a liar out of me." Surprised, I said, "How did I do that?" And he replied, "I said no one could putt poorly and win this tournament." So I guess it's a good thing I didn't have to putt on the seventeenth. Mr. Stranahan was around golf a lot, involved in various golf organizations, and an avid golfer himself. To give him credit, he was right—it was very unusual for someone to putt poorly and still manage to win.

The North and South was a very important win for me, since it was considered a major at the time, and I felt very good about being able to win despite very average putting. I was very happy to have achieved another goal of mine, and the folks at Reading were, too.

In defense of my putting, though, the greens we played from city to city were so inconsistent that we mostly concentrated on getting our approach shots close enough to the pin that we wouldn't have to worry about putting much. Very few of the pros worked a whole lot on their putting. Made more sense to work on your irons or your chipping.

I played all right the next two weeks, finishing tenth at Greensboro and seventh at the Masters, then skipped Asheville, the Met Open, and the Goodall Round Robin. Not because I had to be at the club, but because I had been given another wonderful opportunity to advance in my career as a club professional.

Cloyd Haas, president of the Haas-Jordan Company in Toledo and a member at Inverness, had gone to George Jacobus, my good friend at Ridgewood, and told him Inverness was looking for a new pro. George told him about me, and also suggested he speak with Ben Hogan up the road at Hershey Country Club. Mr. Haas did exactly that, and I guess he liked the way I combed my hair better or something. Anyway, he invited me to come up to Inverness, which I did the next week, and I signed a contract with Ralph Carpenter, president of the club and of Dana Corporation, to come to Inverness in April 1940.

I would be paid $3600 in salary—basically about $600 a month for the time I'd be there, plus I got all the profits from the shop. The club paid the caddiemaster, Huey Rogers, and either all or part of assistant pro Herman Lang's salary. Even then, though I was playing well and winning money most of the time, I wasn't thinking about making a living on the tour. I knew I needed that club job to survive.

My Inverness contract was again an improvement over what I was making at Reading, but also a lot more responsibility, larger membership, and a well-known championship course. As you can imagine, I was flying pretty high. I also signed an endorsement contract with MacGregor in June 1939. Tommy Armour was the pro at Boca Raton, and his clubs were the main ones MacGregor was making then. We pros were all at Boca at the time for a meeting, and afterwards I went to Tommy's pro shop and picked out a set of his irons, called "Silver Scots." Two weeks later, I won the Open with those irons and kept them quite a while—at least till I had MacGregor make some with my own name on them.

The Open that year was held at Philadelphia Country Club, which at that time had two courses: Bala Cynwyd in town, and the Spring Mill Course out in the country, where the tournament was to be held. I felt I was playing rather well, hitting my irons great, and in the practice rounds, I scored close to par. It was normally a par-71 course, but the USGA wanted to make it more difficult, and changed two of the short par fives into par fours, which made it a par 69—about the only time such a "short" course has been an Open site. One of the redesigned holes was the eighth, and the other was the twelfth. This was in the days before clubs would spend money to change a course just for a specific tournament.

You might be interested to know that despite a par of 69, those par fours were far from easy. They were 480, 454, 453, 449, 447, 425, and 421 yards, so you know we were using those long irons a lot.

I was very nervous in the first round and played poorly for the first seven holes. The eighth was a long par 4, slightly uphill. I hit a good drive and a 2-iron on the green and almost birdied it. On the 9th I hit a long iron to within eight feet of the pin and made it, which encouraged me. I really did hit my irons well, though I never holed a chip or pitch the entire time. In the four regulation and two playoff rounds, I hit the pin six times with my irons, from 1-iron to 8-iron.

We played thirty-six holes the last day, and I was paired with Olin Dutra, who'd won in '34 at Merion. We were both well in contention. My friend from Texarkana, J.K. Wadley, was following us, and also knew Olin. After our first eighteen, he offered to buy us lunch. Dutra ordered roast beef with gravy, mashed potatoes and all the trimmings. I said, "I'll have the same," and Mr. Wadley said, "No, you won't." He ordered for me—a chicken sandwich on toast with no mayonnaise, some vegetables, iced tea, and half a piece of apple pie.

That afternoon, it was hot and muggy. Dutra played badly, and I shot a 1-under-par 68, which got me in a tie with Denny Shute and Craig Wood. That taught me a good lesson, not to eat too heavy a meal before going out to play, and I've abided by it ever since.

I was very fortunate to get into that playoff. Snead, who was worried about Shute playing behind him, made a poor club selection on eighteen. He thought he needed a birdie to win when he only needed a par, but he ended up with an 8, so he missed both winning and getting into the playoff.

In the first playoff, Shute struggled to a 76, while Craig and I tied at 68. On the last hole, Craig was leading me by a stroke and tried to reach the green at 18 in two, but hooked his second shot badly, and hit a man in the gallery right in the head. The man had been standing in the rough to the left, and the ball dropped and stayed there in the rough, about thirty yards short of the green. The fellow was knocked out, and they carried him across the green right in front of us while Craig waited to play his third shot. Of course, his ball would have been in even worse trouble if it hadn't gotten stopped, but that didn't make Craig feel any better. He hit a pitch shot then that left him with a six-footer for birdie, while my ball was eight feet away. I would putt first.

As I stood over my ball, suddenly the thought popped into my head of all the times when we were playing as caddies at Glen Garden and we'd say, "This putt is for the U.S. Open." Now I was really playing that dream out, and it steadied me enough that I sank my putt. But Craig left his just one inch short, so we were tied.

That meant another 18-hole playoff in those days, and the committee asked us before we played that afternoon whether we would be willing to go to sudden death if we tied again. We both said, "No, we'll go a full eighteen." They weren't real happy to hear that, because the folks working on the tournament had to get back to their jobs, and of course the members wanted their course back. But we both felt the same way, that we didn't want to win based on just one or two holes. So they agreed.

On the second playoff, I hit a bad second shot at the first hole and ended up in the deep right bunker, but I got up and down all right. On the second, a long par three, we had to use drivers, and had to carry the green. I pushed mine into some deep rough, while Wood's tee shot landed on the green. I got out with my sand wedge and saved par, and Wood two-putted. The next hole I birdied while Craig parred, and on the fourth, I hit a good drive, then holed a 1-iron for an eagle, while Craig made another four.

When I was lining up to play my second shot, I wasn't thinking at all about holing out. But I'd been striking my irons so well, had just birdied the third hole, and I felt I could hit this one close and make birdie again. Sure enough, the ball went straight up to the green and straight into the hole like a rat. There were a lot of folks in the gallery, and they whooped and hollered quite a bit, though they were still quieter than the fans are now. You know, when you're on the golf course and hear the spectators cheering, you learn quickly that the applause for an eagle is different from a birdie, and of course it's even louder for a hole in one. No matter where you are, you can tell by the applause just how good the shot was. What you don't want to hear the gallery do when you're playing is give a big groan—because that means you just missed a short putt.

Anyway, as I walked off the green, I remember thinking very vividly, "Boy, I'm three strokes ahead now!" But I knew it was no time to turn negative or quit being aggressive. I knew I had to continue playing well. As it happened, I then bogeyed a couple of holes but so did Craig, and that three-stroke lead proved to be my winning margin, 70 to 73.

Harold McSpaden—who was really the best friend I had on the tour—walked along with me through both of the playoff rounds, helping me get through the gallery and just being there. Naturally, he didn't say anything, but his presence and support sure were a big help to me.

Mr. Giles, my boss and friend from Reading, was there with quite a few of the members, so you might say I almost had my own gallery. George Jacobus was there too, and was nearly beside himself with excitement. He said to me afterwards, "You remember, Byron, we talked about this, and I said, 'You're going to be the National

Champion one of these days.'" I was kind of in a trance for a few days before I fully realized I was indeed the U.S. Open champion and had accomplished another dream.

After I got back home, the members of all three clubs—Berkleigh, Galen Hall, and Reading—gave Louise and me a wonderful party. They presented Louise with a large silver bowl that had her name engraved on it. Then they gave me a handsome, solid gold watch by Hamilton, engraved on the back "Byron Nelson, Winner U.S. Open 1939–40, Members of Reading Country Club." I still have both of them. They also gave me a Model 70 Winchester 30.06, a mighty fine rifle. That was arranged by Alex Kagen, a member at Berkleigh, who owned a sporting goods store and had once asked me if I hunted. When I told him all I had was a shotgun, he came up with the idea for the Winchester. I used it every time I went hunting, and kept it until just recently, when I sold it to my good friend, Steve Barley.

So there I was, the U.S. Open champion, with a contract I'd signed two weeks before to go to Inverness, just like when I signed the contract to go to Reading one week before I won the Masters. Some people would say I needed an agent to help me capitalize on my wins, but hardly anybody had one in those days. Hagen was the only one I knew of who did—a fellow named Bob Harlow, the golf writer who started *Golf World* magazine.

Shortly after the Open, Ben and Valerie Hogan came to visit and stayed a week. We practiced a lot and played some. I had to work, of course, but Ben played a couple of times with Mr. Giles, and he really enjoyed getting a chance to play with Ben, who was playing much better by then.

As it happened, my next tournament was the Inverness Invitational Four-Ball, which involved seven two-man teams. It was an interesting format, where you scored only plus or minus over seven rounds and four days of play. I was paired with McSpaden, and we tied for first at plus 6, then lost on the first playoff hole. This was my first real chance to see the course and the club where I'd be working the next year, and I enjoyed myself.

One week later, I won the Massachusetts State Open. McSpaden wanted me to come play in it because he knew the course real well, and because we were such good friends. I went, and in the last round,

Harold and I were battling it out pretty tight. Along about the middle of the last nine, there was a long par 3 with a bunker on the right. I pushed my tee shot into the bunker and holed it from there. That kept me going good and I won by four shots. I won $400 plus $250 appearance money. There weren't many events that paid appearance money then, and I'm glad the PGA stopped it, but it sure did come in handy back when most of us were just barely making ends meet.

The PGA that year was at Pomonok, Long Island. The World's Fair was in New York, and my mother came to see me play and see the fair, too. It was the only tournament she ever saw me play in. I beat Chuck Garringer, Red Francis, John Revolta, and Emerick Kocsis—brother to Chuck, a wonderful amateur who still shoots better than his age—to get to the quarterfinals. Then I went up against Dutch Harrison, and either I was playing awfully well or he was way off his game, but after the 26th hole, I was 9 up, and as we came to the 27th hole, Dutch said to me, "Byron, why don't you just birdie this one, too, and we won't have to go past the clubhouse." I thought it was a good idea. As it happened, I did birdie, and beat him 10 and 9.

In the finals, though, I had my hands more than full with Picard. I was one up coming to the last hole, and Picard laid me a dead stymie. It was a short par 4, and I had pitched to three feet. But Picard's shot stopped twelve inches from the hole directly in my line, and since we were playing stymies, you didn't mark your ball or anything—the other fellow had to figure out a way to get over or around you and in the cup. Unfortunately, I didn't make my shot go in, and we tied.

Picard won on the first extra hole, but there's a little story connected with how it happened. This was the first tournament ever that was broadcast on radio. It was just short-wave, and it was done by Ted Heusing and Harry Nash. Ted Heusing was an excellent broadcaster who my good friend Chris Schenkel admired a great deal, and Harry Nash was a fine golf writer for the *Newark Evening News.*

On that first extra hole, Picard hit his drive into the right rough, and Ted and Harry were riding in a sizable four-wheeled vehicle, right close by. They didn't see where Picard's ball had landed, and drove right over it. The officials ruled that he should get a free drop, which was only right, and he put his next shot twenty feet from the hole and made birdie to win.

I took the next week off, missing the tournament in Scranton, to make sure things were in order back at the club and to practice some for the Western Open, another major I had my sights set on. It was at Medinah #3, and I drove exceptionally well—seldom ever got in the rough at all. I won by one shot, and it meant even more to me because the trophy had been donated by my friend J.K. Wadley.

Though the North and South and the Western Open aren't considered majors now—the North and South doesn't even exist anymore—you knew then which ones were more important because the golf club companies would award bonuses for them. I got $500 from Spalding that year for the Western, which was always considered somewhat more important than the North and South because it drew from all around the country. The other was always played at Pinehurst, and a lot of the players from the western part of the country didn't go. Another reason the Western was ranked higher was that the tournament contributed money to the Chick Evans Scholarship Fund, which added prestige and publicity. Evans, an excellent golfer, was always there, too, and his name meant a lot of good things to golf. He'd won the Open himself, and had been a caddie like most of us, so I felt really good about winning the Western.

The next regular tour event I played well in was the Hershey Open several weeks later. The tournament was sponsored by Mr. Hershey himself, who was the president of the club and a very nice man. Par was 73. I was 5 under and leading going into the fourth round, and paired with Ed Dudley and Jimmy Hines. We came to the 15th hole, where you'd drive down the fairway and over a hill. Well, I drove right down the middle of it, but when we got to the place where my ball should have been, it was nowhere to be found. There wasn't any confusion about it, because my golf balls had my name imprinted on them, and everyone there had seen mine go absolutely straight down the fairway and disappear over the hill.

I had no choice but to go back and hit another ball. But with that two-stroke penalty I ended up in fourth place. Afterwards, I was talking to the press in the locker room and told them what had happened. Fred Corcoran was managing the tour then, and always trying to get publicity, so he got all the papers he could to pick up the story.

About ten days later, I received an anonymous letter stating that the writer's guest and friend at the tournament, a young woman who knew nothing about golf, had picked up my ball and put it in her purse. After the tournament, as they returned to New York on the train, the woman opened her purse and showed him the ball she'd found on the course, and the gentleman realized then what had happened. Since these were the days before gallery ropes, people walked all over the course in front of you and in back of you and right alongside you. The young lady had apparently been walking across the fairway at the bottom of the hill after I drove, saw the ball lying there, and simply picked it up.

The letter was postmarked from the New York Central Post Office, and the man included money orders totaling $300—the difference between third prize in the tournament and fourth, where I finished. The money orders were signed "John Paul Jones"—clearly fictitious. I never did find out who did it, but whoever it was, it was a nice thing to do.

I guess I got a lot of media attention for that time but it was very little compared to what goes on now. I was glad for the attention, but since I hadn't talked to the press much after beating Lawson Little in San Francisco in '35 and winning the Masters in '37, it took some getting used to. I was even being interviewed on radio now, though we always had to go downtown to the station to do it.

I've always been fortunate with the publicity I received, and have had very little inaccurate reporting. Might be because I was always a little on the shy side, and didn't really talk very much or very fast, so the reporters couldn't get much wrong. I'd have to say, overall, that I enjoyed the attention. After I won the Open especially, people in the gallery would say, "Boy, you're sure hitting your irons good," or some such thing, and that would encourage me. Then I'd try even harder, because I didn't want to let them down.

With three majors to my credit, 1939 was definitely my best year so far. My official winnings were $9444, making me fifth on the money list. My stroke average was 71.02, good enough to win the Vardon Trophy, which was an added bonus.

The year I'd have in 1945 was a little more unusual, but with the quality of the tournaments that I won—three majors—and the way I played, 1939 was right up there with '45. And naturally, I had no idea what would happen in '45 was even possible. No, at that point, I was simply looking ahead to the winter tour and wanting to do my best for the folks at Inverness the next spring.

So Louise and I packed up and went back to Texarkana, where I practiced and played some with my friends or with the pro there, Don Murphy. Looking back on the whole year, I was more than satisfied with my accomplishments.

SIX

Inverness and the War Years

With my job at Inverness—a wonderful club and wonderful golf course—waiting for me the next spring, I guess I was a little nervous going out on the tour that winter of 1940. I certainly didn't get my game going very quickly. For some reason I can't recall, I skipped several tournaments early that year. I didn't play at Los Angeles, Oakland, or the Crosby Pro-Am; I lost in the quarterfinals at San Francisco, and finished out of the money at Phoenix. Not a very good start.

Back then the tour was different than it is now. A lot of us pros drove from tournament to tournament in a kind of caravan, and right after Phoenix, which happened to end on my birthday that year, we all headed for Texas. Ben and Valerie Hogan and Louise and I liked to stick together, so we'd follow each other pretty closely on the road. You kind of had to do that, because if you had car trouble, it was good to have a buddy nearby to help you fix a flat or whatever.

There was a place in Las Cruces, New Mexico, where we liked to stop for lunch. They had the best tamales and chili we'd ever tasted, with real authentic Mexican flavor. One particular time, we decided to ask if we could buy some to take along with us. The waitress told us,

"Well, the tamales come in a can, and they're made by the Armour Meat Company in Fort Worth." All four of us just looked at her. Then at each other. Somehow, those tamales had suddenly lost their appeal, and we never ordered them again.

On that same trip, the wives of Ed "Porky" Oliver and Harold McSpaden weren't along, so Ed and Harold were driving together. It was a good hard day's drive from Phoenix to Van Horn, Texas, where most of us stopped for the night. McSpaden drove pretty fast, but Oliver was a lot more cautious. They were going along down this two-lane road and had to go through a tunnel at one point. Ed kept telling McSpaden to slow down, but Harold just kept saying, "I know this road like the back of my hand." They got into this tunnel, and the tunnels then were always narrower than the road, and halfway through, barreling along at full speed, they met this fellow driving a wagon pulled by two big old mules. They just barely squeaked by, with McSpaden not slowing down hardly at all, and when they got through, Oliver yelled, "Don't tell me you knew that wagon and those mules were going to be there, too!" I don't know that they ever rode together after that, because it scared Ed pretty bad.

We all made it to Van Horn, including Oliver and McSpaden, and stayed at the El Capitan Hotel, which we always liked because they had wonderful hot biscuits and their food was very good. About dinnertime, we noticed that Oliver had disappeared. When he showed up about five hours later, everyone wanted to know where he'd been. He'd gone to a double feature movie the entire evening. Imagine—after sitting in a car from dawn till dark, he goes and sits in a theatre for four hours more. We couldn't believe it. But it was all part of life on the road, and even though we had to do a lot of driving, we all stuck together and had a lot of fun.

As far as tournaments go, though, the first good thing I remember about that year was the Texas Open at Brackenridge Park. Ben Hogan and I tied at 271. I beat him in the playoff, 70–71, and broke 70 all four regulation rounds. It seems as if I played better against Ben on the average than I did against anybody else. I tried harder against him, because I knew I had to.

After we tied, we were told that a San Antonio radio station wanted to interview us. There wasn't any such thing as a remote broadcast then, so they had to take us downtown to the station. I was asked how I felt about tying for the tournament and being in the playoff with Ben, and I said, "Anytime you can tie Ben or beat him, it's a feather in your cap, because he's such a fine player." Then they asked Ben the same thing, and he said, "Byron's got a good game, but it'd be a lot better if he'd practice. He's too lazy to practice." Ben never did think I practiced enough. But I did manage to beat him the next day, practice or not.

The next tournament was the Western Open at River Oaks in Houston. On the morning of the first round, my head hurt and I felt terrible. I shot a 78. The next day, I tried to play, because I hated to withdraw, but I shot 40 on the first nine and nearly passed out, and just had to quit. It turned out I had the flu and ended up in bed four days. I didn't get the flu often, but whenever I did, it really laid me flat. Jimmy Demaret won the Western that year in a playoff with Toney Penna.

We went on to New Orleans, and I must have still been weak, because I finished fifteenth and won $146. I don't remember much else about that week, except that we were staying at the St. Charles Hotel, and Louise and I were having breakfast in the dining room when she realized she'd left her aquamarine ring in our room. She went up to get it, but it was gone. We called in the manager and house detective and everyone, but it was never found. Louise was very upset about it. The ring wasn't all that expensive, but I had brought it back from my trip to South America in '37, and it had a lot of sentimental value for her.

The spring of 1940 was my first chance to play in the Seminole Invitational, one of the pros' favorite tournaments. In the pro-am, if you won, you got 10% of the money in the Calcutta pool. The pros loved to get invited, because not only was it a wonderful golf course, but they had great food—a buffet every night that had more good food than any of us had ever seen before.

Next was the St. Petersburg Open. I made an eight-footer on the last hole for a 69, finished second to Demaret and won $450. Demaret was two years older than Ben and I, but he never would admit it until it was time for him to collect social security. He always claimed, in fact, that he was actually younger than we were.

In the Miami Four-Ball that year at the Biltmore Hotel golf course, McSpaden and I were partners. In the first round, we beat Johnny Farrell and Felix Serafin, 7 and 6, and then got trounced in the second round by Paul Runyan and Horton Smith, 5 and 4. They were a fine partnership team and outputted us that day. They were always wonderful putters, both of them.

In the Thomasville Open at Glen Arven Country Club in Georgia, I finished second again, this time to Lloyd Mangrum, though I broke 70 all four rounds. Next was the North and South, where I was defending champion. I finished second again at 2 under, won another $450, and lost to Hogan, who had two very fine first rounds and held on to win.

The Greensboro Open was played then at two courses, Starmount Forest and Sedgefield. I shot 68–68 the last two rounds and was third at 280. My philosophy at this point was not to have a bad round, and to have at least one hot round each tournament. I didn't always do it, but that was what I knew I had to do to win or finish near the top.

Next was the Masters. Even then, just a few years after Bob Jones and Clifford Roberts started this wonderful tournament, it was a very prestigious one, and everyone coveted the title. I always loved going, seeing the flowers and Jones and Cliff. Just being at the Masters always got me excited and I nearly always played well there. That year, I finished third at 3 under and won $600. This was when the greens were not only as fast as they are today, but they were hard as rock, too. If you landed an iron shot on the green, it would bounce six feet in the air and roll off nearly every time. You couldn't back the ball up no matter how much spin you put on it. Being able to back the ball up or land it on the green and stop it came about in later years.

Immediately after the Masters, Louise and I drove straight to Toledo. I was a little anxious about how I would do at Inverness. I felt I could handle it, but there were so many more active members compared to what I was used to. At Reading, I had less than a hundred sets of clubs to care for, and not all of those members were real active golfers. At Inverness, I had 365 sets of clubs, all quite active. I replaced Al Sargent, whose father was pro at Atlanta and had been Bob Jones's pro when Jones was a young man. The golf shop at Inverness was in a separate building, about seventy-five yards from the clubhouse and right next to the first tee. In fact, it had been the clubhouse at one time. It was built when the original clubhouse had burned down years before, and served as a temporary clubhouse until the new one was completed. Then it became the golf shop. The caddies' room was in the back, then there was my office, and then the shop itself. It was a nice building with high ceilings, though the shop was a little smaller than I would have liked.

One of the first things I did was to stock shoes. I brought in eighty-four pairs of men's shoes, both street and golf, by Foot-Joy, selected with the help of my friend Miles Baker. Miles told me I was really the first pro to do this. Most pros would have sample pairs of different styles, but the members had to order them and then wait several weeks to get them. My eighty-four pairs covered all the styles in just about all the sizes and widths, which made it very convenient to sell the shoes on the spot.

Next, I talked to Mr. Carpenter and got his permission to put up an 8 × 8-foot square mirror on the wall across from the door. It not only made the shop look bigger, but when the weather was bad or I had time, I'd use that mirror to check my swing. When I had lessons scheduled during rainy weather, I'd put the students in front of that mirror and work with them, have them check their shoulder alignment, grip, stance, where they placed the ball, and so forth. It was really quite helpful.

When I arrived they gave me a locker upstairs, right where a group of the most prominent and influential members' lockers were. That was a big help, because I got acquainted with them more easily. Another thing that helped me greatly was that Huey Rodgers, the caddiemaster, would stand at the door of the shop, and when he'd see the members coming from the clubhouse, he'd tell me who they were. That way, I got to know the members by name very quickly, and it impressed them that I could learn their names so soon—I don't guess they knew Huey was helping me.

One of the first things I found to be different at Inverness was bookkeeping. At Reading, I had been fortunate in this regard. I just kept all the members' charge slips and simply turned them in to the club bookkeeper each month. But at Inverness, it was a whole new world. It was so much busier, for one thing, and then I found I was expected to do my own bookkeeping, which naturally took quite a lot of time. Actually, I didn't know how to go about it at all, and in about six weeks, I had all these boxes full of slips and charges and merchandise orders and no idea how to organize them. I was terribly confused. Finally I asked one of the members what to do, and he recommended

Roy Bowersock, a fine CPA with the accounting firm Wideman and Madden, who got my books straightened out and taught me how to keep them myself. His firm was bought out by Ernst and Young some years later, and they moved Roy to Tulsa about the time I moved back to Texas in 1946. A year later, Roy was transferred to Fort Worth, and did all my bookkeeping and accounting for many years afterwards. I've been pretty good about it ever since—in fact, good enough to get me out of trouble with the IRS many years later.

About this time I was advised I needed to have an official domicile for tax purposes, and I figured Texas would be the best place, because it was one of the few states that had community property laws to protect Louise in case anything happened to me. It was also my home state, and Louise and I had felt for some time that if I ever left the tour, we wanted to settle near Fort Worth, because my family was all there and her sister Delle had married and moved there by this time.

Just as important to me was the fact that I'd wanted to do something for my folks for some time. They were living in Handley, Texas, and my father was running a feed store there. My brother Charles, about fourteen, was helping out, lifting those hundred-pound sacks of feed and doing the deliveries, but it was still awfully hard work for my father. He had bought the feed store some time before from Mr. Magee, the banker, with whom he'd become good friends. Magee was a widower, and talked my mother and father into moving into his home where my mother could keep house and cook for him, and they had lived with him for a few years. But I wanted them to have their own place.

We eventually found a fifty-four-acre farm for sale southeast of Denton. We bought it, and they moved there in October of 1940 and lived there six years. It was a good place for them. The farm gave both my parents plenty to do without overworking them, and made it easier for Charles and my sister Ellen to go to college as well. Louise and I never actually lived there, though it was my official domicile for tax purposes until I left the tour in '46 and moved back to Texas permanently.

But back to Inverness and golf. Naturally, I was so busy those first few months that between the Masters and the Open, I only played in one 72-hole tournament, the Goodall Round Robin. It was at Fresh Meadow Country Club in Flushing, New York; I tied for sixth at plus

2 and won $300. Hogan played beautifully and won with plus 23. Besides being busy, my contract only allowed me to be gone six weeks out of the six months I would be at the club, so unless a tournament was close by that summer, I couldn't play in it. The pros' club contracts differed quite a bit back then. Some pros could go play in tournaments every week, and simply "played out of" a certain club rather than working there every day, while others worked a full week, like me. But I was enjoying my new job and the club a lot more than traveling on the tour, and making more and steadier money most of the time besides. I did play in one local tournament, the Ohio Open at Sylvania Country Club just northwest of Toledo. I shot 284 and won $250, but it wasn't an official PGA event, so it doesn't count on my record. But it served as a nice warm-up for the National Championship two weeks later.

The Open was at Canterbury Country Club in Cleveland that year, about a two-hour drive from Toledo. Not quite close enough to commute. I tied for fifth with 290, but felt very good about how I'd performed, all things considered. Lawson Little and Gene Sarazen tied at 287, and Little won in a playoff. The week after, I played in the Inverness Invitational Four-Ball. I was paired with Walter Hagen, long after the peak of his career. The sponsors then did everything possible to get more people to come watch the tournament, and in those days they didn't invite just the players on the tour, necessarily. Hagen was in his fifties and playing no tournament golf at all, but they invited him to help draw more gallery. Because I was the host pro, they had me play with Hagen because it would have been unfair for the other players to be paired with him as his game wasn't very sharp. We had to walk, naturally, and Inverness was a tough course, so it was a bit much for Hagen. The ninth hole there comes right by the side of the clubhouse, the tenth tee is at the men's entrance to the locker room, and the 13th hole comes back to the clubhouse again. So after we played the front nine, Hagen would say to me, "Play hard, Byron, and I'll see you at the fourteenth tee." This was the only tournament I finished last in after becoming an established player (we tied for last, actually, at minus 14), but it was all for a good cause and it was fun to see Hagen play even then, so I didn't really mind.

The PGA was at Hershey in 1940, but busy as I was at the club, I hadn't played in a tournament for two and a half months. I was playing well, however, playing quite a bit with the members and giving lots of lessons. I had arranged in my contract with Mr. Carpenter that I could play in fivesomes with the members. What that meant was on Saturdays I'd go play a few holes with one foursome and a few holes with the next and so on. It was a good way for me to get to know each of the members, plus I could see what condition their clubs were in and how they were playing, and help them decide what kind of clubs, putters, new bags, or whatever they needed. It helped my sales in the shop, and it helped the members, too. They seemed to like it that I played with them.

About a month or more before the PGA, I started to get in shape for the competition by taking on three members at a time and playing against their best ball. They gave me a one-putt maximum on the first green, so I always started with par or birdie, but after that, I had to really play hard. We'd play once a week. These fellows all shot in the 70's, and their best ball would be 65 or 66. It was tough competition, but I held my own and won most of the time. Some of the fellows I played with were Ray Miller, Eddie Tasker, Bob Sawhill, Alan Loop, and Tony Ruddy. A great group of golfers and good friends.

So I felt I was in good shape when I arrived at Hershey. I did all right in the qualifying and early matches, and made it to the semis without too much trouble. I remember how difficult it was for me to play in the semifinal against Ralph Guldahl, who was a wonderful player and a tough competitor, but who was also very slow and deliberate, while I played very quickly. I had to work at staying calm and not becoming impatient, and I managed to do it, fortunately. Then, in the final against Sam Snead, on the third hole in our afternoon round, Sam laid me a dead stymie* and thought he had the hole won. But I

* We played stymies into the late forties. You see, we weren't allowed to mark, lift, clean, and replace the ball on the greens then like we all do today. So in match play, if the other player's ball was in your way, that was just bad luck. You played around it or pitched over it or whatever you could do to get in or near the hole. A lot of luck was involved, naturally, because you didn't think about trying to stymie your opponent when you were pitching from sixty yards off the green or more. But that was the reason scorecards then were exactly six inches long and had an arrow pointing in both directions at the bottom. If your ball was quite close to your opponent's, you placed the scorecard between yours and his, and if it touched both of them, one of you had to mark the ball. Otherwise, it was a stymie. You didn't think about laying someone a stymie when you were well off the green, but if you had to play over someone's ball, you'd try to.

chipped over his ball with my pitching wedge and holed it and we halved the hole instead with birdies. By the time we reached the 16th tee, I was one down with three to play. On the 16th, I hit a good drive and a fine iron and holed a six-footer for birdie to catch up with Sam. On the 17th, a short par 4, you drove out on to a hill and pitched to a small green. I pitched three feet from the hole and made another birdie to go one up.

Then we came to the 18th, a long par 3, and it was my honor. I'll never forget it. I took my 3-iron, almost hit the flag, and went about ten feet past the hole; I'd be putting downhill. Sam put his tee shot about twenty-five feet to the left of the hole and putted up close, so he had three. So all I had to do was make three to win the match one up. I coasted that putt down the hill very gently and made my three to beat Snead and win the PGA Championship.

As a nice sidelight to that victory, a couple of years ago I received a very kind letter from a man named Charles Fasnacht in Pennsylvania. He wrote that the boy who had caddied for me at Hershey had been a good friend of his, and when I sank that last putt to win, his buddy tossed Charles the ball and he had kept it all this time. He felt bad about it and wanted to send me the ball, but I wrote and told him that if it had meant that much to him to keep it all these years, then I couldn't think of anyone who deserved to have it more.

That PGA was where the story got started about my so-called nervous stomach. Mr. and Mrs. Cloyd Haas came over when I had to play Guldahl in the semifinals. Mr. Haas had gone to the locker room with me before this 36-hole match, and while he was there, I lost my breakfast. He went right out and told Louise and Mrs. Haas. Louise said, "Good!" which Mr. Haas at first thought was very cruel, but he later found out that it was a good sign, because it meant I would play well. I didn't do it all that often, but somehow the story got started in later years that this was why I left the tour. Actually, it was a little more complicated than that, which I'll tell you about later.

A few other members from Inverness had come with the Haases—Hazen Arnold, Mr. Carpenter, the Bargman brothers, and several others, and after I won, I learned they'd made reservations for me and Louise to return to Inverness on the train that night. After dinner, they gave us a wonderful celebration party in the dining car on the way home.

I'd now won every major American tournament plus the Ryder Cup, but had not won the Los Angeles Open, which was considered a big tournament then. But I just didn't feel yet that I'd completed my record. I wanted to win the PGA again, and had hopes of winning the national championship again as well. So I still had some golf to play.

The week after the PGA, I played in the Anthracite Open at Scranton and was second, with Snead winning. Then it was back to Inverness and no more tournaments until after I left the club in the early fall and went back to Texarkana. I finished the year well, though, winning the Miami Open and $2,537.50 at Miami Springs. I shot 69-65-67-70—271 and beat Clayton Heafner by one shot.

One thing I should mention about that year was how I got Cloyd Haas started in the golf umbrella business. Golf umbrellas then were about as bad as golf shoes had been before Foot-Joy started making them for me and McSpaden. Our umbrellas were flimsy, the cloth they used wasn't waterproof and would leak, and if it was windy, the things would turn inside out and the ribs would break all to pieces.

Mr. and Mrs. Haas had taken Louise and me in like their own children, and we went over to their home for dinner quite often. Summers in Toledo were famous for mosquitoes, but they had a nice big screened-in back porch where Mr. Haas and I would go after dinner to sit and talk. We'd talk about first one thing and another, and one evening, I said, "Mr. Haas, you make such wonderful street umbrellas. Why couldn't you make a good golf umbrella, too?" He said, "What kind of a golf umbrella do you need?" I told him, and he got to thinking about it. A few weeks later, I was at the Goodall Round Robin tournament in Fresh Meadow, New York. Mr. Haas was up there in New Jersey at the same time, visiting the factory he ordered his umbrella frames from, so he asked me to come out and meet him there. We talked with the manager about what we needed, and we settled on a double rib design and birdcloth for the fabric. They used my size to decide how big to make it, and it was quite adequate. Those first ones turned out to be a little heavy, but they were so much better than what we'd had before. I had mine made up in British tan and brown, and had one made for McSpaden in green and tan. When we brought them out to the course, all the boys wanted to know where they could get one, too. So Haas-Jordan got into golf umbrellas from then on, and theirs are still the finest, in my opinion.

I worked with Haas-Jordan for several years after that. Mr. Haas made me vice president of marketing, and each tournament I'd go to, I'd visit the large department stores—Neiman-Marcus, Macy's, Bullock's—and give them my card, and just introduce myself. I didn't really do any selling, it was more of a public relations thing. But I got $25 for each call I made, which was nice, plus a generous bonus check each year, which was even nicer. Mr. Haas also had special ties made up for his staff to wear, with all kinds of different designs of umbrellas. I soon became known as "The Umbrella Man," and it stuck for quite a while.

My connection with the Haas family continues to this day. I gave some lessons to Mr. Haas's daughter, Janet, when she was just a college student, and she and her husband, H. Franklin "Bud" Waltz, became two of our dearest friends. Bud has been on the PGA advisory committee for many years.

I started to teach right away at Inverness, and found that I was teaching more of the better players now. I gave lessons almost constantly while I was at the club, and I enjoyed it. It was much easier to make the better players understand what I was saying, because they had a better grasp of the basics of the game.

One of the first good young golfers I met at Inverness was Frank Stranahan, R.A.'s son. He was quite an admirer of my accomplishments, and as he got better at his own game, he began to think he was as good as I was, which led to some interesting stories.

At one point, Mr. Stranahan had signed Frankie up for some lessons with me. Well, I soon found out that this young man wouldn't listen to anything I had to say. He just wanted me to watch him hit balls, and wouldn't change anything or take any of my suggestions seriously. After a few weeks of this, I told him, "Frankie, I'm not going to give you any more lessons. You won't listen to me, and you're wasting my time and your father's money."

Naturally, it didn't end there. A few days later, Mr. Stranahan came into the shop with Frankie in tow, and said to me, "Frankie says you won't teach him any more." I was really on the spot. I certainly didn't want to get Mr. Stranahan mad, because he was very influential at the club. But I had to tell the truth, too.

"Mr. Stranahan," I said, "that's not exactly what I said. Frankie won't listen to me or change anything about the way he plays, and he's wasting your money and my time. That's why I told him I wouldn't teach him any more." Mr. Stranahan looked at Frankie and asked, "Is that true?" Frankie nodded and said, "Yes." So Mr. Stranahan said to me, "If you'll continue to teach him, I'll make sure Frankie does what you say." I agreed to give him another try, and he fortunately changed his attitude as well as his golf swing, and became a very fine player.

I had three assistants during my time at Inverness—Tommy Sullivan, Herman Lang, and Ray Jamison, who I hired from Ridgewood. Ray was an excellent golfer and teacher, and after I left Inverness, he moved on to be head pro at Hackensack Country Club in New Jersey, where he worked for many years. Herman Lang was a wonderful pro too, and was later hired to be head pro at Inverness until he retired and was succeeded by their present pro, Don Perne, also a fine man.

I had quite a few bad last rounds in '40 that cost me some tournaments. I became conscious of this, and it wasn't because I was nervous or choking or freezing up, but I gave some thought to it, and changed my philosophy. Regardless of whether I was behind or ahead going to the last round, I tried to really charge and go all out—not foolishly taking chances, but building myself up for the last round mentally. That's why I began to play the fourth round the best later in my career.

1940 was a little like 1938. I had won four tournaments and added another major, the PGA, to my record, but I couldn't expect it to be as big a year as '39 had been. I was enjoying life in Toledo and my job at Inverness. I finished second on the money list, and I felt very fortunate. It was really a wonderful year, considering how little golf I played.

Louise and I left Toledo for Texarkana at the first cool spell, about the middle of September. I left my assistant in charge of the shop until it actually closed around the first of October. In December, we drove to Miami for the Miami Open again, which I managed to win for the second year in a row. That put another $2,537.50 in the bank, so my total winnings for the year, according to my little black book, were $9696. No, we weren't having to borrow from Dad Shofner any more.

I went deer hunting that November in Uvalde, Texas, with Hogan, Demaret, and the new Winchester rifle I'd received from the folks at Reading the year before. I bagged a beautiful buck with a twelve-point rack of horns, but the game warden decided that since I had an Ohio driver's license and Ohio plates on my car, my official domicile in Denton and my Texas hunting permit didn't count, so he confiscated the deer and I had to pay an $80 fine. It really upset me, because I'd obeyed all the rules, but this fellow didn't agree. And $80 was a lot of money in those days, especially for us.

Very few people today realize what it was like to be on the tour then. You didn't make enough money even if you were a fine player to make a living or ever accumulate anything just playing in tournaments, so it was necessary to have a club job. Certainly, the better you played and more tournaments you won, the better your chances of getting a job at a fine club. Especially if you were toward the end of your career and wanted to settle down and not travel any more, having a good tournament record was a really big help. Being a good player also helped you get more lessons, because people thought if you could play that well you certainly should know something about the game and be able to impart your knowledge to your pupils. That wasn't always true, because some of the touring pros didn't ever spend much time teaching or become good teachers. The best teachers in my opinion were those who had taught themselves how to play, and who also had the ability to take it slow and easy with amateurs and be very patient. A top touring pro could also help increase membership and playing activity. Ridgewood was pretty full when I arrived, but Reading wasn't, because there were a lot of golf clubs in Reading and it wasn't that large a town, so my coming there after winning the Masters and then winning the Open two years later really did increase the membership. Inverness was always a famous club ever since 1920, when they held the U.S. Open there for the first time, so Inverness was also full when I arrived, but I did give quite a few more lessons than the pro before me had done. A couple of other examples of fine touring pros getting jobs at good clubs were Craig Wood at Winged Foot and Claude Harmon after him. No doubt their playing ability helped a great deal, in both their getting the jobs and helping to improve the clubs as well.

There were a few pros, like Hogan and Snead, who were registered at a club such as Hershey for Ben and Greenbrier for Sam, but who never worked there full time, really, though the club got the benefit of their names and the prestige associated with their wins.

But my situation was more like the rest of the fellows out there. I was very busy at Inverness and extremely happy there. I did enough traveling during the winter in California and the southeast that by the time the Masters was over, Louise and I were happy to get back to Toledo and spend the relatively cool summer there. Plus, I was making more money at the club—from salary, lessons, and shop profits—than I could count on making on the tour anyway.

Still, it was hard to keep my game in shape, and essentially, my golf suffered the first three years I was at Inverness. For instance, I started out 1941 pretty rough. Played badly the first two events, with a 302 at the L.A. Open and a 290 at Oakland, and just plain failed to qualify for the San Francisco Match Play tournament. Then I tied for fifth at the Crosby Pro-Am and for second in the Western Open at Phoenix Country Club. On the last hole, I hit a high 6-iron to the pin, which was cut fairly close to the front, over a bunker. I made that eight-footer to tie for second.

We pros always enjoyed playing in Phoenix, because Barry and Bob Goldwater would invite quite a few of us pros out to Barry's house for a steak cookout during the tournament. This was long before Barry ever became Senator Goldwater. In fact, the two brothers owned Goldwater's department store, a wonderful store which they ran quite well. The Goldwaters were very nice people—Barry was a natural leader, a good thinker, and good at speaking. Louise and I always looked forward to that party, and since I had won the tournament in '39, I was on the list of invitees the rest of the time I was on the tour. This must sound at times as though all we pros thought of was our stomachs. The truth is, traveling the way we did, sometimes the food we'd get was all right, sometimes it wasn't very good at all, and once in a while, it would be excellent. We'd all had enough lean times that we really appreciated good food when we could get it, and that wasn't any too often.

The Texas Open was next, and that year it was played at Willow Springs in San Antonio, a tough little course. We had terrible weather, both snow and hail, but we went ahead and played in it. Lawson Little shot a 64 the final round—none of us could believe that—and I tied for fourth, mainly due to my putting. I had streaks of poor putting then; I remember after I'd played in the British Open, someone said that if I had putted well, I could have set a new scoring record. Well, that may be or may be not, but as I've said before, we didn't work on our putting much because of the inconsistency of the greens. We concentrated on getting our approaches close to the pin, which was a lot more effective.

I didn't do too well in New Orleans, either, tied for eighth. Then we went on to Miami for the Four-ball. My partner was McSpaden again, and again we lost to Runyan and Smith in the second round. Maybe that's why Jug and I were called the Gold Dust Twins—because we didn't get the gold, just the dust.

Next was the Seminole Invitational Pro-Am—not an official PGA event, but we loved the course and the food and loved to get to go. My partner that year was a fine amateur named Findlay Douglas. He was sixty-six years old and the 1898 National Amateur Champion. He still carried a 6 handicap, and he was a pleasure to play with. On the last hole, we needed a 3 to win, and a 4 to tie. Well, I made the 3, so that made Findlay pretty happy. Interestingly enough, though my winnings weren't considered official, I did get $232.50 for my two rounds of 64-71, and $571.79 for my share of the Calcutta pool for a total of $803.29. Not bad pay for two rounds of golf, back then.

Then Louise and I headed back to Toledo so I could get things ready in the shop. The golf course wouldn't really open until the middle of April, and there wouldn't be much activity until after Decoration Day—what's now called Memorial Day. But I needed to get things ordered and see that things would be running right when I did return after the Masters.

The next tournament was the North and South at Pinehurst. I played all right, tying for fourth, but had a bad last round of 76. I don't remember what caused it now—sometimes it's a blessing not to have a perfect memory. But the Greensboro tournament started the very next day, and I did better. I had a hot second round of 64 and won, so I was real pleased. A round of 64 can almost make you forget a 76. Another reason I was pleased to win there was that the weather was real bad, and the courses weren't in good condition at all. Playing well in conditions like that gives you confidence. Of course, we pros didn't complain about course conditions then—we were just glad to get to play.

You know, looking over my record for '41, I'm surprised to see how many bad last rounds I had. It's understandable that I didn't win much until I got those last rounds turned around some. The next week at Asheville, North Carolina, I tied for tenth on a very hard course and never scored better than 72, though at the Masters I played very steady and finished three shots back of Craig Wood, who won.

Because my contract limited me to six weeks away from the club, I skipped the Goodall Round Robin in favor of playing in the U.S. Open, which was at Colonial in Fort Worth. They had put new sod on two greens and the course was in terrible shape. There had also been a lot of rain, which didn't help anything. People didn't know what to do then for golf courses like they do now, so we all just played and tried our best. I had another terrible final round of 77, tied for seventeenth, and won $50. You could say I was disgusted with myself. So the next few weeks I worked hard and finished second three times in a row, at Mahoning Valley, the Inverness Four-Ball with McSpaden, and the PGA at Cherry Hills.

A couple of interesting things happened at that PGA championship. I remember in my second match, with Bill Heinlein, I was coasting along through the front nine. Then all of a sudden he got hot and pretty soon I was 2 down going to the 13th. I managed to pull myself together and won 2 up. Next, I dispensed with Guldahl 2 and 1, and faced Hogan in the quarterfinal. I was 1-up going to the final hole. He had a fifteen-foot putt and I had a twelve. He missed his, I made mine, and that was the match. Remember, all of these were 36-hole matches, and the qualifier was thirty-six holes as well.

Next was the semifinal against Gene Sarazen, always a tough competitor. Fortunately I won, 2 and 1. Later he came over to me in the locker room and said, "Nelson, you double-crossed me." Surprised, I looked at him and said, "How did I do that, Gene?" He said, "I've been playing my irons so well, I decided I'd let you outdrive me, then put my ball close to the pin and it would bother you. But you just put yours inside me all day!"

Next came the final against Vic Ghezzi, and one of the most unusual things happened that I ever saw or heard of in golf. I played wonderfully well the first twenty-seven holes and was leading 3 up going to the back nine. But I'd had such tough matches before this one, all of a sudden I just felt like all the adrenalin went out of me. I tried to fight it, but it didn't do any good. After thirty-six holes Vic and I were dead even.

The playoff was sudden death. On the 2nd hole, we drove, then hit our approach shots close to the green. We both chipped past the hole about forty-six inches, and our balls were fairly close together, though mine was about a half-inch further away and his was about eight inches to the left. The referee, Ed Dudley, asked if Vic's ball was in my way, and I said no. But when I took my stance, I accidentally moved his ball one inch with my foot. Well, of course, that was a penalty. In match play, it meant loss of the hole and in this case the match. Naturally, I conceded.

But Vic said he didn't want to win that way, and there was quite a discussion. They decided that I should go ahead and putt, but I knew the rules. In my mind I'd already lost the match and knew it wasn't right to let me putt. I didn't want anyone ever to say I'd won by some sort of fluke. So of course I wasn't concentrating real well and missed the putt, and Ghezzi won, which was only right.

The next tournament I played in was the St. Paul Open at the end of July. It was a six- or eight-hour drive from Toledo, so it was reachable. I tied for seventh and won $278. You see, I really did make more money at Inverness than I could count on on the tour. With my salary, all the income from my lessons, and shop profits, I did pretty well, with the exception of winning the occasional big tournament. This was why, with my commitment to Inverness, I had to pretty much concentrate on the majors and big money tournaments, because anything less would cost me time at Inverness, plus lesson fees and shop income. And if I didn't play well, I could end up losing even more.

So I worked until the first week in September, when I drove to Chicago for the Tam O'Shanter. This was a new tournament put on by George S. May, a "business engineer." That meant he advised other companies how to run their businesses. He was the first to put up a lot of money for a tournament. The first year, 1941, the first prize was $2000, the next year $2500, and it kept going up.

I played well in that first Tam O'Shanter and won the $2000. No, I didn't make that much each week in the shop, but that was just one tournament of four or five that had big purses, and I sure couldn't count on winning all of them. I always did well at the Tam, though. I wish the course were still there—it was turned into a development some years after George May died. The course was fairly hard, and the fairways were narrow. I played well there for two main reasons:

one, it was a big money tournament so I tried harder, and two, I played those clover fairways well. Not that they planted the fairways in clover, but there was a lot of it on the course, and there were no chemicals to control it back then. Having learned to play on Texas hardpan, I always clipped the ball off the fairway and didn't take much turf like some of the other boys. That clover had a lot of sticky juice if you hit very much of it, which would cause you to hit fliers. Fliers have little or no spin and you never can be sure what they'll do, except it's usually something you don't want.

After the Tam, I played in a couple of little events near Inverness, the Hearst Invitational and the Ohio Open just outside Toledo, where I had a final-round 62, one of my lower scores in competition. Then Louise and I took our annual trip back to Texarkana. In December, we drove to Florida again, where I won the Miami Open for the second year in a row. That brought me $2000 prize money, plus an extra $537.50 in pro-am and low-round awards. It was a tough little course and the greens were stiff bermuda with a lot of grain. But in the practice round, I noted which way the grain ran on each hole, and most of the time, I didn't pay as much attention to where the pin was as to which way the grain ran on that green and where I wanted to be when I putted. I was hitting my irons well, so I was able to place most of my approach shots where I would be putting downgrain, because that was the easiest putt you could have on that type of grass.

Right after Christmas, I played in the Beaumont Open and tied for seventh, then won the Harlingen Open with 70-65-70-66. The Beaumont course had the narrowest fairways of any course I ever saw. They were lined with trees, and Chick Harbert, who had trouble keeping his drives straight anyway, would tee his ball up as high as he could and hit toward wherever the green was. He'd say, "If I'm going to be in the trees, I'd rather be closer to the green." Even as straight as I was, I had trouble staying in the fairways. They were the talk of the week.

I finished up 1941 playing in 27 tournaments, and my black book says I won $11,819.12, though Bill Inglish's records say it was a little more, $12,025. The difference wasn't enough to worry about, that's for sure.

Of course, the whole year of '41, there had been a lot of talk and worry over the situation in Europe, and we knew it was just a matter of time before the United States would get involved. Sure enough, that

Byron Nelson, about eight months old.

At age 5½.

Byron with his mother, Madge Nelson, and her parents, M. F. and Ellen Allen.

Byron in 1934.

Louise Shofner Nelson.

Louise and Byron on their wedding day in 1934, leaning against Byron's 1933 Ford roadster.

Taking a lunch break on the final day of the 1936 Metropolitan Open, which he eventually won.

A locust swarm during an exhibition at the Jockey Club in Argentina in 1937. After 3 holes the match was called off.

Playing in the 1941 exhibition match for British relief, Byron nearly holed out after Olin Dutra picked up his ball and placed it on a pop bottle lying nearby.

Bob Hope, Bing Crosby, Byron, Johnny Weissmuller, and Jimmy Demaret have a little fun in Houston during a wartime Red Cross/USO tour.

Left to right:
Ben Hogan, Byron, Bobby Jones, and Jimmy Demaret at Augusta National Golf Club in 1942.

Playing out of the rough on the way to victory at the 1945 PGA Championship.

Celebrating a world record 259 at the 1945 Seattle Open.

Byron with his mother and father on his Denton farm in the early forties.

Feeding the hogs in Denton.

This Ford tractor from the 1940s is still running.

The Masters Champions for the first dozen years, excluding the war years: Horton Smith, Byron, Henry Picard, Jimmy Demaret, Craig Wood, Gene Sarazen, Herman Keiser. (Ralph Guldahl is missing.)

The 1947 Ryder Cup Team. ***Standing:*** *Dutch Harrison, Lloyd Mangrum, Herman Keiser, Byron, Sam Snead.* ***Sitting:*** *Herman Barron, Jimmy Demaret, Ben Hogan, Ed Oliver, Lew Worsham.*

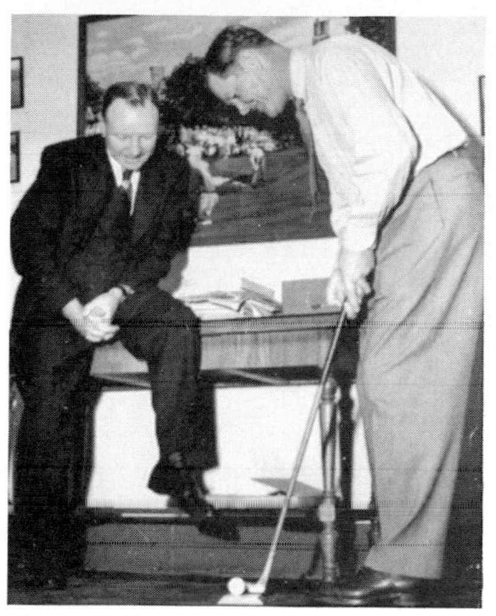

Byron putting in good friend Eddie Lowery's office in San Francisco.

Byron with Babe Didrikson Zaharias in 1946.

Ben Hogan, Byron, and Herman Keiser at Augusta in 1946, just before the final round.

Byron receiving some tips from Ed Sullivan in the early fifties.

With Bob Hope at Pebble Beach in the late sixties.

Byron with President Eisenhower, Ben Hogan, and Cliff Roberts at Augusta in the late fifties.

Arnold Palmer, Byron, Doug Sanders, and Gene Littler at the 50th anniversary of the LA Open in the mid-seventies.

Presenting Ken Venturi with the Sportsman of the Year award after he won the U.S. Open in 1964.

Byron with longtime ABC "Wide World of Golf" partner Chris Schenkel doing a Masters tournament broadcast in the early sixties.

At President Ford's tournament in Vail, Colorado. The President's birdie putt has just lipped out.

Ken Venturi and Byron doing a clinic at Jasper Park Lodge in Canada in 1980.

Byron with winner Tom Watson sometime in the late seventies at the Byron Nelson Classic . . .

. . . and in May 1992 at the same event.

A publicity shot taken in 1981 at Augusta.

Byron and wife Peggy at a local charity tournament in 1992.

Vice President Dan Quayle, Sam Snead, Gene Sarazen, Peggy Nelson, and President George Bush watch as Byron putts on the White House lawn in May 1992.

The 1992 Masters Champions Club Dinner. **First Row:** *Byron, Tom Watson, Gene Sarazen, Jack Stephens, Ian Woosnam, Henry Picard, Herman Keiser, Sam Snead.* **Second row:** *George Archer, Nick Faldo, Doug Ford, Gay Brewer, Billy Casper, Bob Goalby, Art Wall, Ray Floyd, Bernhard Langer, Arnold Palmer, Seve Ballesteros.* **Third row:** *Ben Crenshaw, Craig Stadler, Larry Mize, Tommy Aaron, Sandy Lyle, Jack Nicklaus, Gary Player, Fuzzy Zoeller, Charles Coody.*

December we jumped in with both feet, and everyone's lives changed almost overnight. Most people thought we'd lick both Germany and Japan in six months, come home victorious, and get on with business as usual—but of course, it didn't turn out that way.

All of the men who were able to signed up for the draft, and then we tried to go about our business whatever way we could until our number came up. You know, it's a good thing we really can't see into the future, because if we'd been able to back then, I don't think many folks could have stood it.

Starting out in '42, I tied for sixth in Los Angeles, which kept the L.A. Open on my list of important tournaments I still wanted to win. Then in Oakland I did win, by five shots. This is how I did it: The greens there were quite soft, and all eighteen had a definite slope from back to front. I noticed that we were all hitting at the flag, and our balls were spinning back, sometimes off the green. I changed tactics after the last practice round, and aimed for the top of the flag. Then, when my ball spun back, it ended up closer to the hole. That's the main reason I won. I remember the pro there was Dewey Longworth, brother to my good friend Ted Longworth from Texarkana. He was a good player and a nice man, just like Ted.

Our next stop, the San Francisco Open, was played at the California Golf Club where my friend Eddie Lowery was a member. I played well but putted very poorly and finished eighth. I've already said that most of us pros didn't spend much time on putting, because of the difference in the greens and so on, but I had another reason. I had originally learned to putt on stiff bermuda greens, where you had to hit the putt rather than roll it. I never really got over that, and I didn't work on it enough because we tend not to work on things we're not good at, and that certainly was true for me. I didn't three-putt much, but my bad distance was eight to fifteen feet. Those were the ones I didn't make as often as I should have.

Hogan won at San Francisco, though he was still hooking quite a bit then. On the 18th, which was a dogleg right, Hogan hooked a 4-wood high up over the trees and back into the fairway, because he just couldn't fade the ball or even count on hitting it straight then. Though he hooked it, he used the same swing and did the same thing every time, so he got to be pretty consistent.

At the Crosby and the Western I didn't do very well. I'd occasionally have several weeks when I wasn't chipping or putting well, either one. But I practiced some, and by the Texas Open, I was doing better, finished eighth, then sixth at New Orleans, and second at St. Petersburg. Still couldn't make much headway in the Miami Four-Ball, though—got knocked out in the second round again, this time with Henry Picard as my partner. But at least it was someone else beating us—Harper and Keiser instead of Runyan and Smith.

My game was getting better all along, but of course, so was everyone else's. Our on-the-job training was working for quite a few of the players, from those who had loads of natural talent to those who had some talent and a lot of persistence. There still were no real teachers to go to like the boys have today. Most of the older club pros were still making the transition to steel shafts, or even teaching the old way of pronating and all, so they really couldn't help anyone much. We had to figure things out on our own for the most part, and some fellows were better at it than others. But it was getting more and more important to have most of your rounds under 70, if you wanted to have a chance to win.

After Miami, I played in the Seminole Invitational again, enjoyed all their good food and being with the other players, and won $50. Well, at least the food was free, there was no entry fee, and my caddie only cost $8, so I had $42 more when I left than I did when I arrived.

I did better in the North and South, but had a bad last round of 73, tied for third, and won $500. At Greensboro, I had another poor last round of 74 and tied for fourth. Back then, they sometimes had prizes for low round of the day, and I tied in the third round with a 68, so I got another $25. Then I finished third at Asheville, and won $550. In my last five tournaments, I'd finished second once, third twice, and fourth once. I was definitely getting steadier, despite final rounds I wasn't very happy with.

During that Asheville tournament, I realized there hadn't been any pictures or publicity about me. It seemed the articles were all about the other players. I figured the press had gotten tired of writing about me, and I had gotten just enough used to all the attention that I kind of missed it. Anyway, about the third round, I was playing just so-so and was tied for the lead or leading. On the 16th hole, I put my ball in the left bunker, which was over six feet deep. I got in there and was trying to figure out how to get out and close enough to one-putt, and stuck my head up and looked over the bank to see the pin. Right above the bunker, on the green to my left, was a photographer, getting ready to photograph me as I played my shot. I said to him, "Where have you been all this week? Just get out of my way!" I did get up and down, but I felt bad about what I'd said, so I looked the fellow up afterwards and apologized, and he said, "That's no problem, I shouldn't have been where I was."

Along about this time, McSpaden and I were on a train together, talking about the money to be made on the tour. We figured then that with an interest rate of about 10%, if we could make $100,000 during our careers, we could retire and live quite comfortably on that annual interest of $10,000. That seemed quite reasonable at the time, but it's a ridiculous idea now.

Next was the Masters, but before the tournament started, I played a match there with Bob Jones against Henry Picard and Gene Sarazen. We were all playing well that day, including Bob, and on the back nine, Henry and Gene made seven straight birdies—but never won a hole from us. Jones shot 31 on the back nine that day. Amazing.

Then the tournament began, and fortunately, I played very well, ending the first round with 68. Paul Runyan led nearly the whole first round, and ended up tied with Horton Smith at 67. Sam Byrd was tied with me at 68, and Jimmy Demaret was behind us with 70. The second round, Horton led by himself for one hole, then I tied him with a birdie at the second hole. It was kind of huckledy-buck between Paul, Horton, and me for the next five holes, but I pulled ahead of them both with a birdie at the par-5 eighth. I was leading then for the rest of the second round, when I shot 67, and all through the third, but lost a little steam in the fourth when I bogeyed six, seven, and eight. Hogan had caught up with me when he birdied the eighth himself. He was several groups ahead of me, of course, so I couldn't see how he was doing. I birdied 9 to lead again, and led till the last hole despite bogeying 17.

When I stepped up to hit my drive on 18, I noticed the tee box was kind of soft and slick. As I started my downswing, my foot slipped a little and I made a bad swing, pushing my tee shot deep into the woods on the right. By now I knew Ben had shot 70, and I had to have a par just to tie. When I got to my ball, I was relieved to find I had a clear swing. The ball was just sitting on the ground nicely, and there was an opening in front of me, about twenty feet wide, between two trees. I took my 5-iron and hooked that ball up and onto the green fifteen feet from the pin and almost birdied it—but I did make my par. So you can see why I felt very fortunate to tie.

Then came the playoff. This was one of the rare occasions when I was so keyed up my stomach was upset, even during the night. I lost my breakfast the next morning, which I thought might be a good sign, because I had always played well when I became that sick beforehand, and it always wore off after the first few holes. When I saw Hogan in the clubhouse, he said, "I heard you were sick last night," and I said, "Yes, Ben, I was." He offered to postpone the playoff, but I said, "No, we'll play." I did have half of a plain chicken sandwich and some hot tea, which helped a little, but you can see in the picture that was made of Ben and me when we were on the first tee that I was very nervous and tense.

This was probably one of the most unusual playoffs in golf, in that at least twenty-five of the pros who had played in the tournament stayed to watch us in the playoff. I don't recall that ever happening any other time. Ben and I were both very flattered by that.

Flattered or not, though, I started poorly. On the first hole, I hit a bad drive into the trees and my ball ended up right next to a pine cone, which I couldn't move because the ball would move with it. On my second shot, the ball hit more trees in front of me, so I ended up with a 6 while Ben made his par. We parred the second and the third. Then, on the fourth, a long par 3, I thought the pin was cut just over the bunker, but my long iron was short and went in the bunker, so I made 4 while Ben made 3. We'd played four holes and I was 3 down.

The 5th hole had a very tough pin placement at the back of the green, but we both parred it. The par-3 6th, I began to come alive a little and put my tee shot ten feet away, while Hogan missed his to the left and made 4. I put my ten-footer in for birdie, so I caught up two shots right there.

We both parred the 7th. Next, I eagled 8 and Ben birdied, so now we were even. I picked up three more shots on the next five holes, including a shot on 12 that rimmed the hole and stopped six inches away. But Ben didn't get rattled much. Though his tee shot stopped short on the bank, his chip almost went in for a 2.

When we arrived at the 18th tee. I was leading by 2, and Ben's approach shot ended up way at the back of the green, with the pin way at the front. I played short of the green on purpose, not wanting to take a chance on the bunker, because in those days, a ball landing in the bunker would bury, and then you really had your hands full. But I figured I might chip up and make par, or no worse than 5, while I was pretty sure Ben couldn't make his putt from up on the top ledge. I was right—he two-putted, I made 5 and won by one shot.

Louise and Valerie had stayed together up at the clubhouse during the playoff, and they were both very happy for me. Valerie was a very gracious lady, and Ben was always fine whether he won or lost. It was a great victory for me, and more so because I'd been able to beat Ben, who by then was getting to be a very fine player. The fact that he had come from well behind everyone else here showed that he had a lot of determination and persistence.

Then it was time for us to head back to Toledo and Inverness, where we stayed for six weeks before I played again. The PGA that year was at Seaview Country Club in New Jersey, and I was up against Jim Turnesa, one of the wonderful Turnesa brothers, in the semifinal. Jim was in the service, and naturally, the gallery was pulling for him, which I could well understand. I was 1 up when we came to the 18th hole, and I was short of the green, but chipped up two feet from the hole. Jim putted his stone dead and I gave it to him. The gallery gave him a tremendous round of applause because he'd played so well, and I thought it was one of the nicest things I'd ever seen a gallery do, to applaud like that when they thought he'd lost. I felt I had taken enough time over my putt, but maybe I hadn't waited long enough for the noise to die down and lost my concentration. Anyway, I missed my putt, so we were tied. On the first playoff hole I hit a terrible drive and pulled it into the sticks. I made bogey, so Turnesa won, but ended up losing in the final to Snead. I was very disgusted with myself, feeling I'd just thrown the match away.

Back home, the Inverness Four-Ball was two weeks later, and my partner was Jimmy Thomson. We made a pretty good team, because I was playing well generally, able to make pars most of the time, and he was a good partner because he was so long. I'd hit a good drive and he'd be twenty to forty yards ahead of me. We managed to finish fourth and won $454.

The next week was the Hale America Open at Ridgemoor in Chicago, where I finished fourth and won $475. I skipped the Mahoning Valley tournament the next week in favor of the Tam O'Shanter again, and managed to win it—but just by the skin of my teeth. I was leading by five shots going into the fourth round and playing very well in beautiful weather. It seemed I had the tournament won, though I certainly didn't feel that way. Anyway, on the first hole, I left my approach shot short and the green had a ridge on it with the pin on top. I three-putted for a 5. On the second hole, I hit an excellent drive that landed in a divot. But it was sitting all right and I was sure I could reach the green in two, though there was a creek just in front. Well, I hit it thin, it went in the creek, and I three-putted for a 7. The 3rd was a par 3 with a lake in front of the green; I hit a 6-iron that landed on the edge of the green but rolled back into the water. I'd made one bogey and two doubles, and was five over after three holes. I was out in 42—just terrible. But I pulled myself together and played the back in 35, which put me in a tie with Clayton Heafner after starting the day five shots ahead of the field. You think I don't feel for the boys today when the same thing happens to them? I surely do.

We had the playoff the next day—all playoffs were eighteen holes in medal tournaments, and there were just about as many playoffs then as there are now. But the beautiful weather had gone—it was windy, rainy, and miserable. However, I was steamed up enough to play well, shot a 67 to Heafner's 71, and won the Tam again. That was a good comeback for me, particularly because of the way I'd lost in the PGA just a few weeks before.

I won two other small tournaments that year, the Ohio Open and the Charles River Invitational, but neither of them were official events, so they don't count on my record, though they were good experience for me, and it never hurts to win, even if you're just playing a casual round with friends.

What did happen that year—in fact, the next month—was my professional baseball debut. Growing up, I liked to play baseball and was a good outfielder. At one point, I thought quite a bit about which one I wanted to concentrate on, and chose golf. But I still loved baseball and went to watch a game whenever I had the chance. In Toledo, that meant the Mudhens, a farm team for the St. Louis Browns. Fred Haney was their manager, and he and I had played golf some at Inverness. The

Mudhens had an exhibition game coming up against the Browns, and Fred got the idea of having me play in it to get more people out to the game, which was going to benefit the Red Cross. He advertised it as "Golf Night," and gave me ten days to practice with the team. I remember that catching the ball in the type of glove we had then was making my hand really sore. He told me I could fix it by sitting and tapping my palm with a pencil over and over to toughen the skin, and it worked.

In the practice sessions, I did all right on everything but batting. You just can't believe how fast that ball went past the plate. You really had to be ready to hit before it left the pitcher's hand, and I never quite caught on. Then they got me suited up, and Fred told me it was fortunate I was the size I was, because I wasn't too hard to fit.

The game began, and I started in right field in place of a fellow named Jim Bucher. Milt Byrnes was the center fielder, and he said, "Byron, if you get the ball, just toss it to me and I'll come running and throw it in," because he knew I'd have trouble throwing accurately the distance to second or third or home. Well, the first thing you know, someone hits a grounder right at me. I scooped it up and threw it to second, which kept the runner on first and got me a big round of applause from the fans.

Then it was my turn to bat, and I whiffed. The fans started hollering, "Better stick to golf, Nelson!" and "Put Bucher back in!" Fred kept me in till the fourth inning, though, and then he said, "Byron, you've had enough fun, and I really would like to win this game, so I'm taking you out." That was fine with me. So Bucher goes back in, and strikes out his first time at the plate. Now the fans start yelling, "Put Nelson back in!" And then when we took the field, Bucher tried to catch a fly ball and dropped it, which really got the fans yelling even louder, "Put Nelson back in!" It was a lot of fun for me, but not so much for Bucher.

There's a good follow-up to this story, though. The Ohio Open was a few days later in Cleveland. Marty Cromb, the pro at Toledo Country Club, rode on the train with me to Cleveland, and was criticizing me severely for being so foolish as to play baseball. "You could have hurt yourself—broken a finger, ruined your career," he said. When we got to Cleveland, we were met by a friend of his, Bertie Way, a Scottish pro. Marty got to telling Bertie how crazy I was to play baseball, and how it was going to hurt me playing in the tournament.

Well, Bertie got all fired up and went to see some buddies of his, making bets against me, even though I was the favorite. We had no time to play a practice round, so I went out when the tournament started, scrambled around on the first hole and made par, scrambled again on the second, then settled down and started playing. To make a long story short, I birdied 6, 7, 8, 9, 10, 11, and 12, shot 63, and won the tournament. Bertie was so mad at Marty I thought he was going to kill him. He really thought Marty had set him up.

By this time the war was getting worse, and many of the pros were already in the service. It was becoming more difficult to put on tournaments, and at the end of '42 the tour just plain stopped.

There would be no Masters or U.S. Open for the duration of the war, and none of the regular events were played for all of '43. We did have just a couple of tournaments that had pretty good fields, but most of the boys were either in the service in some capacity or doing exhibitions for the Red Cross or war bonds.

Back in the spring of '42, when the draft was in full swing, I'd had a conversation with Colonel Woolley from the artillery training base at Camp Perry, near Toledo. He had played golf with me several times and thought I had a great eye for judging distance. He knew I had registered for the draft, and wanted me to let him know when my number was coming up, because he wanted to get me to teach his men how to judge distance. I went down to enlist soon after he talked to me, but I failed the physical because of my blood condition. It was not hemophilia, but what was called "free bleeding"—my blood didn't coagulate within the normal amount of time. Later that year my number did come up, and I failed the physical again for the same reason. They could have put me in a desk job of some sort, of course, but I still would have to go through basic training, and the Army didn't want to take a chance on me getting hurt out in the field and not being able to get help soon enough. After I failed the physical the second time, they didn't call me any more. So I was out of it. McSpaden was rejected too, because he had severe allergies and sinusitis. So there we were, looking as healthy as could be, but not in uniform like the rest of the boys. It was an uncomfortable feeling, believe me.

But it wasn't too long after we were rejected that Ed Dudley, who was president of the PGA then, asked if we could do some exhibitions for the war effort, visiting rehab centers and so on. He and Fred Corcoran, who had been managing the tour, wanted golf to do its part. So Jug and I began in late '42 and did exhibitions all through '43 and part of '44. David Fay, president of the USGA, told me recently that we did 110 of them, traveling back and forth across the country. We actually criss-crossed the United States four times doing Red Cross and USO shows, and going to the camps where they had rehabilitation centers for the soldiers. A lot of the camps had putt-putt courses and par-3 courses for the boys. Sometimes we'd go on military planes, sometimes on trains. We got no money, but MacGregor helped pay my expenses and Wilson paid some of McSpaden's. The people at Inverness really supported me during that time too, making sure my shop was being run right while I was gone.

We started in the early spring, working with the Red Cross and the USO to help the boys' morale. There were very few golf facilities, so we didn't do a lot of exhibitions, but we did visit the hospitals and camps and shook hands with the soldiers and told them how much their sacrifices meant to us and to the whole country. Most of the patients were ambulatory, so when there were golf facilities available, we'd show the soldiers the fundamentals of grip, stance, and so forth, or hit some drives and other types of shots to demonstrate the basics. One time we went to a camp near a rocket-testing site in New Mexico, I believe, and they shot off a few rockets for us to see. It was impressive—and scary.

Because of all the gas rationing, we traveled on restricted types of orders. We'd be put on troop trains or planes where they'd always feed the servicemen first, which was only right. We weren't neglected, you understand—just hungry a lot. Once, I remember they ran out of food before they got to us, so when we stopped at a little station near El Paso, Jug and I jumped out and ran in to see if we could get a sandwich. Well, the man said, "These are for the soldiers," but after we explained what we were doing and why we were on the train, he finally let us have one sandwich apiece.

It was tougher on McSpaden than on me in a way, because he really did love to eat and could eat a lot more than I could. Once, in Seattle, we stayed at a hotel and at breakfast, McSpaden had half a cantaloupe with ice cream, ham, eggs, toast, and tea. I had what you'd call a more normal breakfast. When he was done, he asked the waitress to bring him another half cantaloupe with ice cream. The waitress said, "Are you kidding?" and Jug replied, "That's what I ordered, isn't it?" She brought the cantaloupe, put it down on the table very carefully, and then backed away like she was expecting him to explode any second. That fellow really could eat.

On the trains, once in a while we'd have a berth to sleep in, but mostly we just slept sitting up like a lot of the soldiers. Even though we were pretty young ourselves, most of the servicemen seemed like kids away from home for the first time. But their morale was quite good. I'd have to say the whole experience was enjoyable for us, but very tiring with all the travel, and it wasn't easy to see those young boys going off to war or coming back all busted up.

In the middle of July, we did have a tournament called the All American, played at George May's Tam O'Shanter course. The purse was $5000. I tied for third, thanks to a final-round 68, and won $900. I was one shot back of McSpaden and Buck White, a pretty good player who wasn't around too long on the tour. McSpaden beat Buck in the playoff. In August, I played in the Chicago Victory Open. I started off with a 68, then did three 72's in a row and finished fifth. I didn't win any money because they paid only the first four places. Then there was the Minneapolis Four Ball at Golden Valley, which I played with McSpaden. We finished second at plus 8. They also had the Miami Open in December, but I didn't play in it, most likely because I was doing an exhibition somewhere to raise money for the war or the Red Cross.

I did, however, play in and win the Kentucky Open that year. It was played at a course called Whittle Springs, and I remember it well because I was presented with my winning check by Sergeant Alvin York, the much-decorated hero of World War I. That was quite an honor for me.

We also had sort of a substitute Ryder Cup tournament that summer, called the Ryder Cup Challenge. I was selected to be on the Ryder Cup team, and Walter Hagen captained the "Challengers." We played at Plum Hollow in Detroit. McSpaden and I tied Willie Goggin and Buck White in the foursomes, plus I beat Goggin in the singles, 4 and 3. We beat Hagen's team overall $8\frac{1}{2}$–$3\frac{1}{2}$.

Sometimes we'd pick up other people who'd play these exhibitions with us—people from golf or the entertainment field like Bob Hope or Bing Crosby. We didn't always play eighteen holes, usually only nine, but they'd build a platform near the clubhouse at whatever course we were at, and whoever was in charge of raising the money for the Red Cross or selling the war bonds would get up on the platform, and it would be almost like an auction. A man would say, "I'll give ten thousand dollars if Bing will sing 'White Christmas.'" Or "I'll give five hundred if Hope will tell a joke." We'd raise tens of thousands that way. It was exciting at times, and I really believe we contributed more to the war effort that way than if we'd been accepted for service. Another benefit was that it kept my game in tiptop shape for when the war was over and the tour started again. Fortunately for some of the pros who were in the service, they had the opportunity to play quite a bit, too. Sam Snead was in the Navy, stationed at La Jolla, California, and he played nearly every day with the admirals and such. Horton Smith, Ben Hogan, and Jimmy Demaret also had quite a few opportunities to play—not just at the bases where they were stationed, but in whatever tournaments there were, too. By the end of '43, we'd played at quite a few camps where our fellow pros were stationed. So despite the fact that the tour was canceled, we did get to see the fellows from time to time and play with them a little.

Once we did nineteen days in a row with Hope and Crosby, who were great. Bing would sing and Bob would tell jokes, and the crowd loved it. They were both just as you imagine them, born entertainers. Bob was always telling jokes, and Bing was quick-witted, too, plus he was completely natural at all times. The people loved them both. On one of these stops we were staying at a hotel and to avoid the crush of autograph seekers they ushered us in through the back door and up the elevator. But some of the fans had seen the elevator going up and where it had stopped, and they all trooped up six flights of stairs to our floor. Bob and Bing were so impressed with the fact that these kids would climb all those stairs just for an autograph that they signed every single one of them.

One other time, I was with Hope and we were on an Army plane. Sometimes there wouldn't be any seats—we'd sit on a bucket or a box or just on the floor. Anyway, they had picked us up in Alabama and we were going to Memphis. Ed Dudley was going to meet us and we were to put on a show there. When we landed, the runway was very narrow, plus it had rained a lot, the ground there was very muddy, and the plane slipped off the runway and into the mud up to its hubcaps. It took forty-five minutes for them to get a vehicle big enough to pull that plane out of the mud. But we got there and did the show just a little late and everyone seemed happy.

I did have one pretty scary experience during this time. I was with Bing Crosby in San Antonio, and a man picked us up at the train station and took us to an army base—I don't quite remember which one—where Bing was to perform. There were a lot of restrictions then, and when we arrived at the gate, there were two sentries with rifles guarding it. But this fellow who'd picked us up just drove past them without even stopping. There was another pair of sentries a little further on, and when they saw us drive past the first sentries they immediately raised their rifles and ordered us to stop. I was in the front seat and Bing was in the back, and when we saw those rifles go up, Bing hit the floor and I ducked as best I could. We truly thought we were going to get shot at. Of course, the driver had to stop then and explain who we were and what we were doing there, and they finally did let us through, but they really gave that fellow a tongue-lashing for not stopping at the first gate. And you know, that man never did even apologize to us. Just acted like nothing had happened at all.

I've been asked whether we got much criticism for not being in the service, and I have to say we got far less than I expected. Mainly, I think it was because what we were doing for the war effort with our Red Cross and USO exhibitions and so forth got plenty of publicity, and every write-up that I can recall was sure to mention that we had been rejected for military service for physical reasons. We were fortunate to have that kind of positive press; there were plenty of other men who had also been refused for physical reasons that no one else could see who were unfairly criticized.

The only complaints I did get were about gas rationing. I was still the full-time pro at Inverness all through 1944, but because I had to travel so much to do all these exhibitions, I needed more gas stamps than most people. Fortunately, I was able to get them without too much difficulty, because the people in charge of the various exhibitions would take care of it for me most of the time. But sometimes people would see me driving along here and there and think I was doing something wrong. Once the rationing board called me in about it because a man in Toledo had complained, but when I explained what I was doing and showed them my stamps, which were all legal and proper, they said it was all right.

Naturally, Louise couldn't be with me on any of these Red Cross or USO exhibitions. She mostly stayed at her folks' place in Texarkana, her sister Delle's in Fort Worth, or else in Denton at the farm I'd bought for my parents in 1940. It was a difficult time for her, and I sure didn't appreciate the separation myself, but fortunately it didn't last forever.

By 1944, the tour was alive again with twenty-three events, not quite as many as there had been before the war. Still, many of you who read this will be surprised that there were even that many. I was, too, really. The PGA had used golf in any way they could to help the war effort, but the people interested in golf had reached a point where they were hungry for news of any sports, including golf. Ed Dudley and Fred Corcoran deserve a lot of credit for not only what they did during the early war years, but for getting the tournament back on its feet again in '44. Many of the tournaments in '44 were renewals of ones that had been going on before the war, but a few were new ones, and some of the older and bigger ones still weren't back in operation, including the Masters and the U.S. Open. What Louise and I were happiest about was the fact that we could travel together again. McSpaden was okay as a traveling partner, but I definitely preferred Louise.

As I said earlier, my game was in good shape because of all the work I'd done during 1943, so I started out in '44 with some good pro-ams. We still played pro-ams then with just one partner and used no handicaps, which meant we always got good partners. Just like today, your partner would be someone who had helped sponsor the tournament. Anyway, at the pro-am at Hillcrest I won with 65. Then I won with 67 at San Gabriel Country Club in Los Angeles, and with 64 in Phoenix.

Another thing worth noting about the Phoenix tournament was that it was the only time my good friend Harold McSpaden beat me head to head. It was in an 18-hole playoff and we were even, going to the 17th. He had a twenty-footer, I had an eighteen-footer; he made his, I missed mine, and we both birdied the last hole, a par 5, so he beat me by one shot. I think that's the happiest I ever saw him in golf, because the rest of the time, I just happened to be fortunate enough to sneak out on him one way or another.

Of course, I was still at Inverness all this time and working hard, but I was playing every tournament my contract would allow. By now, Frankie Stranahan had become a pretty good amateur golfer, and from time to time wanted to take me on. I was too busy with the shop and my own tournaments, so I turned him down a few times. Well, one day he came in the shop with a couple of the boys he usually played with, and wanted me to play him. Something about the way he said it intimated that I was afraid to play him, and I guess it kind of got under my skin, because I said, "Okay, Frankie, I'll play you. Not only will I play you, but I'll throw in your two buddies and play all three of you, right now, best ball!" I was hot. We got out on the course and I was nicely steamed up and shot a 63, a new course record, beat Frankie and his friends, and Frankie never bothered me again.

So much has been written about 1945 and what I did then that my performance in '44 has been kind of overlooked. I played in twenty-one of the twenty-three tournaments and won eight of them—some record books don't include the Beverly Hills Open—which is a little better than a third. I was second five times, third five times, fourth once, and sixth twice. My winning margin was from 1 to 10 strokes, and I was also runner-up in the PGA. So '44 was a good year for me also.

One of my most memorable wins that year was the Dallas Victory Open at Lakewood Country Club where I won by 10 shots, which was a pretty nice margin of victory for me. It was the tournament's first year, and it drew a very good field. I won it the first year, Snead the second, and Hogan the third. Hogan was in the military in 1944 but played in the tournament, though I don't recall where he finished. Then it wasn't held again until 1956. I did some writing for the tournament during my newspaper years and always kept my eye on it, and it turned out to be the predecessor of the Byron Nelson Classic that is still going strong today.

Another interesting note about '44 was that I won twice in San Francisco, once in January and once in the fall, and both times at the same club, Harding Park. It was a fine municipal facility, and the pro there was Kenny Venturi's father, a good pro and a nice man. This was where Kenny learned to play as a young boy, and I guess he was about twelve at the time. I won by six strokes in January and by one in the fall. Kind of unusual, I thought.

Something else kind of unusual happened in that tournament. Seeing Nick Faldo with his ball up in the tree at Pebble Beach in 1992's U.S. Open reminded me of it. It was the last round, and I was fighting it out with Jim Ferrier. Ferrier was a pro from Australia and his wife was unusual among the pros' wives of that time in that she followed him every time he played, walked the course every hole with him. Anyway, we were on the 16th hole at Harding Park. The hole goes downhill and doglegs right. I was one stroke up and hit a good drive. Jim pushed his tee shot and his ball went into a tree, where it stayed. But you could see where it was, just kind of resting on this big branch. After a bit, Jim decided to try and play it out, and got someone to boost him up. He knocked it off that branch and out into the fairway, then onto the green, where he holed his putt for one of the most unusual pars I've ever seen.

That year Jug McSpaden and I played together in the Golden Valley Invitational in Minneapolis. It was a round-robin type of tournament, with seven teams. We played eighteen holes Thursday, then thirty-six holes Friday, Saturday, and Sunday for a total of 127. It was best ball of the team, but they gave plus or minus scores, plus being good and minus being bad. So if you lost the first round 5 down and won the second 6 up, you'd be plus 1. McSpaden and I had a wonderful tournament and finished 66 under par for the 127 holes, which is an average of a little better than a birdie every other hole. Not bad hacking around, but still we only won by three shots, so the other boys were playing pretty well too. My back was very bad that week, but somehow it didn't bother me when I played, and it even seemed to help me play better, because I played like gangbusters.

The next week after Golden Valley was the Beverly Hills Open, which I also won with a score of 277. Then came the PGA, where I started off well by being medalist with 138. In those days there was some extra money if you were medalist, so many of the boys would play in the qualifying rounds even if they didn't have to in order to have a chance at that extra prize money. I then made it to the finals against Bob Hamilton but lost on the 36th hole. He played very well and holed a great putt for birdie on the last hole after I had made a birdie trying to get even. There were some players still in uniform, and some who were just about done with their tour of duty. Lloyd Mangrum was the only pro I know of who actually saw combat. He was injured and awarded the Purple Heart, I believe.

Yes, 1944 was a good year. My average score was 69.67, and I was over par only three times in the twenty-one tournaments I played; my total was under 280 ten times. I was reasonably well satisfied with my performance, and very happy about winning over $37,000, which was more than twice as much as anyone had won before then. I was also given a great honor by being voted the Athlete of the Year by the Associated Press writers, and that topped it all off, for sure.

There was a major change in my job situation that fall—one that made it possible for me to have more freedom and play even better in '45. What happened was that some of the members at Inverness were becoming uncomfortable over how much money I was winning as well as what I was making at the club. This was along about the fall of the year, and fortunately, Mr. Haas warned me about it ahead of time. I must admit I was a little surprised by it, because I had worked hard at the club and the members had seemed pretty well satisfied with me. It was the first time I had had any problems in my working life as I had moved from Texarkana to Ridgewood to Reading and then to Inverness. Most people understood that young folks wanted to better themselves in those days.

Well, I was thirty-two, I had already realized I didn't want to play tournament golf forever or be a club professional all my life, and I'd been thinking about leaving Inverness before this came up, so it gave me a perfect excuse to resign, which I did.

Though I had done well that year on the tour, I also had another source of income besides Inverness. Mr. Haas had made me a vice president for Haas-Jordan. I had been able to be of great help to Mr. Haas during the war years when they were unable to get material for their umbrellas. On one occasion I happened to be playing golf with a fellow in the East who owned a fabric company, and I put him in touch with Mr. Haas. That made it possible for Haas-Jordan to get the material they needed.

Leaving Inverness made it possible for me to enjoy for the first time the freedom the pros in the sixties and later knew, of being able to play in as many tournaments as you wanted and concentrate solely on your game, with few distractions and worries. It was another part of what made the year to follow as memorable as it was.

SEVEN

1945 and the Streak

PEOPLE HAVE ASKED ME A LOT OF QUESTIONS ABOUT 1945. What happened? How did you come to play so well? How bad was the pressure? and so forth. There were several reasons for my good play that year. Mainly—and this seems unconnected to my golf, but it's not—I had thought for quite some time that I wanted to have a ranch someday. It had been my dream for years, really. And since Louise and I had grown up and lived through the Depression, we didn't want to borrow any money to buy a ranch. We wanted to pay cash for it. Actually, Louise didn't really like the idea of a ranch at all, because I didn't know very much about ranching, and she was afraid we couldn't make a go of it. But it was my dream, and she knew I'd done well in everything else I'd tried, so she decided to go along with me as long as we didn't have to borrow any money. That meant I had to make enough from my golf, and 1944 was the first year that I made enough to think I could make my dream of a ranch come true within a few years. All I had to do was continue to play well enough to keep winning or at least finishing in the top ten.

The second reason I did so well in '45 had a lot to do with something I did in '44, when I won nearly $38,000, played in twenty-one of twenty-three tournaments, won eight, and averaged 69.67 per round. During that year, I kept a record of my rounds and whether I played badly or what club I used, also whether I chipped badly, drove bad, putted terrible, or whatever. When I got through with the year, I went back over that book—which I don't have anymore, though I wish I did—like a businessman taking inventory.

I found two things that were repeated too often during the year, and they were "poor chipping" and "careless shot." The word "careless" was written in there quite a few times, which often was due to poor concentration. Or sometimes I would have a short putt and walk up to it and just kind of slap at it and miss it. So I made up my mind, like a New Year's resolution, that for all of 1945 I would try very hard to avoid a careless shot.

One other thing I should mention. My game had gotten so good and so dependable that there were times when I actually would get bored playing. I'd hit it in the fairway, on the green, make birdie or par, and go to the next hole. The press even said it was monotonous to watch me. I'd tell them, "It may be monotonous, but I sure eat regular." But having the extra incentive of buying a ranch one day made things a lot more interesting. Each drive, each iron, each chip, each putt was aimed at the goal of getting that ranch. And each win meant another cow, another acre, another ten acres, another part of the down payment.

Finally, I had one other incentive. I wanted to establish some records that would stand for a long time. I wanted to have the lowest scoring average—lower than when I'd won the Vardon Trophy in '39, when it was 71.02. And though I'd won eight tournaments in '44, I knew that the way some of these boys played, that number wouldn't stand up very long. I also wanted the record for the lowest score for an entire tournament. At that time, the record was 264, held by Craig Wood and a few others. I also wanted to be the leading money winner again. So you see, I had a whole collection of goals I wanted to reach, and every good shot I hit supported all of them. I guess I was fortunate to have so many goals, because to focus on just one, like a tournament scoring record, probably wouldn't have worked for me. But the ranch was my number-one, overriding dream, and that was what kept me going even in tournaments where I didn't play particularly well or finish where I wanted to.

Actually, I had played so well in '44 that it gave a great boost to my confidence, and it would have been unusual for me not to have done the same the next year. So I started off very positively in '45. In January I was second at the L.A. Open by one shot; that just gave me more determination to try and win it next year. At the start of the tournament, Bing Crosby—who by now I considered a good friend—was there on the first tee. I asked him, "You going to go with me some?" And he said, "I'm going to follow you till I feel you've made a bad shot." He was with me the whole first round when I shot 71, which was par, and he showed up again on the first tee the next day. On the 11th hole, I hit a drive and a 6-iron to the green, but pushed the ball to the right, and it landed short in the bunker. I happened to look around then and saw Bing leaving, waving his hand and saying, "I'll be seeing you!"

The next week I won the Phoenix Open by two, then was second—again by one shot—at both the Tucson and Texas Opens. My second win of the year was by four shots in the Corpus Christi Open in early February, where I also tied the low tournament scoring record of 264. While it was nice to have played so well and tied Craig and the others, I couldn't help but feel it would be even nicer to set a new record, so that remained one of my goals. Then I won my third tournament of '45 the next week at the New Orleans Open, this time by five shots in an 18-hole playoff with Harold McSpaden. Actually, Jug had a chance to beat me. In the last round, he had to birdie the 18th to win, but he hit a bad drive and we ended up tied. By the way, a lot of people don't know this, but McSpaden set a record that year himself—he finished second thirteen times.

I dropped back to second the next week, losing at Gulfport, Mississippi, by one shot in a sudden death playoff—one of the few times sudden death had been used on the tour at that point. I had tied with Sam Snead, who was just back on the tour. (Both he and Ben Hogan were released from the military early in the year and played quite a few tournaments. Hogan played in at least eighteen, and Snead twenty-six.) The playoff was to begin on the first hole, which had a creek running across the fairway at just about driver range. All through the tournament, we'd all been laying up in front of the creek with 3-woods. Well, I didn't realize that my adrenalin was up, and I hit that 3-wood absolutely perfect and it rolled into the creek. When Snead saw my ball go in, he put his 3-wood back in his bag and laid up with a 1-iron. I made bogey to his par and that was that.

I slacked off a little more the next week at Pensacola, finishing second to Snead by seven shots, though I played pretty well, shooting 69-69-71-65. Then at Jacksonville I played just plain terrible—for me—and tied for sixth, nine shots back, mostly because of a bad third round of 72, which was par there. Well, that must have gotten me a little steamed up, because it was the next week that I got started on what everyone today calls my streak, though of course I didn't have any idea at the time it was going to happen or keep my name alive in golf for so long.

It began with the Miami International Four-Ball the second week of March. I was paired with McSpaden again in what had never been a good tournament for either one of us. But it must have been our turn, because we finally did win. We beat Willie Klein and Neil Christman 6 and 5, Hogan and Ed Dudley 4 and 3, Henry Picard and Johnny Revolta 3 and 2. Then to finish it off, we walloped Sammy Byrd and Denny Shute 8 and 6. Harold and I were 21 up in our four matches, so we weren't exactly squeaking by.

Next was the Charlotte Open at Myers Park a week later. Snead and I had tied after 72 holes. This time it meant an 18-hole playoff, and on the 18th hole of that playoff, a long par 3, Sam was leading me one stroke. He put a 1-iron just on the front edge of the green, which was two-tiered and quite long. So he was a long way from the hole. Now, I was getting a little tired of having Sam beat me, and I thought, "There's a chance he just might three-putt from there." So I reversed what had happened at Gulfport. I changed from a 1-iron to a 3-wood and knocked the ball onto the upper level of the green about twenty feet from the hole. Sure enough, Sam three-putted and I parred, so we were tied and went into another 18-hole playoff the next day. This time I really concentrated and played better than Sam, shooting a 69 to his 73; I knocked in a thirty-foot putt for a birdie 2 on the final hole. That gave me a lot of confidence and made me feel my game was in tiptop shape. I was driving very well and putting even better than I had the year before. From there on, I just kept going and playing well and it seemed everything was going my way.

Of course, it wasn't going as well for some of the other players, and it was common knowledge that some of them were unhappy that

McSpaden and I were winning so many of the tournaments and so much money. During the Charlotte Open, in fact, Willie Goggin, one of the older pros, suggested that the PGA redistribute prize money in the tournaments so that there would be more money available for players who finished farther down the list. I could see his point, but I have to admit I sort of liked things the way they were.

The next tournament was the Greensboro Open, which the press would one day call "Snead's Alley," after he won it a record eight times. Sam had a wonderful following, and there were times that if it looked as if his ball was going over the green, the gallery would just stand there and let it drop right in the middle of them, which often made the ball end up closer—though sometimes his lie might not be as good where the grass was all trampled. However, I felt real good that week, and managed to win by eight shots to go three in a row. That particular year the tournament was played completely at Starmount, which was nice for the players, because the other course, Sedgefield, was clear across town, so it saved us all a lot of driving.

The following week we were at the Durham Open playing the Hope Valley course, which was a very good one. We played two rounds the last day, and the 18th hole was a slightly uphill par 3 of about 210 yards. In the morning round, I used a 1-iron, put the ball four feet from the pin, and made birdie. In the afternoon, I started out one shot behind but shot 65 to win by 5. Toney Penna finished five strokes behind me at 270. The icing on the cake was when I reached 18, got out my 1-iron and made another birdie.

Talking about that tournament reminds me that in 1990, the 45th anniversary of my streak, I was greatly honored by a party at Durham. My good friend Buddy Langley, then head of GTE Southwest, got together with the folks at Hope Valley, who in turn contacted the other nine clubs still in existence (Tam O'Shanter was gone, unfortunately—it had been sold and made into a development), and invited them all to come and celebrate. They had a beautiful plaque made to commemorate the event and installed it at the 18th tee. There was a little scramble tournament and a party that night, and everyone had a very pleasant day. I'm always amazed that people think so much even today of what I did so long ago. I guess it's a good thing they do, or I might think I dreamed it all up.

By now, having won four tournaments in a row and tying the record set by Johnny Farrell, I of course wanted to break that record, too. My concentration had gotten so good that I was in sort of a trance much of the time. That's about the only way I can really explain it. When I did hit a bad shot, I never thought anything about it, just went ahead and played the next one and it never bothered me or upset my ability to focus. I wasn't hooking at all, just had a good, normal flight to the ball that landed it softly on the greens. I was swinging just enough from the inside, and the ball flew straight until its velocity slowed to a certain point and it would fall slightly to the left, though I could go right if I needed to.

Next in line was Atlanta, a par-69 course, where I finally broke the scoring record with a 263. But I could have done better. The last hole was a long par 3, and I put my tee shot on the green, tried too hard to make birdie, and three-putted. That's a funny thing about golf—even when we play well, we know there are shots we missed. I remember that even Al Geiberger, when he shot his 59, said he missed a couple of short putts or he would have had a 57. Still, I had also broken the record of four consecutive wins and I won pretty decisively—by nine shots—so I didn't feel like I should complain very much.

After I'd won the fifth tournament in a row, someone from the company that made Wheaties approached me about doing an ad for their cereal, which was of course known as the "Breakfast of Champions." I never had an agent so I just talked to them myself and they put my picture and some statistics about me on the box and paid me $200 plus a case of Wheaties a month for six months. I had to give most of the cereal away; because although I liked Wheaties fine, you can only eat so much of it. I don't know if any of those boxes are still around—I sure don't have any, and back then, people didn't collect or save such things like they do now. Even during my streak, for instance, I signed very few autographs, though you might find that hard to believe.

To add a little to my story, a few years back I went to WFAA's studio in Dallas to talk with Bryant Gumbel on the morning news show. We chatted a bit about my record and the Nelson Classic, then Bryant asked if I had done any commercials in those days. I told him about the Wheaties ad and he said, "Pete Rose just signed a contract with Wheaties for $800,000." Well, we both had a good laugh. But considering where Pete Rose is today, I think I was better off with my $200.

But after Atlanta in early April, pressure from the press and fans was starting to build. Up to that point, there had been only a couple of other players who had won four in a row, so when I passed four, the writers and fans started saying, "He's got four, can he make it five?", then "He's got five, can he make it six?" One way I dealt with the pressure was to simply not play practice rounds, which kept me away from the press and the fans to some extent. That sounds foolish, but many times I played my best golf when I hadn't even seen the course, just went out and played. I was blessed with wonderful sight for many years and was an excellent judge of distance, which was a great help on an unfamiliar course. I'd just look down the middle of the fairway and try to hit it there, and I wasn't worried about getting into trouble because I didn't know where the trouble was. But by this time, too, I was familiar with most of the courses on the tour anyway.

Quite often, I'd play an exhibition at another town on the way to where the next tournament was and make $200–$300 for one round of golf, which was nice and helped a lot. That kept my game going well, besides helping me get closer to my goal of buying a ranch one day. That was another reason why I might not get to some tournaments until it was time to actually start playing.

There was a two-month break on the tour at this time—I have no idea why, just that no one was holding a tournament. So Louise and I went back home, worked on my parents' farm in Denton some, and visited her folks in Texarkana. That's where I practiced, hitting a bucket of balls every day or so. I wasn't working on anything in particular, just keeping my muscles limbered up.

I also did a couple of exhibitions during this time, and even played in something called a "Challenge Match" against Snead. There was a lot of talk going around then because Sam and I were both playing so well. Some folks thought Sam was better, some thought I was, so they had this match to supposedly decide the thing once and for all. It was in Upper Montclair, New Jersey, and it was a 36-hole match, with the first 18 being medal play and the second 18 match play. Sam shot 69 and I had 70 the first day, but the second day I beat him 4 and 3, so they figured I won.

But back to the streak. Next, in June, came the Montreal Open at Islesmere Golf Club in Montreal, where I finished 20 under par and won by 10 shots. Jug came in second with 278. I made just one bogey the entire tournament, on the par-3 14th hole in the last round, when I hit a 1-iron through the green and took three to get down. At that party in Durham in 1990, the nice folks from Islesmere gave me a beautiful silver tray that was engraved, "The greatest display of sub-par golf ever witnessed on a Canadian course." That made me feel pretty good, even forty-five years later.

Now I had won six in a row, and I was enjoying myself despite the pressure. The next week we were playing in the Philadelphia Inquirer Invitational. McSpaden lived there, and Louise and I were staying with him and Eva. We were both playing well, but starting the last round, McSpaden was leading by two shots. At that time, remember, they always didn't pair according to who was leading going into the last round. They tried to spread the gallery out among the players. That was why very often the leader might be playing a couple of groups or more ahead of the ones going off last. That was true in this case, because McSpaden was leading the tournament starting the fourth round, but was several groups ahead of me.

Now, Leo Diegel was a club pro who also lived in Philadelphia, and he had always liked me, called me "Kid," in fact. He came out to see how I was doing that afternoon, and I was getting ready to drive on 13. He said, "How you doin', kid?" And I said, "Well, I've got par in for 68." And he said, "That's not good enough." I said, "Why isn't it good enough?" He replied, "McSpaden just shot 66." He was leading me two shots before we started, so standing there on the tee I said, "That means I have to birdie nearly every hole but one to beat him." He laughed, and I did too, not thinking very much about it.

But as it happened, I did birdie all but one hole on the way in, shot 63, and beat Jug by two. On the last hole, I'll never forget it, I hit a driver and 6-iron and knocked the ball one foot from the hole, made my birdie, and Jug was right there watching me. He was so mad at me he called me every dirty name you can think of. When he accepted his check, he said, "You not only beat my brains out, but you eat all my food, too!" Still, he'd beat me in that playoff in '44 at

Phoenix, so I couldn't really understand what he was so upset about. That 63 was the most unusual thing I did that whole year—knowing I had to birdie the last five holes to win, and being fortunate enough to be able to do it.

The eighth tournament in my streak was the Chicago Victory Open at Calumet Country Club at the end of June. I don't remember a lot about it, except that I played very steady there, though the fairways were quite narrow and the rough pretty heavy. I shot 69-68-68-70—275, 13 under par, and won by 7 shots. McSpaden came in second again, tied with Ky Laffoon at 282. Sometimes people are surprised I don't remember more about all these tournaments, but as I said, I was in a trance of sorts, so a lot of the events and people and so forth were all kind of a blur to me.

However, the next tournament is one I remember quite clearly—the PGA Championship at Moraine in Dayton, Ohio, a city that would prove to be very important to me some time later. First of all, I tied for medalist with John Revolta in the qualifying rounds. I didn't have to qualify because I was a former champion, but in those days they gave a cash prize for medalist, and I wanted that money—all of $125—to go toward another acre or two for my ranch.

Some people think of match play as being easier than medal play, but there was a whole lot of pressure every round. And most of the PGA championships were 36-hole matches after the qualifying rounds. You had to sometimes play ten rounds of good golf just to make it to the finals, and it was nearly always played in August, the hottest time of the year. It was tough.

In my first match I took on the Squire himself, Gene Sarazen, and managed to top him 3 and 2. I was told later that he had asked Fred Corcoran to pair the two of us in the first round, because he wanted to either get beat early or stay a long time. I guess he got half his wish, but I don't think it was the half he really wanted.

My second match was against Mike Turnesa, one of that great family of golfers. He was playing well too, and putting beautifully. So well, actually, that he had me 2 down going to the 15th tee in the afternoon round. The 15th was a par 3, about a 4-iron shot, and he put his ball on the green about ten feet from the hole. The way he was putting, I thought, "Man, if I'm ever going to get out of this match, I've got to get the ball closer than where he is." And I did it, put mine just inside of Mike's. He putted first and I thought sure he'd made it, he hit such a beautiful putt. But it rimmed the hole on the high side and stayed out. I was fortunate to get mine in, so I got one back.

Now I was one down with three holes to go. On the 16th at Moraine, you drive over a hill and pitch up to a little old dinky green. It's a tough little shot. The hole is short, but you have to hit the ball straight and have it in the right position. Well, I made a birdie there while Mike parred, so I got even.

The 17th was a par 5. I'd outdriven Mike a little bit, and he put his second shot just on the front of the green. I put mine closer, about twenty-five feet from the hole. He putted up very close, and I gave it to him, so he had a birdie. Well, I scrambled around and made my putt for an eagle. Now I was one up, and the last hole is a drive and 2-iron par 4. Fortunately we halved that one, so I managed to beat Mike one up. His brother Jim was playing another match the same time we were playing ours, and he lost, too. They were Italian, and afterward they were kidding around in the locker room, saying, "We'll have to eat our spaghetti without the meat sauce for dinner tonight."

Then I played Denny Shute, who'd won the PGA twice, and beat him, too. That gave me confidence, because if I could beat those three fine players, I might have a chance to win. Next came the semifinals, where I played Claude Harmon, a wonderful player who became one of the greatest teachers of the game, and who had won the Masters as well as several other tournaments. But I shot 65 and Claude shot 68, and afterwards he said, "I know what you've got to do to win a match—you've got to shoot better than I've been doing. Because when I shoot 68 and lose three down, the game's too tough for this old man."

Now I was up against Sam Byrd, a wonderful player who was making a career out of golf after being a fine baseball player for the Yankees. In the morning, he finished with four birdies in a row, then chipped in from about forty yards off the green on the last hole to put me 2 down at noon. Starting off in the afternoon, he birdied the fourth and I was 3 down. Everybody said it looked like I was going to lose in the finals again. The wind was 35 miles an hour that day, so besides playing a tough opponent, I was playing under tough conditions as well. But I had grown up in Texas and was a much better wind player than Sam, fortunately. I managed to make a two at the next par 3, and from there to the 14th hole, where the match ended, I was 6 under par.

That PGA was one of the best match play tournaments ever for me, because I played some very difficult matches and very wonderful players. It was the most strongly contested championship of match play in my career. These were all 36-hole matches, remember, so by the time I won, I had played 204 holes and was 37 under par. That was a lot of golf, especially in July in Ohio, and there were more than 30,000 in the gallery. Fortunately, for the first time, each hole was roped off and the crowds were controlled with the help of soldiers from nearby Wright Field.

My back was beginning to bother me some by then, and I was having heat and massage and osteopathic treatments every night during the championship. A couple of weeks later, I went to the Mayo Clinic and had them check me out, which took about three days. All they told me was that I had a lot of muscular tension, which wasn't much of a surprise, and they recommended that I find some way to relax, which was next to impossible right then.

But bad back or not, I was on the tour again two weeks later at the Tam O'Shanter All-American Open in Chicago and shot 269. I won by 11 shots, adding $10,200 to our savings for the ranch. It was one of my best tournaments that whole year—including my 259 at Seattle. The course was tough and the prize money of $10,200 brought out all the top players, including Hogan and Sarazen, who tied for second at 280. I may have said this before, but one reason I always did so well at the Tam was that I had learned to nip the ball off the fairway—I didn't ever take much turf. This was important in Chicago because the Tam O'Shanter fairways were nearly solid clover, and when that clover got between the ball and the club, the clover had a lot of slick juice in it. You never knew where the ball would go, but most of the time, you'd hit a flier. Because of the way I nipped the ball, I didn't ever hit many fliers, especially not at the Tam O'Shanter.

An interesting sidelight to that victory concerns George May, the fellow who put on the Tam. He liked to drive around the course in a cart and be very prominent in front of the spectators, doing whatever he could to promote interest in the tournament. In the first round that year, I had a 34 on the front nine, and George was waiting for me on the 10th tee. He bet me 100 to 1 that I couldn't shoot 34 on the back.

I could only lose a dollar, so I took him on. I started with an eagle 3 at 10 and a hole in one at 11, so I was four under after two holes. I parred the rest of the way, shot 32, and got my $100.

George loved to make those kinds of bets, and he especially loved to bet with Joe Louis, the great prizefighter. Joe was a pretty good golfer, but was really too muscular through the chest and shoulders to be as good as he wanted to be. One time on the first tee at the Tam, which was just to the left of the clubhouse—a long, low building about twenty yards away—May came up and bet Joe he couldn't break 80 that day. So Joe got all fired up and took a swing at the ball, hit under it and off the toe, and we all watched it sail right over the clubhouse. So there went his chance to break 80 and make a little money off George.

Getting back to my streak, by this time the pressure from the press and the fans really was getting to me. Another thing that added to it was that I was expected to make a talk at some sort of civic club luncheon nearly every city I played in, since I was a leading player and these folks were doing the pros a favor by putting on the tournaments. I didn't get paid, just got a free lunch, but it all added to the pressure, believe me. I got so sick of it that I just wanted to get it over with. Before I went out to play the first round at the Tam, I told Louise, "I hope I just blow up today." When I came back in, she asked, "Did you blow up?" I replied, "Yes, I shot 66."

So it went on. A week after the Tam O'Shanter I played in the Canadian Open, and that was really a test. The Canadian PGA had gone to work to make the Thornhill course really difficult, and they succeeded. Snead said the first seven holes were the hardest seven holes in a row he'd ever seen. According to an article written before the tournament, those seven holes were lengthened specifically because of me—and some of the other fine players, I'm sure—and par was changed from 71 to 70. I guess a few of our friends across the border weren't happy about my playing so well at Islesmere in June. My friend George Low, a pro famous for his wonderful putting, even bet that no one would break 70. But I shot 68-72-72-68—280 and won by four shots, ahead of Herman Barron at 284 and Ed Furgol at 285. So I think I gave everyone their money's worth—except maybe the folks who bet against me.

As you can imagine, though I was playing very well, I was also getting very tired. The next week we went to Memphis, and that was where the streak was broken by an amateur named Fred Haas—no relation to my friend Cloyd Haas of Toledo. I read recently that Fred was supposed to have been wearing shorts during the tournament, but I surely don't remember that he was. We weren't allowed to then any more than the boys are now. But regardless of what Fred was wearing, I had gotten very tired and made some foolish mistakes and ended up fourth at Memphis.

Now comes a strange thing. I was definitely and genuinely relieved when the streak was broken, because it took so much pressure off me from the media and the fans. But the fact that I had played poorly at Memphis made me kind of hot, and I went out and won the next two tournaments. One of them, the Spring Lake Invitational in New Jersey, doesn't count as an official tournament now, but I played and won $684.74 in the pro-am and $1500 in the tournament itself, so it counted as far as Louise and I and our bank account were concerned.

I went back to work at Knoxville, winning the pro-am with a 66 and the tournament by 10 shots with 67-69-73-67—276. Sammy Byrd was second with 286 and Ben Hogan was third with 287. After that came Nashville and the Chickasaw Country Club. I shot 70-64-67-68 and finished second. I had a good caddie, and in the first round on the back nine, I pulled my tee shot into the trees. When I got to the ball, my caddie was there ahead of me. I saw that I had a clear area for my swing and a clear shot to the green, so I said, "That's all right." The caddie said, "I was praying it would be all right." Now, I have to explain that I've been a member of the Church of Christ since I was twelve, and quite a few of the fans knew that I was. We preferred to be called simply Christians, but sometimes were referred to as Campbellites, because a man named Alexander Campbell had begun the Restoration movement that resulted in the Church of Christ being brought back to life as we feel it was begun in the Bible. Anyway, a man in the gallery overheard the caddie and me, and said, "Your caddie must be a good Campbellite, too." It made me feel good to realize I'd gained a reputation for not only being a good golfer, but also for being a Christian.

Next I played the Dallas Open, where I was third, then Southern Hills in Tulsa, where I was fourth. I didn't drive well there, and at Southern Hills, you must drive well. The greens were bermuda, but for some reason I wasn't negotiating them well. I was getting a little weary and feeling a little burned out by all the excitement and pressure of the whole year. Things were slipping a little, more than I liked, so I decided to try and put a stop to it when the tour went to the Pacific Northwest the next week. I did a little better in the Esmeralda Open at Indian Canyon Country Club in Spokane, sponsored by a local hotel called Esmeralda. I shot 266 and won by seven shots—McSpaden was second with 273—but there's more to that story. Before Louise and I arrived in Spokane, I had made reservations at the Davenport Hotel. We got in very late, nearly midnight, and they didn't have our reservation. The night clerk told me, "All our rooms are reserved for the golfers." Obviously, he didn't recognize me as being a golfer, which I could understand, but we were tired and I was somewhat put out by the confusion and the fact that they had no rooms at all. We called Fred Corcoran, who was staying at the other large hotel in town, the one that was actually sponsoring the tournament, and he managed to get us a room there. Louise was even more upset than I was at the situation, and before I went out to play the next day she said, "I just have one favor to ask. I want you to play well enough in this tournament that they'll know who you are!" Fortunately, I did—though we never went back to that hotel anyway, so I'll never know if they figured out who I was or not.

At the Portland Open the next week, Ben Hogan played the best tournament of his life and shot a new all-time record of 261, 27 under par. He obviously was playing quite well, and had been that entire year. I might have been happier for Ben if I hadn't finished 14 shots out, even though I was only in second place. I remember the press asked me how long I thought Ben's score would hold up, and I said, "Well, you don't know in this game. It could be forever, or it could be broken next week." As it turned out, I was two weeks off.

The next tournament was at Tacoma, Washington, the first weekend of October, on a course called Firecrest. I wasn't on fire at all, finishing third, 8 shots back. I was still fuming at how I'd played the week before and that upset my concentration so much I had my worst finish all year, ninth place. Tacoma and Tulsa were the only two tournaments that whole year that I finished over par, by a total of seven shots. But that wasn't much comfort right then. I was getting steamed about the way I was playing, and I really got hot the next week at Seattle, when I shot the easiest 259 you ever saw, 62-68-63-66. Jug

McSpaden was again second, tied with Harry Givan at 272. I liked the Broadmoor Golf Club's course, and I drove well and played my irons exceptionally well. Didn't have to hit many putts of any length at all, and in the first round I had two eagles. The last round, I was leading by so many shots that someone said, "All he has to do is make it to the clubhouse and he'll win." But I knew by the middle of the last round I had a chance to go for the record, and I was able to keep focused and do it. I really was pleased, especially after the drubbing I'd taken from Ben at Portland. In fact, I was so embarrassed by having Hogan beat me by 14 that I might not have played as well at Seattle if I'd only been two or three shots back at Portland. That 259 held up for ten years, till Mike Souchak shot 257 at Brackenridge in the Texas Open.

The tour was still going on, but I was pretty tired at that point and needed a good, long break. After all, by this time I'd won seventeen official tournaments and the pressure from the press was constant. After we got back from the hunting trip, I worked quite a bit at the farm in Denton and kept busy with first one thing and another, but my only other tournament that year was the Fort Worth Open at Glen Garden, my old stomping ground, and I was fortunate enough to win it.

It was in December of '45, just a week before Christmas. We were on our way to Glen Garden from our place in Denton. On the way there was a bridge with some ice on it, and a car was stopped on the bridge. As I started to go around the other car, mine skidded off the road into the ditch and turned over. We weren't hurt, but in the back seat we'd had a box of about 140 eggs we were taking to Louise's family and some friends. When the car rolled over, it threw all those eggs into the front seat on Louise. She was a mess, with eggs dripping off her hair and everywhere. Fortunately, a man with a wrecker was coming down the road to help the car that was stuck on the bridge, so first he turned ours over and fortunately, it was driveable. Another man came along then, and he kindly took Louise back to Denton and straight to her beauty shop. Her hairdresser said, "This is one time you've really gotten an egg shampoo." But we never could get the smell of those eggs out of that car, so we didn't keep it for very long. Guess that's why I played so well in the tournament—I knew we'd have to be getting another car soon.

It was actually the worst golf I'd played to win that whole year. The sub-freezing weather was terrible, and the greens were frozen each morning and hard as rock. The first round, you absolutely had to run the ball up because if you landed it on the green it would bounce as high as if you'd hit the sidewalk. There was a cold wind that blew nearly all the time, and it never did get very warm. I did have a 65 in the second round, though, with a 30 on the back nine. I finished with five straight 3's—remember, there are four long, tough par 3's the last five holes—by birdieing the par-4 16th and parring all the par 3's, so it made an interesting finish to that round. Jimmy Demaret, in his first tournament since his discharge from the Navy, was second with 281, and Harold was third at 282. The local paper the next morning called me "the Man O' War of golf," one I'd never heard before.

Really, it was a remarkable year. My scoring average was 68.3, I had eighteen official wins, eleven in a row, finished second seven times, and had nearly 100 official sub-par rounds, my best being 62. I set new records for most wins in a row, most in one year, lowest tournament score, and lowest scoring average. Not too many "careless shots"—in fact, my New Year's resolution had knocked off 1⅓ strokes per round. Looking back, I realized that even though I had all those goals in mind, I never expected to do so well, especially against the competition I had. And despite the fact that some of the boys were still in uniform for part of the year, most of them were playing at least part of the time. Snead played in twenty-six events, Hogan eighteen, Dutch Harrison at least thirteen, and so forth. But beyond the fields I played against most of the time, I think that 68.3 speaks for itself.

Louise was very happy about what I had done and very happy for me, though she was realizing one thing about our situation that didn't especially please her. Because I had become something of a celebrity, Louise became simply "Byron Nelson's wife" to a lot of people, rather than Louise Shofner Nelson, and at times that was a little awkward for her. It's a shame the way the world can be about such things, though on the other hand, when she wasn't with me, she could go wherever she wished anonymously, while I no longer had that option very much—and that's become even more true today.

One thing that helped her feel better happened late that fall. The city of Denton wanted to honor us for all the good publicity we had brought to Texas and especially Denton, so they surprised us one day by presenting us with a pair of beautiful horses on the courthouse steps. They were half Tennesee Walkers, so they made good riding horses for our 54-acre place there in Denton and eventually for the ranch in Roanoke. But Louise definitely got the better part of the deal. Her horse, Linda, was not only beautifully gaited; she had a wonderful disposition. You could do just about anything with her. My horse, Rex, a gelding, never was anything like Linda; he was quite fractious at times and we eventually had to sell him. But Linda was a joy to us for a long time, and it was certainly a wonderful honor from the folks in Denton.

It was now December. I had begun my career with the goal of winning every important tournament in the United States at least once. I already had the Masters, the U.S. Open, the PGA, the North and South, the Western, and the Tam O'Shanter. The only one left was the L.A. Open, which once again had eluded me in 1945. I ended the year feeling very satisfied in some respects, but I still had at least one goal left in golf—and still had to save up enough money to buy that ranch I'd been dreaming of.

Speaking of money for the ranch . . . . in 1945, I made more than I ever had before, but because so much of it was in war bonds, it's been reported in the press for years and years that I won much more than it actually turned out to be. You see, Fred Corcoran, who was running the tour at the time, wanted golf to do as much as possible toward the war effort, and we were all glad to help. So he got the various tournament committees to have the prize money in war bonds. In case anyone doesn't know, they were similar to our savings bonds and CD's today. You bought, say, a $1000 bond for $750, and if you held on to it for ten years, it would actually be worth $1000. Most of the tournaments paid totally in war bonds, a few paid in a combination of cash and bonds, and once in a while one would pay totally in cash.

Well, none of us were making the kind of money where we could hold on to those bonds for ten years, so we cashed them in immediately, which meant at about 75% of their face value. When you look at the official records and see where I won $1,333.33, for instance, that meant it was actually $1000 in cash. According to the press, I won somewhere between $60,000 and $66,000 in '45, but according to my black book where I kept records of each tournament played and what I really won, my winnings were closer to $47,600. In fact, my IRS records for that year show that I made $52,511.32 from golf, but that includes such things as exhibitions and pro-ams and sometimes a portion of the gate receipts, which once in a while you would get if you were in a playoff. It's very confusing for anyone trying to get all those figures to make sense, because the PGA didn't keep the best records then, and sometimes even the press reported things inaccurately. But that's about the best I can do at straightening it out as far as my own golf winnings are concerned. I know for sure that Louise and I didn't hold on to any of those war bonds—we couldn't afford that luxury!

EIGHT

Golf for the Fun of It

EVEN THOUGH I'D HAD A WONDERFUL YEAR IN 1945, I still had that goal of winning every important tournament in America at least once. But that Los Angeles Open had gotten away from me every year. I felt I'd just plain thrown it away a couple of times. All golfers have certain areas of the country where they play better—especially on the greens—than others. I negotiated the greens beautifully in Chicago, where I won six tournaments, and San Francisco, where I won three. So I was always comfortable playing in both those cities. But I never could get the hang of the greens in Los Angeles. They were poa annua then, and everyone told me the greens always broke toward the ocean, but half the time I couldn't figure out which way the ocean was. We had caddies, but they were just kids, most of them, and in that day and time, nearly all the players depended on themselves to judge distances and read greens.

So the Los Angeles Open was still on my list to win, and I set myself to win it that next January, just a couple of weeks after I'd won the Fort Worth Open at Glen Garden. I was still hitting my irons very well, and I remembered that the 10th hole at Riviera was a very demanding one. It was more than a dogleg, it just went dead right at the landing area. You had to drive on the left side of the fairway, because the green sloped to the left and you had to approach it from the left to have any chance to make par. So I was very sure to drive to the left, and I believe I even made a couple of birdies. Fortunately, I played very steady on the other 17 holes as well, shot 284, and won by 5 strokes. That was very satisfying, to win a tournament that had escaped me so many times. I was bent on playing well, of course, and I was leading going to the last round anyway, but I finished five shots ahead of Sam Snead, thanks to a birdie on the 18th hole. That birdie gave me a great deal of satisfaction, being in front of quite a large gallery and coming at the end of a tournament that had eluded me so many times. Maybe it meant more to me because southern California was where I'd done so poorly when I first turned pro, and I was determined to make up for it. In any case, it was an excellent tournament for me, and another goal checked off on my list.

At the San Francisco Open the next week, my score was one shot better—283—than at L.A., but I got a little more distance between me and the field, partly because of the course conditions. It was terribly wet and cold all through the tournament. The ball did not roll at all; in fact, the players were allowed to lift, clean, and drop the ball if it plugged in the fairway. I hit some of the best iron shots of my career in that tournament, and beat Ben Hogan by nine. What I liked best about it was the tenth hole, a very demanding par four. I hit driver and 1-iron all four rounds and made two birdies and two pars, and won by 9 shots. Under those conditions, that was pretty good. The other satisfying thing was that the tournament was held at the Lakeside Course of the Olympic Club, which is my favorite course outside of Riverhill in Kerrville, Texas.

I was scheduled to play at Richmond just outside San Francisco the next week, but by now I was starting to think about retiring. I really felt I had played all I wanted to play. I'd achieved all my goals and then some, and the traveling was getting pretty old. I wanted to settle down and do something different with my life. I'd been doing nothing but golf since I was twenty, and it's a hard life in many ways, even though it has its exciting and glamorous aspects—especially if you're playing well. But fourteen years was enough.

During December of '45, Louise and I had talked some about my quitting golf someday, and she said that would be fine with her. I knew she was as tired of the travel and so forth as I was. But we had to talk seriously, because this was a complicated decision. I had a contract with MacGregor, we hadn't found the ranch yet that we wanted to buy—there were a lot of things to consider. But at least we had quite a bit in the bank, and we needed to stop and think about what we wanted to do and how we would do it.

So I withdrew from the Richmond tournament and telephoned Louise. She and Eva McSpaden had already caught a train to Phoenix for the next tournament, and Jug and I were to meet them there after we played San Francisco and Richmond. The girls were staying at the Westward Ho Hotel, and when I reached Louise and told her I had withdrawn from the tournament at Richmond, she was really worried. She asked me three or four times if I was all right. When I finally convinced her I was, I told her I was catching a train and would pick her up in Phoenix and that I wanted us to go home and do some serious talking about the tour. I asked her not to say anything about it, even to Eva.

We started talking as soon as we both were on the train in Phoenix and began figuring things out. The first thing to think about was my contract with MacGregor. It was a pretty good one, and in all fairness to the company, when I decided to quit I would have to renegotiate it, which would naturally mean less income we could count on. We finally decided I would have to go back and play on the tour until all the problems were worked out. So as soon as I got home, I called Henry Cowan at MacGregor and told him I wanted to talk to him. I went up to Cincinnati and told him I was going to retire and needed to renegotiate. He was upset that I was leaving the tour, but we worked out an agreement where I would take the same amount of money for the three-year period of the contract and spread it out over ten years. Then I went back out to play.

One very funny thing happened after I withdrew from the Richmond tournament. I didn't find out about it until nearly forty-five years later, but Prescott Sullivan, a fine sportswriter for the *San Francisco Examiner,* had written a column about me after I'd left San Francisco after winning there in '46. He talked about how the other players were pleased that I wasn't playing at Richmond because I'd been winning all the money on the tour, it seemed like, and they were tired of it. In fact, Willie Goggin, who'd brought this up before, had again tried to get the tour to change the prize distribution. The article ended by saying that I was "knee-deep in greenbacks" down there in Texas. My good friends Bud and Janet Waltz of Haas-Jordan showed me the article just a couple of years ago, and I don't know if I ever laughed so hard in my life as when I read that.

Knee-deep in greenbacks or not, I skipped not only Richmond, but Phoenix and Tucson too. So my first tournament after that was at San Antonio on the Willow Springs course. We had terrible weather—it snowed and hailed. I was third, which wasn't bad considering all that was going on in my head. One big distraction was that we had found the ranch we wanted to buy. It was 630 acres in Roanoke, a small town 22 miles north of Fort Worth. There was already a bid on it, but this was to be a cash sale, and our agent didn't think the buyer could come up with that much money that fast. He said we would know in a month.

So, all excited about buying this ranch, off I went to New Orleans, where I pulled myself together and won by five strokes. We played City Park again, a fine municipal facility that I always liked. I always played well there, and especially liked the long par threes, since I was a good long-iron player. I was a little behind Hogan starting the last round, and birdied the first six holes, as I remember it, to pull ahead of him, so that felt good. Now I was really counting the extra acres and cattle that I could get with my winnings if we were able to buy that ranch.

Next was Pensacola, but with everything on my mind and being all keyed up about the ranch and all, I played terrible. I shot 286, tied for thirteenth, and won $152.50. That wouldn't buy much ranch. But this was the first of March. My real estate agent back in Texas, Mr. Ray, was supposed to have called me by this time and I hadn't heard from him at all, so it was upsetting me. Louise and I got packed and she was sitting in the car, waiting for me to drive us to St. Petersburg, when I decided to call Mr. Ray right then and there. When I got him, he told me he was just getting ready to call me. He'd just found out that the deal hadn't gone through, so I had the opportunity to buy it. I told him, "I have to leave right now for St. Petersburg, but I'll call you as soon as I get there." I was really excited.

All the way on that six-hour drive, Louise and I talked it through. Louise was willing to go along with the idea of the ranch, but she insisted—and I agreed—that we shouldn't dip into any of our investments to buy it. We had to do it strictly with our cash savings, and the purchase price was $55,000, which we were still somewhat short of. We figured if I did well enough through the rest of the year, we'd have just enough to buy the ranch, plus a little to live on and buy cattle with and so forth. When we got to our hotel room in St. Petersburg, my mind was made up. I didn't even unpack, just got on the phone immediately and told Mr. Ray I'd send him the check for the escrow money right then.

With that load off my mind, I played a little better at St. Petersburg, finishing fifth and winning $650. Now my winnings meant more than a ranch "someday"—they meant "very soon." I played in the Miami Four Ball next partnered with McSpaden, but we weren't as lucky as we had been in '45. We did make it to the semifinals, though, and won $300, which was better than getting poked in the eye with a sharp stick.

After that, I took a few weeks off to come home and begin to get some loose ends tied up. Earlier in the year, Otis Dypwick, a sportswriter from Minneapolis, had contacted me about writing an instruction book to be called *Winning Golf,* and I'd agreed to do it, so now it was the middle of March and warm enough in Texas to take the pictures we would need. We did them out at Colonial, and after they were done, I worked with Otis on the copy to go with each picture. One funny thing—in quite a few of the pictures, my hands look darker than you would expect, especially for that time of the year. It's because I'd been painting fences just before we did the pictures, and we didn't have products like they do today for taking paint off your hands, so I still had quite a bit of that red paint on my hands. But red hands or not, I've always been proud of that book. I call it "the primer of golf," because it's quite simple and easy to understand.

Another thing I needed to do was to find out whether my parents were willing to move to the ranch, because I knew I would need a lot of help, and my father was a good hard worker. When I talked to them, my father was willing to move, but my mother wasn't too eager about it. But she agreed to do it and it worked out fine. There was a smaller house next to the ranch house where they could live, along with my brother Charles. Ellen, my sister, had married and moved out by that time.

Finally, I had to start learning how to be a rancher. I wasn't about to jump into buying cattle or much of anything for the ranch until I really had some idea of how to go about it. I set myself to studying and working on it the whole rest of that year. I read everything I could get my hands on, and talked to anyone I could find who had some knowledge on the subject.

But in the meantime, it was back to work on the golf course. My next tournament was the Masters, where I finished seventh. I wasn't very happy with that performance, but my heart just really wasn't in it anymore. I had achieved my goals as far as the Masters and the other majors were concerned, though I still hoped to win the Open again.

For several months then, I would go out and play a tournament, then go back home and study up on ranching. A month after the Masters, I played at Houston and won by two shots, adding another $2000 to our savings. That tournament was interesting in that it was the only one I can recall of all the times we played together through the years that Hogan, Snead, and I finished in the top three spots. I was first, Hogan second, and Snead third. You'd think, as well as we all played then, that something like that would have happened more often, but it didn't. There really were quite a few fine players around then, and they didn't just let us walk all over them much. I think part of the reason I played so well was that, except for Houston, I had won every important Texas tournament, and some not-so-important ones as well. I'd won at Dallas, San Antonio, Fort Worth, Beaumont, even Harlingen, but never Houston. So that was sort of a minor goal for me, and now I had achieved it, which made me feel good.

The following week I played in the first Colonial National Invitational in Fort Worth and finished in a tie for ninth place. That whole year, I would have a spurt of being able to get fired up for a tournament or two, and then run out of steam. The excitement and tension of 1945 had taken more out of me than I had actually realized. But I never did play well at Colonial—my best finish was a tie for third with Harvie Ward some years later, and I really was making just a guest appearance to help the tournament get going and receive some publicity. It's a fine course, but I just never was able to play it very well, though it's difficult to say whether I might have done better had the Colonial gotten started before I'd made up my mind to leave the tour.

It was about this time that Louise and I closed the deal on the ranch. Because the owner had cattle to sell and equipment to get rid of and so forth, we wouldn't be moving in till the end of August, so it was back on the tour for a few more weeks.

Next was the Western Open in St. Louis. I didn't play well, shot 280, and only won $516.67. Then I went to Winged Foot in Connecticut for the Goodall Round Robin, but before the tournament started, I played a 36-hole exhibition called the "International Challenge Match," against Richard Burton, the British Open champion. My good friend Eddie Lowery was the referee, and I beat Burton 7 and 6 and won $1500. Then, in the tournament itself, I finished third at plus 22, and won $1150. Not a bad week, all things considered.

I didn't play at Philadelphia, because I wanted to save my energy for the U.S. Open at Canterbury in Cleveland, which came right afterwards. Also, by this time I was making quite a few appearances promoting *Winning Golf,* which had just been published, and that took quite a lot of time. You might be interested to know that I got 25 cents for each book, which sold for $2.50. That doesn't sound like much, but it was on the best-seller list for several weeks and sold 130,000 copies, and that 25-cent royalty enabled me to buy my first fifty head of Hereford cattle when I did finally get to start ranching.

Canterbury was a good course, and as usual for the national championship, it was tough. The rough was long, the fairways narrow, and I knew inside that this was going to be my last shot at really trying to win it again. I was playing well, hitting my irons as well or better than ever before, including the Open in '39. In the first round, on the front nine I never missed a fairway or had a putt more than ten feet for birdie, but I two-putted every one and had nine straight pars.

In the second round, Cliff Roberts and the great writer Grantland Rice were in my gallery. On the 15th hole, you drove into a valley and had a blind shot to the green. I got up there in good position for birdie, hit my putt perfect, but the ball swung in and out of the hole. I was walking toward it thinking I'd made it, and couldn't believe it didn't go in. I was told later that Rice said to Cliff right then, "He'll never win." When Cliff said, "Why? He's playing beautifully." Grantland said, "Yes, but the ball's not rolling right for him. He's not getting any breaks at all." As it turned out, he was right, but not because the ball wasn't rolling right.

In the third round, on the par-5 13th hole, I hit a good tee shot and a good second, but I laid up on it a little because if you hit it too far you'd be on a downslope. As soon as I hit it, naturally, the caddie went quickly toward it. Remember now, they didn't have the fairways roped off then for most of the tournaments—the only ones I recall for sure were the '45 PGA and the Masters. The spectators would walk right along with you till you got to your ball, and the marshals would then put a rope up to hold the fans back just enough to give you room to swing, really. Sometimes, if the crowd moved too fast, the marshals couldn't get there ahead of them, and that's exactly what happened this time. My caddie got there and ducked under the rope the marshals were holding, but the rope was too close to my ball; my caddie didn't see it, and he accidentally kicked it about a foot. Since I was leading the tournament at the time, Ike Grainger, one of the top USGA officials, was there as my referee, and we talked about the situation and what it meant. We were both pretty sure it meant a penalty stroke, but Ike said he preferred to talk to the committee before he made a ruling, though he said I had the right to have the decision right then. I said it was okay to wait, which was my mistake, and in my mind that was what cost me the tournament, not the delay itself. Because then I was trying to play with all that on my mind. I was pretty sure I would receive a penalty stroke, but not having it settled right then, I played two over par from there in, and then had the penalty stroke added on besides.

I didn't make up any ground the last round, though I had a good chance or two. On the 17th, a long par 3, I hit my 3-wood just beautifully, but it went over the green and ended up on the fringe—actually, in a lady's hat she had put on the ground next to her. Back then, they allowed people fairly close to the green itself, much closer than they do now. They ruled that I could pick up the ball so the woman could remove her hat, then replace it with no penalty, but the lost time and distraction of all this made me lose my concentration again. I chipped from there and it rimmed the hole, spun out three and a half feet, and I missed the putt. I was a little upset by that, and my tee shot on 18 went down the left side of the fairway, where it landed and bounced further left and into the rough, which was really tall and thick. It was only about a foot into the rough, but it was so thick that I had to use an 8-iron to get out. Then I got to the green and missed a twelve-footer for par, so I ended with two bogeys to tie with Lloyd Mangrum and Vic Ghezzi.

One other unusual thing happened there—we three were in and already tied, but on the 72nd hole, Ben Hogan and Herman Barron were on the green with medium-long putts for birdie to win. Both of them three-putted, but if they'd even two-putted, there would have been a five-way tie.

Now we were in the playoff, and on the 4th hole, the first par 3 on the course, Vic and Lloyd both had thirty-footers. They both made theirs while I missed my own ten-footer. I made up that stroke, but we all played very steady golf and ended up tied again at 72. In the second playoff, on the par-5 9th hole, Mangrum hit his drive out of bounds on the left. He got disgusted with himself, hit again, then put a fairway wood on the green and made an 80-foot putt. He ended up with a 71 to Vic's and my 72's. I'd have to say it was the best I played to lose a tournament my whole life. My concentration was probably not as good as it should have been, because I'd made up my mind ahead of time that if I won I would announce my retirement then and there, so that may have been too much on my mind.

One thing I'd like to say here is that Lloyd Mangrum was the most underrated player of my time. He won twenty-one tournaments, including the '46 Open. He was a fine player, but he had a kind of unusual, funny sarcasm that he used, and if you didn't know him and understand it, it made him sound kind of tough. Some years ago, Susan Marr was doing some radio during the tournament at Westchester, and she asked me to go on the air with her. She said, "I've been asking people all day who are the seven pros who've won twenty-one or more tournaments, and nobody's been able to name them all. Can you?" I said, "I'll try." I'd been doing a little studying for my own broadcast work and got through all of them, including Lloyd, and she said I was the only one who'd remembered Mangrum. I won the prize, which was a "Thank you."

Here's a funny story about Lloyd that most people don't know. He was born in Grapevine, Texas, near where I live now in Roanoke, and he was delivered by the father of my good friend Dr. Dudley Wysong. One time, "Dr. Dud" and his mother were visiting us and discussing that fact, and Mrs. Wysong said, "His daddy ain't paid for it till yet!" The next time I saw Lloyd, I told him what she'd said and he almost died laughing. He thought maybe he should go ahead and send her a check for $25, which was what it cost for a delivery in those days.

The next week in Toledo, back in my old stomping grounds, McSpaden and I played together again—for the last time, really—at the Inverness Invitational Four-Ball. We played pretty well, finished second at plus 14 to Hogan and Demaret, and collected $850 apiece.

I took a week off, then played the Columbus Invitational at Columbus Country Club in Ohio and won it, adding another $2500 to our bank account, which came in very handy. Next week, at the tournament in Kansas City, I tied for third (Frank Stranahan came in first) and won $1,433.34.

Here's a very curious story that I hope someday we find the answer to. As I recall, in the summer of '46 I was playing in a tournament in Kansas City at Hillcrest Country Club. There was an electrical storm going on but we kept playing because the rules said we had to. I was standing on the ninth tee with Horton Smith and Jug McSpaden, when we saw lightning hit back of the ninth green and kill several spectators. I was checking on this story recently with my good friend Bill Inglish though, and he said there was no account in the papers of any such thing happening. So I called Tom Watson, who asked his father, Ray Watson, about it. Ray remembered it distinctly, because he was sitting on the clubhouse porch across from the first tee, which was right next to the ninth green, and Ray saw the lightning hit. Only trouble was, Ray said it happened in 1938, and so does the written history of Hillcrest Country Club. This got my curiosity going, so I called McSpaden, who remembered it the same way I did and also said it was much later than '38, because he was at Winchester in Boston then and never got to play in Kansas City that year. I wasn't in Kansas City in '38 either, according to Bill Inglish's records.

However, it wasn't until 1948 that the USGA made the rule about being able to stop play as soon as any of the players see lightning. Up to that point, even though lightning was visible, you couldn't stop playing until the tournament officials said you could, which wasn't very satisfactory. Still, it's a mystery to me why there's no record anywhere of that other lightning strike, when both McSpaden and I have such a clear memory of it. But wherever we were, if our memories are right, Horton Smith birdied that ninth hole, which really impressed me. Guess he wanted to get out of there as fast as he could.

Louise and I had been on the road now for six out of the last seven weeks, and we were both homesick. As soon as I finished playing in Kansas City, we drove all the way home, had one full day there, then drove all the way to Chicago the Wednesday before the Chicago Victory Open tournament started. With all that driving, it was amazing I played as well as I did, but I managed to win. It was played on Medinah #3, which everyone knows is a very tough course. I drove exceptionally well, shot 279, and won by 2 shots. What I remember best about it, though, was that in the first round I was paired with Tommy Armour, the famous Scottish pro. Tommy and I were having breakfast, and he was known to have too much to drink now and then and he was a little hungover that morning. So before he ate anything, he fixed himself a Bromo-seltzer and drank that. It was the first time I'd ever seen anyone do that before breakfast, and I never forgot it.

The Tam O'Shanter that year was called the All-American for some reason, and I genuinely didn't want to play in it. For one thing, I'd already won there four times, and for another, that year they had begun a promotion deal where the winner was almost duty bound to play at least fifty exhibitions the next year, at $1000 apiece. Well, the money was nice, of course, but that type of thing can be hard on your game. Lloyd Mangrum did it one year, and never played as well afterwards. Anyway, I tied for seventh, winning $1,233.34, so I didn't have to worry about it.

I took off again the next two weeks and then played in the PGA at Portland. I won three matches and made it to the quarterfinals against Porky Oliver. We were tied going to the 18th hole, a long par 5 that had a lot of left-to-right slope on the green. I was thirty feet from the hole and Ed was forty. He had to borrow five feet or more for his putt to break, and he made it, while I missed mine. So much for the defending champion.

I went home again after that, and the first thing that happened was we moved to the ranch on August 26. It took only two carloads to get all our things from Denton to the house in Roanoke. We had no furniture of our own, because we had rented already furnished homes the entire time I played on the tour. Fortunately, Louise's sister Delle had some things of hers in storage because her husband was still in the service and Delle was living at home in Texarkana. We used her stove and refrigerator and a few pieces of furniture till we could get started with our own, and when everything was settled, we found we had $2500 to live on, which we figured we could make last six months.

This was also when I prepared to formally announce my retirement. I did it a few days before I played in something called the "World's Championship" at the Tam O'Shanter course in Chicago. I had mentioned a couple of times already that I was thinking of gradually retiring, but hadn't said anything definite yet. I told the press then that I was formally retiring from tournament golf, that after 1946, I would make only a few token appearances, mainly at Augusta and at the Texas PGA.

Now comes a strange thing. After I made my announcement, I played in a "World's Championship" with Snead, Mangrum, and Barron. It was just two rounds, and I finished second two shots behind Snead, but apparently it was a winner-take-all event, because Snead won $10,000, and the rest of us didn't get anything but our expenses. But the most amazing thing is that I don't recall one single thing about playing in it whatsoever. I guess the fact that I didn't win a dime kind of made me want to forget the whole thing.

At this point, taking a break from everything, Jug and I went on a wonderful hunting trip with Seattle businessman Ralph Whaley, one of the most remarkable men I ever met in my life. We had gotten acquainted with Ralph the year before when I had that 259 in Seattle, and during the tournament he'd invited McSpaden and I and our wives to his house for dinner. Ralph was 6'4", a strong-looking man with a wonderful engineering background. He had helped build Hoover Dam, but mainly he was an outdoorsman and a hunter. He'd bagged various wildlife specimens for the Smithsonian, and in his home there, he had a room fixed up exactly like a cabin where he'd spent a lot of time in the Rockies when he was doing a lot of hunting and trapping. He also was a wonderful shot; he did a lot of exhibition shooting for Winchester and he got so good at it that it got boring, so he started hunting with a bow and arrow instead.

As you might guess, he wasn't bashful at all and started telling us about some of his hunting trips and so forth. He said he was very good with a tomahawk, that he could throw one a long way and stick it in a tree or cut a man's head off if he needed to. To prove it, he took us into this "cabin" room, and hanging on the wall was a tomahawk. Ralph took that down and threw it clear across the room. It landed deep into a wooden post between two big picture windows that looked out over the Broadmoor golf course. Next, because it wasn't dark yet, he took his bow and arrows and we walked outside, where he shot several arrows into the air. We couldn't see any of them after they went off, but he told us exactly where each one would land in the fairway, and he was exactly right. Later, he told us about playing a round of golf against a couple of very prominent pros where he played their best ball. But on each hole, instead of hitting a wood or iron, he would shoot an arrow to the green, then chip or putt from wherever it landed. He played in fifty-seven "shots," so it was no contest.

We were quite impressed with Ralph, and that's why we ended up going hunting with him. He'd already arranged an exhibition in Moscow, Idaho, for which we got no money, but the people putting on the exhibition paid for all the stuff we needed for a hunting trip to this secluded area of Idaho. The amazing thing about Ralph was that when you listened to him talk, you thought he was exaggerating, but when you got out into the woods with him, you found he could actually do everything he said and more.

We hunted elk and I killed one. These elk were on the mountain across from us, and I sighted on this big bull and pulled the trigger. I didn't think I'd hit him, but Ralph said, "You got him—I saw his legs buckle." The bull then took two or three steps and all of a sudden raised up on his hind legs and fell backwards so hard his antlers stuck in the ground. I had his head mounted and shipped to Louise's father, and Dad Shofner hung it on a big post in his grocery store for many years.

My final tournament that year was the Fort Worth Open, which I'd won the year before at Glen Garden. I was somewhat obligated to be there since I was defending champion, but I didn't do well at all and finished seventh. It was the last money I won that year, $550, and brought my total to $22,270.

What a relief it was to have it all over with. I packed up my clubs, sent them to MacGregor, and told them to keep them till I asked for them, which wasn't going to be for a long time. That way, if someone asked me to play even a casual round of golf, I could just tell them I didn't have my clubs, and that would get me off the hook.

Now I could get serious about my ranch. Besides the studying I was doing, I had to do quite a bit of repair work. The fences on the place were in pretty sad shape, so all that winter I worked on rebuilding them. If you've ever done fence work, you know it's hard, but I enjoyed it. I enjoyed everything I did at the ranch—except raising hogs.

I had figured I could make some money on porkers, and I'd read enough about it and gotten enough advice to feel like I could do it. So as soon as I got some of the fences fixed, I bought thirty-eight piglets and fed and watered them till they weighed 220 pounds, the proper weight you had to get before you took them to town to sell. I loaded up those hogs and took them to Fort Worth. Well, it so happened that the price on pork wasn't too good right then, and I made exactly one dollar per animal—$38.00 for thirty-eight hogs. Those were the last hogs I ever raised.

Once I'd left the tour, I really expected that people would more or less forget about me, but that didn't prove to be the case. Oh, I knew at least a few of my records would stand for a good long while, but I was very much surprised and gratified, really, to find that people still wanted me to be involved in golf. I knew I wasn't going to make enough money off my ranch to really live on, and I had planned to continue doing exhibitions and making appearances, so it was fortunate for me that folks still did want me to be part of golf.

For the next few years, I began to spend my time doing a whole variety of things. I did a series of instructional articles for *Popular Mechanics* magazine which dovetailed nicely with my *Winning Golf* book. And after the Masters in '47, I also began to do quite a few exhibitions. As much as I wanted to get away from tournament golf, I did want to remain involved with the game, and to give something back to the sport that had done so much for me. Leaving the tour made it possible for me to do that.

For instance, I'd already been doing a little work with Fred Cobb, the golf coach at North Texas State in Denton, and now I could do more. I worked with the team up there quite a bit over the next few years, and they brought along some pretty good players like Don January, Ross Collins, and Billy Maxwell. Cobb was the best thing that ever happened to golf up there. He had the ability to get the best out of every player he had. Unfortunately, he died at a relatively young age in 1953, and the golf program there has never reached that level since.

I also began to do an occasional appearance or exhibition for MacGregor, and I can honestly say I enjoyed it. Playing exhibitions without the pressure of the media and thousands of fans, but with everyone relaxed and enjoying themselves, was quite a different thing, and a lot of fun as long as there wasn't too much of it.

About six weeks before the '47 Masters I received my invitation to play. I'd had enough time off from golf that I was looking forward to it. I called MacGregor, had them send my clubs back, and started practicing. As part of my routine, I would go play at Brookhollow in Dallas with my good friends Jim Chambers and Felix McKnight. I worked at the ranch till noon, then drove over and played. They used to laugh at me because I'd complain about being so sore and I played just terrible at first. They said, "You think you can be digging postholes all morning and come over here and not be sore trying to play golf?" We played at Brookhollow so much that the club finally made me an honorary member, which was a great privilege.

But I got tuned up well enough for the Masters, at least so I wouldn't embarrass myself, and off Louise and I went. We stayed at the Richmond Hotel, and I can still remember the hot biscuits and country ham you could get there every morning. I didn't have the ham a lot because it was too salty, but it sure was good.

It was an unusual tournament for me in a way. Everyone at Augusta National was glad to see me, and I surprised myself by playing as well as I did. I was 14 under par on the par fives, and I had three eagles: one on 15 in the third round, and two on 13, in the first and second rounds. It was a record at the time, and held up till 1974. I don't recall who I was paired with or very much about the tournament, but I finished tied with Frank Stranahan for second, so I was very pleased. There was a point during the tournament when I realized I was playing well enough that I had a chance to win, but it really didn't matter to me one way or another, which may be why I didn't try harder. Though I played well on the par fives, I played the par threes poorly and putted badly, so there wasn't one particular hole where I could say, "That was where I lost it." The fact was, I really didn't care anymore. I enjoyed seeing our friends there, and Augusta will always be a special place for me, but playing there in '47 showed me once again that I was definitely through with the tour. I had no desire to go back out there. It was behind me.

But I did start to do more in other areas of golf soon after the Masters. In June, I went to St. Louis for the Open, but instead of playing, I wrote for one of the press services. That was interesting and fun, kind of being on the inside and the outside at the same time. Less than two weeks later, I played an exhibition at my old post, Ridgewood Country Club in New Jersey, where I proceeded to set the course record of 63. The next month, I began a series of exhibitions in cities like Flint, Michigan; West Bend, Wisconsin; Elgin, Illinois; and even Chisel Switch, Kansas. I did thirty-five exhibitions in two months, shot between 63 and 68, averaged 67, and made enough to keep the ranch going a while longer. Besides being a nice relaxed way to make some decent money, exhibitions made me realize I really enjoyed putting on a show for the fans, especially doing the clinics. Without the pressure of an upcoming tournament to worry about, I could laugh and joke with the crowd, and I found out I actually had a sense of humor.

All that exhibition work also prepared me well for the Ryder Cup matches that year in Portland. It was a great honor to be selected for the team again. I had been selected a couple of other times since 1937, when I'd first played in the Ryder Cup. But with the war on, we never really played until '47, so it was gratifying to get to do it again, since I had a feeling it would be the last time I would get picked for the team. It was an interesting situation. The British, who were just barely starting to recover from the war and all the bombing, were not allowed to take any money out of England. A man named Robert A. Hudson, a successful businessman in the Pacific Northwest and a golf nut, paid the expenses for the British team himself. In fact, the great British player Henry Cotton was able to come and play in the Masters that year only because Eddie Lowery loaned him the money—which Henry paid back immediately.

I remember one funny thing about that Ryder Cup. Herman Barron and I were playing in our alternate-shot match. I was the captain of our twosome, and we were one up going to the 17th, a par 3. I put my tee shot eight feet from the pin, and the British were fifteen feet away. Herman was a wonderful putter and I had complete confidence in him, so when we walked on the green, I got this idea in my head that I would give the other guys their putt, which I did. Barron looked at me like I was completely crazy, and said as much to me. But I just said, "Herman, I have no doubt at all that you'll make this putt." Which of course he did, and we ended up winning the match nicely.

After '47, my appearances in tournaments such as the Masters, the Colonial, and occasionally the U.S. Open were purely ceremonial. With only a few exceptions, I never did play particularly well in any of them, though I certainly enjoyed seeing the people and knowing that they liked seeing me again. For quite a while, I enjoyed playing in a tournament without having the pressure. I could relax, just amble along and enjoy the good shots, but sit back and realize it didn't matter to me if I finished fifth or twenty-fifth. And of course, I didn't play in any of these beyond where I could put on at least a good show. I was the first to play 100 rounds at the Masters, though, which I'm pleased about.

So from that point on, my career in golf is of little interest to most folks except for an occasional story. One funny thing happened in 1948, at the National Celebrity tournament at Columbia Country Club in D.C. I was paired with Snead, who happened to hate cameras. Snead would always look around the gallery before he hit to see if anyone was taking pictures. Well, that day some guy was following us. He was standing about thirty yards down the fairway, and had this camera hanging around his neck—there weren't any rules then about cameras on the course during a tournament. Sam saw him and watched him every hole, though he never once took a picture or even acted like he was going to, so Snead could never say anything to him. But Sam played poorly and I shot 67 and was low pro. I always wondered whether that fellow knew how much Snead hated cameras and had bet against him that day.

Then came one of the most moving experiences of my life. It was the summer of '48, and my brother Charles had been married to Betty Brown of Gainesville, Texas, for several years. Charles had just gotten out of the service, and Betty was seven months pregnant. Then Charles came down with a fever. For a few days we thought it was the flu, but they finally diagnosed it as polio. We took him to the Veterans' Hospital in Dallas, but we didn't feel he was receiving the best treatment. I wanted to take him out of there myself and get him to a civilian hospital. But Charles refused; he knew they wouldn't release him, then he'd be AWOL and that would cancel his Army benefits, so he stayed. My parents drove over there from Denton every single day. They didn't think he'd ever live because he had bulbar polio, the most serious kind.

Well, he did live. After their baby was born, which they named Byron III, Louise invited Betty to come live with us. When Charles finally got out of the hospital, he lived at the ranch with Betty and the baby until he could find work. Now, Charles had a wonderful singing voice, a beautiful, deep, bass-baritone. He had been song leader at the Pearl Street Church of Christ in Denton and when he got well enough, they told him he could come back. When it was announced that he was going to start leading the singing again, the church was packed full, and our whole family was there. He was sitting on a bench with his crutches, behind the podium, but when he got up, he fell. Absolutely flat on his face. But he told everyone not to help him. Then he crawled to the podium and pulled himself up, while the whole church was silent. When he finally stood up, Charles hit the first note of the first song full bore, and off he went. There wasn't a dry eye in the house, and I don't know if any of us were singing very well right then. Even though he's my little brother, Charles has always been an inspiration to me, and I can never remember that moment without getting pretty emotional.

I bought my first herd of Herefords for the ranch in the fall of '48. I bought the cows from a Dr. Wiss in Keller, and the bull from Dr. Alden Coffey in Fort Worth. The bull was from the bloodline of Prince Domino Returns, one of the greatest Hereford bulls ever. As far as I was concerned, the day those Herefords arrived was a lot more important than any tournament I played in that year. My father and I did a lot of the work on the ranch ourselves. We had one hired hand most of the time, and the three of us hauled manure, cut and baled hay, dug post holes, and built fences—whatever there was to do, we did. It was also during these years that I started raising turkeys. Two things started me on them. I knew I wasn't going to be able to make much money on our cattle because the ranch was really too small for that. But I knew you could make money on either turkeys or chickens. We had eaten store-bought turkeys the year before and remembered they hadn't had much flavor because they were too lean. A fellow I knew, Claude Castleberry, was in charge of all the food for the Texas State College for Women in Denton. He played golf, and also had a cafeteria in the school where townspeople could come and eat. When I asked him where he got his turkeys, he said mainly just big producers like Armour and Swift. I was going to raise a few just for our friends and us, but when I told him I was thinking of raising turkeys he said, "If you do, I'll buy them." Between the college and the cafeteria, he would use 400–500 a year. So I got going and built a turkey building right next to my cattle barns, and some roosting racks outside for when they outgrew the building. Then I fixed some brooders in the cattle barn, and raised about a thousand turkeys at a time. They were called "Texas Bronze" because of the bronze coloring at the end of their feathers. I passed the word around to our friends, and I finished the turkeys on corn the last couple of months to fatten them up. The toms weighed an average of over twenty-four pounds, and the hens fourteen. Back then, you could take them to regular eviscerating plants to get them cleaned and dressed, which I did. Then I would deliver them myself, door to door, to our friends and family in Fort Worth and Dallas.

You'd have to use a big pan to roast them because they were so juicy, and everyone said those were the best turkeys they ever ate. I did make a little money on those birds, but I worked hard for my dollar. Things went along all right for a few years, but then in '53, Claude Castleberry left TSCW and someone else took over the buying. Their policy had changed and now they had to take bids, but naturally I had to get more money than the big poultry producers who didn't finish their birds on corn. So I couldn't compete, and I got out of the turkey business. But I have to say you can buy a better turkey now than you could then. Today's turkeys are excellent.

The chicken business was next. Again from playing golf, I'd met Joe Fechtel, president of Western Hatcheries in Dallas. I knew he was in the chicken business and he knew about my turkeys, so one day he asked me if I'd ever thought about producing fertile eggs to sell to a hatchery. He told me his company would furnish the chickens and roosters and show us what to do, then they'd buy the eggs from us. They would pay 65 cents a dozen, cleaned and cased. Then they'd put the eggs in an incubator under my name, and for every percentage point above 65% fertility, I'd get an extra penny, but if I was under

65%, I'd get docked a penny. I'd always liked chickens, and my mother knew a lot about them, so I liked the idea. I invested over $20,000 in the buildings, the refrigerated egg house, and all the automatic feeders and waterers we needed. We had over 17,000 laying hens at one time, and in all the ten or so years we had those chickens, we never had less than 65% fertility. More than any other one thing I did with the ranch, the chickens always made me a little money, enough to fool with, anyway. But in the early sixties, things began to change again. The chicken business started moving to Arkansas, where the summers weren't so hot. Joe told me when he was going to move, and my operation was the last one he closed out with before he moved.

All this chicken talk reminds me of a golf story. One day in June of 1949, I got a call from my good friend Eddie Lowery in California. Eddie had been a fine amateur player as a youngster. In fact, he got started as a caddie, just like I did, only about a dozen years earlier. And Eddie always was serious about golf. He was small, about 5'9" or so and 150 pounds, but he had very large hands. He won several championships in New England, from the time he was sixteen on, and by the time I met him, he knew everyone in golf. He served on the USGA board for many years, and was an amazingly energetic man. He didn't always use the best language, but you couldn't help liking him, he loved golf so much.

Anyway, after we'd chatted a bit he said, "How are you playing, Byron?" I'd been playing well, so I told him, "I'm playing pretty good, Eddie." He talked a little more then said again, "Are you really playing good?" I replied, "Yes, I'm playing good, Eddie—why?"

He said, "I've been playing out here at Santa Rosa Country Club with the Buzzini brothers, and they're picking me like a chicken. I want you to come out here and play them with me. I'll set up a few exhibitions for you, but first we'll play these guys." George Buzzini and his brother worked as the pro and assistant at Santa Rosa. George especially was a pretty good player and did well in all the local tournaments, though neither he nor his brother ever played on the tour as far as I know. But I told Eddie I'd come out there.

Louise and I got there, and after dinner we went to Eddie's house. He took me up to his bedroom where he had this practice putting gadget and a whole bunch of putters lined up against the wall. Now, Eddie never did think I was a very good putter. He was right to some degree, as I've explained before. He just never thought I was as good as I ought to be. So he picked out this putter, a MacGregor Spur, and had me start hitting some putts with it. I had a little trouble at first, but then started hitting it pretty good. Eddie said, "That's the putter I want you to use tomorrow against the Buzzinis." I said, "Eddie, I've got my own putter and I'd rather use it." But Eddie said, "It's my money we're playing for, so you use that putter, not yours." I finally agreed, so we were set.

The next morning, I started off a little slowly and scrambled around and made a par, then another par, then pretty soon I started making birdies. The Buzzinis began pressing, but I kept on making birdies with that putter. To make a long story short, they finally quit pressing, because I made 12 birdies and six pars and shot 60. Eddie got all his money back—with interest.

He had me take that putter home and said, "If you ever use anything but that putter, you're nuts." I used it for two more months and never made another putt outside of four feet, and finally sent it back to him. When he got it back, he phoned me and called me every name in the book, but I told him, "Eddie, I think I used up all the putts in that club when we played the Buzzinis!"

A couple of years ago I got a call from a young man who'd been hired to do a book on the history of the Santa Rosa Country Club. He'd come across a clipping about my 60 and couldn't believe it, wanted to know all the details. It *was* pretty unbelievable—particularly since that putter quit working so soon after that match.

While I was working on getting the ranch going and keeping it going, Louise was very busy getting the house in shape. It was quite a mess when we moved in. The previous owners had dogs that they apparently kept inside the house, and the first night we were there, we had to sleep on a mattress on the living room floor. The first thing we knew, we were getting bitten by all these fleas that were in the carpet, so we had to get the whole house treated the next day. As soon as we could afford to, we hired an excellent architect and set about making the place over. We did it pretty much room by room, starting with the back porch, which we made into a good-sized kitchen, then taking what was the kitchen and dining room and making it just one big dining room. What's now the den or trophy room used to be the bunkroom for four children. It had a little old metal shower in the corner and a fake fireplace and just a couple of little bitty windows. It was quite a project those first few years, but Louise loved it. She had a real talent for decorating and an eye for beautiful things, and because it was our first real home, it made me happy that I could finally afford for her to make our home exactly the way she wanted it to be.

We were so busy with ranching and redecorating that I wasn't thinking about golf much at all. But my friend Eddie Lowery didn't seem to ever think about anything *but* golf. One day in the late forties, Eddie called and had this idea that he'd like me to go on Ed Sullivan's television show and give some brief golf instructions. Back then, the show was sponsored by Lincoln-Mercury, and Eddie, who was a very successful Lincoln-Mercury dealer, was on the panel that coordinated the advertising. I'd known Sullivan and had played golf with him since my early days at Ridgewood. In those days, Ed was a sportswriter and did a radio show called "The Talk of the Town."

So off I went to New York to try this out, and what I did was go on stage with a golf club chosen for whatever the tip was going to be about. The first time we had only two minutes, and of course you can't say much in two minutes. Remember, this was all live TV. Ed introduced me, then he stood very close to me, so close I could hardly swing the club. He apologized later and explained that many newcomers on the show would freeze up when they got out in front of the audience and had all those bright lights nearly blinding them. I didn't have that problem, fortunately.

That first golf tip was reasonably well received, and a few months later, Ed had me on for five straight weeks. They didn't use real golf balls, but light plastic ones, sort of like the wiffle balls they have today, and on one show, Ed saw a friend of his sitting in a box seat not too far from stage, so Ed asked me to hit one of the balls to his friend. I hit it too hard and a little thin, and it hit a lady in about the third row right on her forehead. She wasn't hurt or anything, but after the show she brought the ball up to us and you could still see the dimple on her forehead from where it had hit. Fortunately, in those days we didn't have to worry about being sued, but still I decided to start practicing with those balls, and learned if you didn't hit it hard it would go a lot farther. After that, Ed would often have me hit to someone or a certain place in the audience, and I did all right—at least, I didn't hit anyone else in the head. I enjoyed it, but I enjoyed more getting to see the performers backstage and how they got made up and their nervousness and all they'd go through to get ready to go on stage. It was something to see.

During that five-show stint, one day Louise and I were walking down the street in Manhattan after a show I'd done the night before. We happened to pass by a group of about five men standing together who didn't see us because they were arguing about the way I'd said to do something on Ed's show. Louise said, "Why don't you go over and interrupt them?" but I was a little shy yet about doing such things, so we just kept going.

Along about this time, when I wasn't doing something with or because of Lowery or working on the ranch, I was often invited by Cliff Roberts to play at Augusta. One time in '49 or '50, I was there playing when a fellow named General Dwight David Eisenhower walked in. As it happened, Augusta's pro, Ed Dudley, was Ike's teacher, and Ike was there to take some lessons from him. Cliff set it up for us to play together, and it was fun. Ike was a good man to play golf with. He liked to chat, was very friendly-like, and when he'd hit a good shot, that expressive face he had would just beam all over. But when he hit a bad shot, he'd fuss at himself just like the rest of us. He hit a lot of good shots and was good around the green, but had trouble on his long shots, which faded off to the right a lot.

One of the best compliments I ever had came a few years later when President Eisenhower asked Cliff if I had time to come down to Augusta and play with him, shortly after the election in 1952. Of course, I made time whether I had it or not, and we played several rounds together, one of which made the President very happy. On the second hole, the left side of the fairway slopes downhill toward the green pretty severely. I had driven to the right where it was flat, while Eisenhower drove to the left. It was quite a good drive and when his ball did stop, he had outdriven me a good bit. On the 10th, the same thing happened, and he outdrove me again. I never thought anything about it, but some months later, after he was in the White House, he had a dinner one night for a few of us pros. All of us were in the dining room waiting for him, and he came in and asked us to sit down. Then, before he sat down himself, Ike pointed at me and said, "I want you all to know that I played golf with that man last year and outdrove him *twice!*"

Usually he'd ride in a cart at Augusta, and I would drive. But he was like a cricket, he'd jump out of the cart before it stopped, every time. It made me nervous, so I finally said, "Mr. President, I wish you'd wait till I stop the cart before you get out, because it would look terrible in the newspapers if it said, 'Byron Nelson Breaks President's Leg.'" He laughed and said he would, and he did wait the next time, but after that he never waited again. I didn't mention it again, though.

One other time, Louise was at Augusta with me and wanted to meet him, so when she saw us coming to the 18th, she went out and sat down there by the clubhouse. She had practiced and had it all set what she was going to say to him when I introduced her, but when he saw Louise, he surprised us both by rushing right up to her and introducing himself and saying how glad he was to meet her. She did fine, said something or other to him, but she told me later, "I know I just stood there with my mouth hanging open." That evening, we had an early dinner because we had to leave, and as we got in our car outside the clubhouse, Ike came out to our car. He asked how far we had to drive and told us to be careful. That's how warm and nice he was.

Then, in the fall of 1950, Jim Shriver, a salesman for MacGregor's Northwest territory, called just before he was starting on his fall sales tour. He said he'd like to book me for some exhibitions in his area the next spring. He thought he'd be able to book quite a few and I'd get $300 each, so I said, "That sounds all right, Jim." Unfortunately, when he got back from his fall tour, he called and said, "Byron, I booked a few, but not enough for you to come out for." Well, I was disappointed, because the money sure would have come in handy.

Fortunately, Bing Crosby called me that December and wanted me to come play in his pro-am in January of '51 with Eddie Lowery, George Fazio, and Bill Ford of the Ford Motor Company. I said I would, and as soon as I hung up, I remembered my conversation with Shriver. I realized that I hadn't been doing anything to get publicity and my name was fading fast out there. I made up my mind right then that I was going to try hard to make people aware I was still around.

We flew out to Pebble Beach on Thursday before the tournament started, and I went out and practiced—but only from 100 yards in.

My long game was fine, but my short game wasn't as sharp as it ought to be. By the time the tournament started, my short game had jelled and I was doing quite well. I won with three good rounds, 71-67-71. The weather was very poor that year, with both wind and rain, so one round was washed out completely.

My strategy worked, though. Two weeks after the Crosby, Jim Shriver called again and said, "I've got twenty-six matches booked for this spring. Every town I talked to wants you to come out and play." Well, that was great, so I went on the road for a month. But just to show the difference between then and now, here's what I did for that $300. I had to go to a luncheon at the country club or Kiwanis headquarters or whatever, then go to the course, put on a clinic for thirty minutes and play eighteen holes with the local pro, top amateur, or whoever was trying to beat me that day. Finally, I'd stay and have dinner with everyone that evening, give a talk, then jump in my car and drive that night or in the morning to the next town. So I earned every penny of that $300. I played quite well too.

The next fall, Jim wanted to know if I'd do it again in '52, so I did. I played exactly the same places, twenty-six matches in thirty days. That spring I played some of my best golf ever. My highest score was 68 and my lowest 59. The 59 was at Olympia Country Club in Olympia, Washington. It was a par-72 course, and I shot 31-28. I was playing real well, and was 5 under on the first nine. Then on the 10th, I hit driver and an 8-iron and holed it for a 2. On the 11th, a par 3, I made 2. On the 12th, a good par 4, I had a good drive and 6-iron and holed my putt for a 3. The 13th was a par-5, 520 yards, and I hit driver and 2-wood and holed my putt for eagle, so I used ten shots for four holes.

When I did these exhibitions, as I came to the 18th green I always stopped and thanked the people before putting out. This time they were really enjoying the show, so I said, "You may not know it, but I have this putt to make for 28, and if I do that I'll have a 59, which I've never shot before in my life." Then I sank the putt, fortunately, and they really did cheer me.

While I was playing those Pacific Northwest exhibitions in '52, The National Amateur was being played at Seattle. Eddie Lowery called me and said there was a young boy named Kenny Venturi who had qualified for the Amateur and Eddie wanted me to take a look at him. Eddie felt Ken showed great promise, which was enough recommendation for me. I went out and watched him play his first match with Mason Rudolph, and Mason beat him. Eddie introduced us after the match was over, and I asked Ken when he was going back to San Francisco. I told him I was going there too, and said for him to have Eddie get in touch with me and we'd have a game. We played at San Francisco Golf Club, where Kenny played a lot. He shot 66 but didn't play very well—he made a lot of bad swings. But he pitched and putted great and shot a better score than I did. He was expecting me to brag on him (I knew that from my own experience playing with Bobby Cruickshank when I was Kenny's age), but instead I said, "Kenny, Eddie said he wanted me to work with you and if you're not busy tomorrow, you come out early, because we've got six things we've got to work on right away." He looked at me kind of funny but said, "Okay, I'll be there." Kenny proved to be an excellent pupil. He listened very well and paid close attention, which wasn't easy because we talked about quite a few things.

Not too long after that, Eddie told me he had a fellow working for him, another amateur golfer, Harvie Ward—a young man who could hit the ball a long way and basically had a very good game. But Eddie told me, "He can't work the ball left or right." So I worked with him a few times on it. He could draw or fade after a fashion, but he wasn't going about it right, and was doing too many things wrong to get the results he wanted. When I showed him how to do it correctly, he caught on real quick and told me, "I didn't know the game could be so easy." This was before he won the American and British Amateur Championships. Later, when we were paired together in the Colonial tournament in '54, he was trying really hard to beat me, but in the last round he faltered on a few holes and we came to 18 even. I put my ball inside of his, and Harvie walked up, looked at me and smiled, and knocked his ball right in. Then I did the same thing, only I smiled *after* I made my putt.

Now for a story about a horse of a different color. It was also that summer of '54 that Waco Turner, an oilman in Ardmore, Oklahoma, called me. He wanted me to come up and play in his tournament there. It was a pretty big money event for those days, plus Waco was offering extra money for birdies and eagles and such. I wasn't really interested, but then he said he'd give me a beautiful palomino horse just for coming up and playing. I'd always thought palominos were awful pretty, so that got my attention and I agreed to go. As it turned out, I played very poorly, didn't make hardly any birdies at all, let alone eagles. So I didn't get much extra money.

But sure enough, I did get that horse. When the tournament was over, the sheriff of Ardmore rode up to me at the 18th green on this beautiful palomino mare. I got up on her, but I could tell right away she and I weren't going to get along. Still, my father knew a lot about horses, and I thought he could work with her. When I got back to the ranch he took one look at her and said, "Son, she'll never have a decent disposition." She was wall-eyed, and that's never a good sign in a horse. I kept her for a year, but she wasn't ever any good. Once, I took her to a plowed-up field and worked her and worked her, but it never helped a bit. Finally, I gave her—with fair warning—to a good friend who lived south of Fort Worth, and a month later he told me, "You were right—we can't handle her either." She probably ended up as dog food. What's that they say about not looking a gift horse in the mouth? Well, I sure should have thought twice about that one. It was the last time I played for Waco Turner, I can tell you.

Every once in a while in golf you run up against an odd ruling situation. In October of 1954, I was playing in the Texas PGA at Oso Beach Country Club in Corpus Christi, Texas. I had shot 63 the first round, but in the second for some reason I was just helpless and ballooned up to an 81. That just happens sometimes, as every golfer knows. Still, I had a good third and fourth round and had a chance to win when I ran into this peculiar situation. It was the 18th hole, and a fellow named Jack Hardin had to make a four to beat me. He hit his drive way to the right, over by the equipment barn, and everyone said it was off club property, which meant it would have been out of bounds. But there were no OB stakes, so the committee ruled his ball wasn't out of bounds. Jack managed to scramble for his par and beat me one stroke. I didn't have any bad feelings about it, though later the committee said they should have had stakes there, because without them no one can determine whether your ball is out or not.

I was the captain of the Texas Cup matches several times, and one time I remember very well was in '54. That's the year when Don January and Billy Maxwell, who were in college and still amateurs, were

11 under par for the first ten holes against me and Fred Hawkins at Dallas Country Club. I shot 66 and Fred helped me some, but with January and Maxwell playing like they were playing, we both felt like we weren't doing very well at all. They had two eagles, and it seemed like they were birdieing or eagling every hole.

In January 1955, Eddie and I were partners again in the Crosby Pro-Am. In those days you played at Monterey the first round, and this time we had a good score, 64. We played Cypress the second round, and because we'd started so well, we were right in the thick of the tournament. We came to the 17th hole, where the wind was blowing very strong off the ocean, quartering from the right. Eddie had pulled his drive way left, and mine ended up back of a group of trees, about 175 yards short of the green. I was too close to the trees to go over them, so I was looking at my ball, trying to figure out what to do. Then Eddie missed his second shot and was in the trees on the left and short of the green, so there was no way he could make par. With that strong wind blowing, I decided I could hit my ball against it, hook it, and let it draw back over the ocean to the green. As I took my stance, Eddie could see where I was aiming, and he started yelling and running toward me, but I couldn't hear him because of the wind. I went ahead and hit, and my ball sailed out over the ocean pretty as you please and landed about 15 feet from the hole. Eddie never congratulated me or anything, he just jumped all over me and swore at me and said I was crazy for taking such a chance. He must have decided I couldn't be trusted, because in the third round, which we played at Pebble Beach, Eddie was sensational. He used every one of his eight strokes despite the fact that there was terrible rain all day, and we shot 63 and won.

That must have given him a lot of confidence, because shortly after the Crosby, Eddie called and said he was going to go over and play in the British Open at St. Andrews. He wanted me to play too, and wanted Louise and me to go with him and his new wife, Margaret—it was their delayed honeymoon. (Eddie's first wife, Louise, had died of cancer several years before, and he had recently remarried.) I said, "Well, that sounds okay, Eddie, but you need to talk to Louise." Louise got on the phone then and she told Eddie, "We'll go on one condition—that after the Open we do some sightseeing, maybe even go to Paris." So we went.

We flew over and back on a TWA sleeper plane. At that time I was bothered by claustrophobia some, plus we ran into a bad electrical storm with hail and the whole works. Also, I wasn't a good flier then because of that experience in South America way back in '37, so I was really miserable. I couldn't stay in bed, I just lay there and shook. I was so scared I finally got up and sat and watched the pilot the whole rest of the way. The trip took fourteen hours, and though there really were no problems as far as the plane and the pilot went, it was just a terrible trip for me. Fortunately, when we came back home the weather was fine, and we returned in the daytime, which made it even better.

When we got to St. Andrews, Eddie had set up a practice round with Leonard Crawley, who had been a wonderful player and then became a good golf writer. I'd met Leonard before and Eddie thought he knew more about St. Andrews than anyone. As it turned out, Leonard didn't play, but he did walk the course with us and told us where to go on every hole, what you had to know about the many blind shots, and where the best place to approach the green was.

Now, I had heard and read all my life how hard and fast the greens were at St. Andrews, but even though it rained the first part of the week, I negotiated those greens all right and qualified with 143. Unfortunately, Eddie didn't make it. Then it turned hot—81–82 degrees, which was very hot to those folks—and people were getting sunburned and almost having heatstroke. But the worst part was that the grass started growing real fast, which made the greens very slow, and I never could get that through my head. I averaged 37 putts per round and finished twelfth. I played great from tee to green, hit more greens than anybody, but hitting greens doesn't mean that much on St. Andrews. Peter Thomson won by 5. That was my second and last showing in the British Open.

Now comes the good part. Unbeknownst to Louise and me, Eddie had entered both of us in the French Open the next week when we were going to be in Paris. He'd done it during the British Open after talking to a good friend of his, Jacques L'Eglise, who was president of the French Federation of Golf and was there at St. Andrews. Eddie didn't have the nerve to tell us what he'd done until the day the tournament ended, and with good reason. Louise was very upset with him, but he promised that we really would do some sightseeing after the

French Open—and he did finally keep his word. So we flew to Paris the next day and checked in at the Ritz, where we had a two-bedroom suite. Eddie was paying a lot of our expenses, so I made a deal with him that since I had to play in the tournament, whatever I won we'd put on the hotel bill.

When I went to register at the French Federation of Golf, it was on a street called Rue Byron, which made me feel lucky. As it turned out, Eddie didn't qualify, but I played very well. I broke 70 every round until the first nine of the fourth round, when I shot 38. Eddie was gone that morning; he'd had some business meetings and he got back just as I had turned nine. I wasn't playing well at all and was only a shot or so in the lead, with Weetman and Bradshaw chasing me. I was whining about how bad I was playing, and Eddie jumped all over me and called me all sorts of names. He made me so mad that if we hadn't been such good friends I'd almost have wanted to hit him. But what he said must have helped, because I shot 32 on the last nine and won—the first time an American had won the French Open since Walter Hagen in 1922. My prize money was 10,000 francs, but it wasn't even enough to pay our hotel bill!

Then we finally got to do some sightseeing. Of course, Eddie and Margaret were on their honeymoon, and they wanted to go out every evening. One night we went to the Folies Bergere, where the show was full of half-naked women, and the next night we went to another place where it was the same thing, though the food was good. But after that, Louise said, "Byron, I've seen all the naked women I want to see." I agreed with her, so that was the end of our nightclubbing. All in all, though, it was a very good trip, and that really was the last time I played golf to amount to anything much.

We got back home and settled down a little bit—as much as my life ever settled down, I guess—till that fall. For most of '54 and '55 Kenny Venturi had been in the army, but he got out that October of '55. As soon as he came home, Eddie took him out to Palm Springs to play. When he saw what Kenny was doing, Eddie called me and said Kenny was scoring pretty well but his swing was all off. Eddie wanted me to come out to Palm Springs and work with him, so I agreed. First, we went out and played a round at Thunderbird. Kenny played terrible, scored in the mid-high 70's. So we started practicing that day and worked hard the next three or four days, and the last round we played before I came back, he shot 65. One of Kenny's greatest strengths as a player was that he had the ability to make sudden, fast changes in his game when it was necessary. I felt pretty confident when I left that his game was back where it should be, which gave me an idea.

That year, the former Masters champions had the right to invite one player of their choice, pro or amateur, and I knew Kenny hadn't been able to play at Augusta in '55 because he was in the service. So I began canvassing the former Masters winners about Kenny, and they agreed that he ought to be invited to the Masters the next year, so I was happy about that.

It was early March of '56, and Harvie and Kenny had just played in the San Francisco city championship at Harding Park, where Kenny beat Harvie 6 and 4. There were at least 15,000 in the gallery at that tournament. Shortly after that, Eddie and I were in Pebble Beach for the Crosby Pro-Am, and so were Kenny and Harvie, playing as amateurs, of course. Louise and I and the Lowerys were invited to dinner one evening at George Coleman's home before the tournament started. During dinner, George said to Eddie, "Your two kids really played well in San Francisco." Eddie was feeling pretty good and he said to George, "Yes, they can beat anybody, those two kids." Then they got into a discussion. George said, "Anybody?" Eddie replied, "Anybody—yes, they can beat anybody!" George kind of baited Eddie a little bit and said, "Including pros?" And Eddie fired right back, "Yes, including pros." So George said, "Well, I've got a couple of pros I'd like to have play them." And Eddie said, "That's fine, they can beat anybody." George said, "What do you want to bet on that?" And Eddie said, "Five thousand."

Now all this time, Eddie hadn't yet asked Coleman who his players were. When he finally said, "Okay, George, who are your players?" George looked straight at him and said, "Nelson and Hogan." Well, that sure took me by surprise. But Coleman knew I had worked with both Kenny and Harvie and that I'd love to play with them anytime, so it was fine with me.

Eddie kind of swallowed and looked at me, and finally said, "They'll beat them, too!" Well, Ben wasn't at the dinner, so George first had to call Ben, and he said yes, he'd play. The match was on for the first thing in the morning. By the time we got to the course—which happened to be Cypress Point—the bet had gone down from

$5000 to just a friendly wager, fortunately. But word had gotten out that we four were playing, and we had quite a gallery, about a thousand people. We didn't waste any time getting started—the birdies started at the first hole. They made them, we made them, and sometimes we all made them together. We finally went one up at the 10th, when Ben holed a full wedge on a par 5 that you couldn't reach in two. Then I made a 3 with a drive and 2-iron and one-putt at the 11th, but they birdied too, so we halved that. Starting at 14, the hole up the hill through the trees, we both made 3, and we both made 3 at 15. At 16 I made 2, so we were two up at 17, and they birdied but we didn't. Now we were one up. They birdied 18, but so did Ben, so we won 1 up. The four of us were a total of 26 under par, and many of the people who were there said later that it was the greatest four-ball match in history. It would be interesting to see a couple of the good pros and amateurs play a match like that today.

As for the Masters that year, Kenny played wonderfully well and was leading the tournament four shots going to the last round. I had been paired with the last-round leader since 1946, but Cliff Roberts and Bob Jones decided I shouldn't play with Ken because I was his teacher and it might cause controversy. They had him play with Snead instead. Whether it was just because he couldn't play with me, or simply the pressure of being the one and only amateur to ever have a chance to win the Masters, he stumbled badly that last round; he shot 80 and lost. Four years later, in '60, Ken was in the clubhouse and they already had him in the winner's circle when Arnold Palmer birdied 17 and 18 to beat him by one stroke. So he just missed winning the Masters two times.

Somewhere about this time, I was in Wichita Falls for a large junior tournament. One night at a party, I got to talking with Rufus King, a fine amateur golfer, and his brother Charley, who was in the film business. Rufus was saying, "You know, Byron, you ought to do some instructional films—short ones, for television." Charley agreed and added, "If you could do about thirteen of them, that would be a good package to work with, and maybe I could find someone to help finance it." We all knew that Bob Jones had done some many years before that were sometimes shown in theaters in the early thirties. We talked about it two or three other times and I suggested that Rufus have Charley get in touch with Eddie Lowery. Rufus and Eddie knew each other from amateur golf, so Charley called Eddie and he did help finance it. We called the series "Let's Go Golfing," and did all the filming up at Wichita Falls, Texas. We had a very small crew—just a cameraman who also did the directing, and a couple of assistants. I enjoyed making the films. I'd talk and hit a few shots and talk some more—it wasn't much different from giving a clinic or a lesson except for the part where I'd be indoors, introducing the show or signing off. I never did know whether they really weren't any good or were just ahead of their time, but unfortunately, they didn't sell very well at all.

My golf by now was all right for the most part, though I continued to play just for the fun of it, and at the Masters in 1957, I had almost more fun than I could stand. On the 16th hole in the fourth round, I put my 4-iron tee shot in the water. So I went up to the front of the tee box, about thirty yards closer, and hit my 7-iron good and solid. The ball was sailing towards the hole just perfect, but it hit the flagstick on the metal section about a foot above the cup—back then Augusta had wood-and-metal flagsticks—and it bounced straight back into the water. It was the only time in my whole career that I hit the pin and ended up in the water. Next I went to the drop area, where the gallery sits now, got on, and two-putted for a 7. When I finally did get my ball in the hole, I got the biggest round of applause you ever heard anybody get for a quadruple bogey.

The next year, 1958, I began a minor career as a consultant on golf course design. It started at Brookhaven in North Dallas with Bob Dedman, who now owns Club Corporation of America and is successfully running more than 200 golf clubs. For Brookhaven, I was hired to help the architect, Press Maxwell, shape the fifty-four greens on the course. I greatly enjoyed it, and was able to rely on my experience in playing so many courses across the country. We used what natural landscape there was, didn't move a lot of dirt, and ended up with three good golf courses. I received $10,000 for the whole job.

That was the good news about 1958. The bad news was I had to have back surgery. You know, the peculiar thing about golf is that most golfers who have back problems find it begins bothering them when they're putting more than any other time. In April of '58, I was on the practice green at Augusta, and when I straightened up it hurt quite a bit, though it didn't bother me in the tournament other than when I was putting. After the Masters, my back kept on hurting and getting worse. The pain was going down my right leg; it was so painful to walk on that I could hardly stand it. I finally went to Dr. Brandon Carrell, a golfer and a wonderful orthopedic surgeon. He took X-rays and told me I had a disc problem in my lumbar vertebrae, numbers three, four, and five. Next, he made an appointment for me to see Dr. Albert Durrico, a fine neurosurgeon. Dr. Durrico tested my right leg and found I had lost about 50% of the feeling in it; I couldn't raise my toes on my right foot at all. So in August, they both operated on me at Baylor Medical Center in Dallas. It was then they discovered I'd hurt my back falling off that roof when I was a kid. But I got along just great, and the sixth day after surgery, I walked down the hall to the elevator and out to the car and Louise drove me home. It was good to be free of that pain, though I knew I had to be very careful and couldn't play any golf for a while.

After I'd recovered quite a bit, I called Dr. Carrell and asked him when I could play golf again. He told me I could start with a few little short shots, and work my way up gradually to the longer clubs. A few weeks later, he asked me to meet him at Brookhollow and watched me hit for a little while. Then he said, "I think you're ready to play—and I'll play with you." I'd always given him three strokes but he said, "It's been so long since you played, I'll play you even." Well, I shot 73 and beat him and he said, "Byron, if I ever get you on the operating table again, you'll never beat me any more!"

There was some more bad news that year, but it turned out all right in the end. In '55, when we'd won the Crosby, Eddie Lowery had bought us in the Calcutta pool. He won quite a nice amount of money, which he didn't keep for himself but gave away to his family and friends. Eddie was always a very generous man, and quite often when I went to a tournament he'd pay my expenses and those of others he'd invited, too. He was also quite generous to his brother and sister. The only problem with the money he'd won in that Crosby Calcutta was that he didn't report it to the government.

As it happened, about that time Eddie had a salesman who also played golf. This fellow got to where all he wanted to do was play golf and not work. Eddie called him on the carpet a few times, but finally had to let him go. Then the man got mad and told the IRS that Eddie had made all this money at the Crosby and hadn't reported it. The government picked up on it and in 1958 Eddie was called in on a special

IRS investigation and charged with fraud. Naturally, since my name had been connected with his for many years and I had played with him in the Crosby, they subpoenaed me for the trial. But the day before the trial began, Eddie's attorneys took me to dinner. They never mentioned what they wanted me to say or anything like that, but said, "We see no reason why we can't use you for a witness, too." I said, "Fine." They said, "You need to start thinking about all you want to say, because you'll be asked a lot of questions." When the trial began the next day, the defense was the first to call witnesses, and they called me as a witness first thing, which made the prosecution come right up off their chairs. Then they all had a confab with the judge, who decided I could be used as a general witness, rather than just for either the prosecution or the defense. They questioned me most of that day and the next. It was difficult, but luckily I could recall a lot of what Eddie had done for me and all the particulars, and my testimony helped to clear him. He had to pay the tax on that money plus a penalty, but he was cleared of fraud.

You'd think that would have been the end of it, but the next year I got called in on a special investigation because of my testimony, and the IRS went back five years into all my financial affairs. Fortunately, I was able to identify every deposit in my checking account and every check, and the agent said he'd never seen that done before. But even though they never found anything of any importance, every year they did a special audit on me, until finally my wonderful CPA, Jon Bradley, told them they were harassing me and threatened to take them to court. Things have been fine ever since.

I owe a lot of my financial success in life to golf. Not just because of the money I won—in fact, that was the least part of it—but because of all the wonderful people I met who have helped me in so many ways. Really, it's one of the best things about the game, that you can meet so many excellent people. As I said earlier, I've been a blessed man all my life, and one of the greatest blessings I have is my friends. And it just has always kept getting better and better.

NINE

Television and My Own Tournament

AS YOU CAN SEE, THOUGH I'D RETIRED FROM TOURNAMENT golf, I was just about as busy as I ever wanted to be, what with one thing and another. I was still doing exhibitions and a little radio, raising cattle, farming hay, working those eggs, writing for the *Dallas Times Herald* with my friend Jim Chambers, and occasionally helping to build a golf course somewhere. Then too, I was still working for MacGregor; that continued until 1962, when I switched to Northwestern and stayed with them for sixteen years. So I wasn't exactly finding time hanging on my hands.

I'd even done a little film work. Besides the instructional films I did in Wichita Falls that never got off the ground, I'd had a very small cameo part in a Dean Martin-Jerry Lewis movie back in the fifties. When I say "small," I mean a long-distance shot of me off hitting a ball somewhere, and I never heard anything about it after I did it, though they did put my name in the credits. Ben Hogan was in it, too, but he had a larger part than me, because his name was more prominent at the time.

By then, television was already showing sports such as football, baseball, and basketball. They had even begun doing the golf majors then—the U.S. Open, the PGA, and the Masters. I'd never thought about being part of all that. But in 1957, all of a sudden I was.

As I found out later, Cliff Roberts was having a discussion early that year with Frank Chirkinian, who produces CBS golf and has always produced the Masters telecast. They got to talking about the color commentator Cliff and Bob Jones wanted to use for the Masters. Frank had used various ones, both on radio and then on the first telecast in '56, but Cliff wasn't satisfied with any of them. Cliff and Bob wanted to keep the Masters from sounding as commercial as some of the other tournaments, so there were some restrictions an announcer needed to abide by. For instance, they didn't ever want you to mention the size of the gallery, the prize money, or how much money any of the players had won. You had to keep all that sort of thing toned down. So Frank asked Cliff, "Well, who do you want to use?" And Cliff finally said, "I know Nelson pretty well. He won't go off half-cocked and he'll do what you tell him to do. Why don't you ask him?" Frank called right away and asked me and I said yes, though I was quite nervous about it. Live broadcast announcing wasn't anything like the film work I'd done, nor was it really very much like radio. I knew they had used Vic Ghezzi, Gene Sarazen, and some others before, but I was out on the course playing and had never heard or watched them, so I didn't have an opinion of how they did or the opportunity to learn from them what I would be expected to do. It wasn't going to be easy, and I didn't want to let Cliff or CBS down. But one thing did make me feel better, and that was when they told me I would be working with Chris Schenkel. Chris was already quite well-known for his wonderful ability on television and as a speaker and master of ceremonies at dinners and so forth. Really, he was much more of a celebrity than I ever thought of being, and he still is today. I felt Chris would be good to work with and would help me a lot.

What I didn't realize was that Chris would help me get started on a whole new career. Even better, this became the start of my long friendship with Chris. It was another fortunate thing in my life that came about simply because I'd played good golf some years before and had gained a reputation for knowing something about the game. But when I first talked to Chris about it, I told him, "I'm afraid I won't know what to say." He encouraged me. "All you have to do is tell what's going on in the picture on the television screen in front of you, and you know golf well enough to be able to explain what the player is doing or has to do. You just do the golf, and I'll do the announcing." He helped me tremendously, and instead of being so nervous, I found I really did like doing the Masters because of being at Augusta and working with Chris.

That first year, 1957, we were in the tower back of the 16th green. I don't really recall any outstandingly good or bad shots on that hole, but I remember Doug Ford won when he holed out of the bunker on the 18th. The hardest thing to learn was not to talk about the play on 16 right in front of me, but rather to discuss the play being shown on television. Another difficult thing was to be talking on the air with the earpiece in my ear and Frank talking to me at the same time. Frank would say, "In two minutes we'll go to the twelfth and it'll be so-and-so on the screen." It was hard to remember at first and very disconcerting, but I got used to it reasonably easily.

Since I was just starting in television, I was very fortunate to have Frank Chirkinian as executive producer. When I first met Frank, he struck me as a man who was never at a loss for words, but also had good intuition about when to "move"—from one camera shot to another—to pick up a certain player. He could move from one player to another more quickly and smoothly than anyone I ever worked with. Most people have never seen him, but Frank is short, with dark skin, brown eyes, and very curly hair. He speaks very fast and is very pleasant to work with if you do your job, though if you don't, you're liable to catch a few choice words. But because he moved and spoke so fast, you really had to keep alert. If you weren't tuned in every minute to what was going on in your ear and on the screen, you could easily get caught flat-footed. It took a lot of energy.

We always prepared for the actual show on the weekend by doing a rehearsal during the practice rounds, which in a way was more complicated than the actual telecast. The public didn't hear or see this because it wasn't on the air, but Frank took it just as seriously as if it was. He'd say, "All right, you guys, we're going to do this short and sweet, but we're going to do it like we're on the air, only very fast. So be on your toes, because I don't want to have to tell you twice." He'd get uptight sometimes—you could hear his voice get a little more high-pitched, but you couldn't tell it unless you knew him real well.

The thing that helped me so much, even more than Frank's expertise, was that when the show would be thrown to us, Chris would lead me in at the right time and make it very simple. Also, if I were talking and he needed to say something, he'd just tap my leg to signal me that he needed to take over. I really feel that if I had not been assigned with Chris and later worked with him so long at ABC, I never would have been on television the length of time I was. He really did train me and helped me tremendously.

Apparently Cliff Roberts and Bob Jones weren't unhappy with my performance, because they asked me to come back the next year. This time, though, Chris and I were at the 18th hole, the command center for the tournament, which was considerably different from being at the 16th. After that we did the Masters together for several more years. In between, I also did a little freelance work for NBC and ABC, and in 1963, I signed my first full-year contract with ABC. Chris stayed with CBS till 1964 when he came to ABC. I was very happy about that, because I'd enjoyed working with him so much. Chris told me recently that I was the first professional golfer to do television commentary on a regular basis, so I guess I pioneered in that area, too.

When I first started, Arnold Palmer was on his way up; by the early sixties, he was in his heyday. I felt just like the gallery did. He was one of the most exciting golfers I ever saw. He really was a charger—he hit quite a few bad shots, but he had a knack of recovering with some wonderful shot to make up for his mistakes. Chris and I would always go watch him whenever we could. It was always fun to watch Arnold play.

I was still getting my feet wet in television work, just doing the Masters with Chris, when another film opportunity came along called "Shell's Wonderful World of Golf." Fred Raphael, who helped start the first seniors tournament in Austin—now called the Legends—was the producer for the Shell series, and he called me in the summer of 1961. He explained what the series was all about, that the matches were to be played with various players on courses around the world, and that he'd like me to play the first one with Gene Littler, the U.S. Open champion that year. The match would be at Pine Valley in New Jersey, and the winner would get $3000, the loser $1500. It sounded like fun, so I agreed to play.

Since this was the first match, the film crew was still learning what was involved, so it was very slow. They had a station wagon with a camera on top of it and some other small vehicles with cameras on them so they could get around where the wagon couldn't go. Gene Sarazen was the commentator for our match; he alternated on the series with Jimmy Demaret.

I played rather well, but Gene had a lot of trouble at the fifth hole, which is one of the most difficult par threes I know. You play uphill across a ravine, and a gravel road runs across the fairway quite a little ways short of the green. It was a driver for me from the back tee, about 227 yards, but I put it nicely on the green. Gene missed his tee shot badly and his ball went into these short, thick, stubby oak trees at the bottom of a hill to the right of the green. After he'd hit three times, I still couldn't see him. Finally I hollered, "Are you still down there, Gene?" He said, "Yes, but I'm not making much progress." Finally, he put his next shot on the bank at the side of the green and made 7. I had a pretty nice putt for a birdie but missed it and made 3, so I gained four strokes on Gene there. He shot 42 on the front and I shot 37.

They talk a lot about slow play today and it is a problem, but this match was ridiculous. We started as soon as it was light enough, but it took all day—ten solid hours—to film ten holes, and most of the next day to do the other eight. Slowest round of golf I ever heard of in my life. It bothered me some even though I played all right.

When we were finished for the day, Gene and I went in to shower and change clothes. I'd known Gene a while and after we'd already started to undress he said, "Man, I played badly today, Byron. What in the world was I doing?" He had respect for my knowledge of the golf swing, and I told him that when he played well, he set the club perfectly at the top of his swing. But that day, because of the slowness of the filming, he rushed his swing and wasn't getting set at the top. He asked me, "Do you mind if we go hit some balls?" I said, "Sure." So we got dressed again and went out to the practice tee, and the next day when we played the final eight holes, he put the charge on me and ended up with 34 on the back nine. I played the back nine well, but he made quite a few putts and came within two strokes. On the last hole, a tough par four, they had to stop filming for one thing or another three different times. Then the whole thing had taken so long that they ran out of film. When they finally got the film changed, it was time to hit my second shot, but I hit it real thin, put the ball in a deep bunker in front of the green and made five, while Gene made four. For the full eighteen I had 74 and Gene 76, which wasn't too bad considering it was the longest round of golf either one of us had ever played.

The way the series worked, whenever you won a match you'd play another one. So the next year, I had the pleasure of going to Holland and playing Jerry DeWitt, Holland's champion and a fine player. Unfortunately I had the flu and felt terrible, which isn't an excuse for the way I played, but Jerry did beat me that day. Before the match Sarazen, Demaret, Raphael and I had a wonderful luncheon with the president of Dutch Shell in his private suite. Gordon Biggers, the man from Shell who was responsible for arranging and producing all the shows, was also at that luncheon, and I got very well acquainted with him. After Shell stopped doing the series, I asked Gordon why and he said, "It was very well-liked, but Shell didn't sell any more gasoline because of the show, so we had to drop it." I've had many people tell me about seeing that match because so many golfers like Pine Valley, and they really did enjoy all the shows. Besides being about golf, they were kind of travelogues, showing the sights to see in the area around the golf courses where the matches were played—and of course, they always promoted Shell's products.

In 1963, the year after my match with Littler was shown on television—which incidentally was on my fiftieth birthday—I signed my first contract with ABC. As anyone who's ever heard me talk knows, I have a fairly strong Texas accent, and when I first started doing television, I not only had the accent but a lot of Texas expressions and pronunciations to go with it. Roone Arledge, our producer, right away started telling me I needed to change the way I spoke and quite a few of my expressions. But Chris told me, "Don't pay any attention, Pro. People who know you know the way you speak, and you speak very plainly. It wouldn't be you if you tried to speak like an Easterner." So I pretty much ignored Roone and only changed the way I pronounced one word, bermuda, which Texans used to pronounce "bermooda." No one seemed to mind that I didn't change much, and even Roone kind of got used to me after a while.

That first year with ABC, 1963, the PGA Championship was played at Dallas Athletic Club. I was working with Jim McKay and doing the color commentary. Jack Nicklaus won; it was his first PGA championship, and I remember the 18th hole well. Jack drove in the rough to the left and had to make a 4 to win. There was water in front of the green and he had a bad lie, so he played a smart shot and laid up in front of the water, knocked his third stiff and made 4. Besides it being Jack's first PGA, the other unusual thing about the tournament is that it was and still is the hottest week on record in Texas. The temperature hit 113 degrees and even the air conditioning in the clubhouse went out. There were people fainting everywhere; some almost had heatstroke, and it was very serious. I know the heat hurt attendance to some degree.

The next year, 1964, a couple of great things happened. The first was that Chris Schenkel came to ABC and I got to work with him again. Chris and I had a lot of wonderful times working together, and one of the funniest happened when we were doing the World Series of Golf at Firestone Country Club in Akron, Ohio. I was still pretty new to television, and one of the problems I had in those early days was keeping my voice low enough so the players on the green in front of us wouldn't be bothered as they tried to putt. Both of our voices carry quite well, but Chris had more experience at lowering his voice almost to a whisper, while I never really did learn to do it like he could. Quite often, the players or their caddies would be looking up at us on the tower and waving for us to hush.

But sometimes they listened real well. This particular year, Billy Casper was getting ready to putt for a birdie on eighteen, with his ball twelve feet back of the pin. I was describing the putt and spoke into the mike as quietly as I could, "No one has played quite enough break on this putt. Everyone has missed it on the low side." Billy was standing over his putt, but suddenly backed away, looked at it again, then walked up and knocked it in. I saw him later in the clubhouse and he said, "Thanks, Byron." I said, "What for, Billy?" He said, "I heard you talking about my putt on eighteen and I'm glad I did, because I didn't see that much break. I would have missed it otherwise." Shortly after that I suggested they put a plexiglass screen in front of Chris and me, so we could talk in a more normal tone of voice without the players being able to hear us.

Besides getting to work with Chris again, the second great thing that happened to me in '64 was Ken Venturi winning the U.S. Open after a terrible struggle. In the early part of the year, I'd had a few conversations with Ken about his golf game. He was playing very well then and I'd encouraged him and told him he was doing great. I didn't work with him at all, just talked with him on the phone. That June, the Open was at Congressional Country Club in Washington, D.C. Kenny did well the first two rounds despite the heat and humidity, which were very bad. But the real test came when they had to play the last thirty-six holes on Saturday. Kenny wasn't used to that kind of weather, living in San Francisco and having already had some recent health problems that had seriously affected his golf game for a while. Chris and I thought even during the third round that Ken wasn't going to make it. It looked like he was out on his feet just walking down the fairways. After he played the morning round, a doctor took care of him all during his break for lunch and followed him quite closely the rest of the day.

When he went back out in the afternoon, Kenny just played absolutely automatic, thinking more about just finishing than what he was doing as far as playing was concerned. Fortunately, he was playing with Ray Floyd, an excellent man to be paired with and a super nice person. I can still see how Ken looked on that television monitor. I couldn't believe he was still on his feet. When he made his putt on the last hole, I don't think he could have gone another step. Ray Floyd was so moved by Kenny's performance that there were tears in his eyes when he picked Kenny's ball out of the hole. I'd have to say that those 36 holes were the two most unusual rounds of golf I ever saw. What's more, they proved what a great player Kenny really was.

It wasn't very long after the Open, though, that Ken began to have trouble with his hands. A golfer's hands are pretty important, and Kenny's hands got so bad that he finally had to have them both operated on in June of 1965. I was concerned about what this might mean to Kenny's career in golf, and my concern became considerably stronger when Kenny was selected to be on our Ryder Cup team. The rest of the team included Julius Boros, Billy Casper, Tommy Jacobs, Don January, Tony Lema, Gene Littler, Dave Marr, Arnold Palmer, and Johnny Pott.

It was a good team, I felt, and I had just begun to wonder who the captain would be when I got a call from Warren Cantrell, president of the PGA, who happened to be from Amarillo, Texas. Warren said,

"Byron, I talked to the players on the team and asked if they would like you as captain, and they said 'Absolutely!'" There wasn't one dissenting vote, which made me feel very happy and very honored. Warren's call took me right back to the days of the 1935 Ryder Cup at Ridgewood when I was assistant pro. While I knew then that I wanted to be on the team one day, I never dreamed about being captain. This wasn't even on my list of goals when I was on the tour.

It was certainly one of the greatest honors in my career, but I wanted it to be more than an honor—I wanted it to be a victory. The Americans had held sway for quite a while, but I knew the British players were getting stronger and were looking forward to the chance to trim our sails. In those days, the captain had nothing to say about the selection of the team—it was all done on the basis of points earned by winning or playing well in various events over the two-year period between the matches. When my captaincy was announced, it was only three months before the matches, so I didn't really have much time to work with the team.

Because of the lack of time, right away I began thinking about what I could do to help the team before we went over to England. Our opponents were still using the smaller British ball and we would have to use it too, so I got some for the team to practice with when we all met in New York before flying to England. I made arrangements with the good folks at Winged Foot, and as soon as the team arrived, we went out there to practice. They were amazed at how differently that British ball behaved. Because it was smaller, you didn't get as much ball on the face of the club, so it didn't have as much backspin and it wouldn't fly as high as the American ball. Also, the heavier, wetter air they would encounter in England would affect the ball even more. I'd always felt that was why the British played more pitch-and-run shots than we did, because the small ball lent itself to that type of shot more.

I already had Venturi's hands on my mind, and then during the practice round that afternoon, Johnny Pott got a stitch in his right side that was hurting quite a little bit. But we had a doctor examine him who decided it was only a pulled muscle and shouldn't be a problem. That relieved me considerably, because Venturi had only recently gotten back to playing and was just now at the point where he could play without gloves, so he was somewhat of an unknown quantity.

There were several parties for us before we left, and the biggest one was on the last night, when the PGA gave a wonderful one at the Waldorf-Astoria. There we were, dressed in our dark blue suits, white shirts, and striped ties, all matching, and each of us had a complete Ryder Cup wardrobe right down to our golf bags, shoes, and windbreakers, just like when I'd been on the team in '37 and '47. Bob Hope was there, I think Bing Crosby was too, plus the Governor of New York, the Mayor, and many golf dignitaries from all across the country. Everyone wanted to give us a big sendoff and encourage us to play well, which we all appreciated.

We had a good flight over on BOAC and landed in London, then boarded a smaller plane which took us to Southport, near the Royal Birkdale course. When we'd recovered from the trip and began practicing, it soon became apparent that Johnny Pott's side wasn't any better. As it turned out, he never so much as hit a ball. That cut me to nine players, and I knew Venturi's hands wouldn't allow him to play every match, so I had to figure very carefully how I would use him and the rest of my team. What's more, Tony Lema had not come over with us because he'd been competing in the Canada Cup matches in Madrid, where he'd played poorly because of a sore elbow. That didn't reassure me any, but during the practice rounds, Tony came to me and said, "Byron, I'm driving the ball badly—I need help." He had a lot of confidence in me because he'd watched me play a lot at the California Golf Club when he was the assistant caddiemaster there in the fifties, and we'd played some together, too. I went out on the course to watch him, and I saw right away he wasn't setting the club right at the top of his backswing. We had a little discussion about it, I told him what he was doing, and he began playing better immediately.

Despite our situation with Pott and Venturi, when there was a press conference that afternoon, I was not about to let the British know my concerns. The British captain, Harry Weetman, had his say first. By now, we had become the underdogs in the British press, so Harry announced that the British definitely had the stronger team and would win the match. Then it was my turn. I got up, looked at him and said, "Harry, we didn't come three thousand miles to lose."

It's very awe-inspiring to represent your country in the Ryder Cup, and I'll never forget the feeling of pride and excitement as I raised our country's flag at the start of the matches. The Prime Minister, Harold Wilson, was there and welcomed us, Harry Weetman and Warren Cantrell made some remarks, and the match was on.

Most of the matches were very exciting and quite close, except for Davey Marr and Arnold Palmer's showing in the morning foursomes on the first day. It was Dave's first time to play in the Ryder Cup and he was very nervous. I watched him and he hardly got the ball off the ground the first seven holes. Obviously, even Arnold couldn't overcome that and they lost to Dave Thomas and George Will, 6 and 5. However, I'd noticed that Dave finally settled down and was playing real well at the end, so I got an idea. Since this was the second match that morning, I figured Harry would move Thomas and Will to the first match that afternoon, so I did the same thing with Dave and Arnold. When I announced at lunch that Palmer and Marr would be playing Thomas and Will again, Arnold and Dave didn't even finish their food, they jumped up from the table and charged off to the practice tee. My guess was right, because in the afternoon they shot 30 on the front nine—a remarkable score at Royal Birkdale, where par is 73—and they turned the tables completely, winning 6 and 5. We were all pretty happy about that, and I think it was the most exciting match of the whole tournament.

Though Tony was playing well and Arnold and Davey had come back, at the end of the first day we were tied at 4 points apiece. Kenny had not played well in his first two matches, so I had him rest during the morning of the second day. That was when we played the alternate shot format properly known as four-ball. In the morning we won two matches, lost one, and halved one, so we were needing to do better in the afternoon. For the last match of the afternoon I decided to pair Ken with Tony because they were good friends; they were both from San Francisco, and I knew they enjoyed playing together. They went up against Hunt and Coles and came to the last hole, a par five, deadlocked. It was Kenny's turn and he hit a good drive, then Tony pulled the second shot and the ball ended up left and short of the green, back of a small shallow bunker. I was standing back of the green and knew we needed a point badly. The British players left their second shot short but on the right side, with only a simple chip to the green. Prime Minister Wilson was standing next to me and he said, "I say, sir, it appears as though we have the advantage." I answered,

"Yes, Mr. Prime Minister, it appears that way, but of all the people on my team, I'd rather have Venturi playing this shot than anyone else." Then Kenny gripped down on the club, used a little short firm motion, and chipped close to the hole. The British chipped short and missed their putt and we won, 1 up. At the end of the second day we had taken the lead, 9 to 7, and went on to win decisively.

When the matches were over, I was talking to some of the British golf officials. They were wondering why it was that the Americans seemed to play better golf and a different type of golf. I told them it was in great part due to the different ball we used, and after I explained my ideas, quite a few of them agreed. A year or so later, they changed their ball to the same specifications as ours, which was a good thing for the game altogether.

It was a very emotional moment when the matches were over. The bugle corps played "Taps" as Harry Weetman and I lowered our country's flags, and everyone had tears in their eyes. We had a beautiful flight home and we were a very happy group, believe me. The PGA officials had a celebration party for us when we arrived, and it was an occasion I will always remember, for a very good reason.

All through the matches, I had wanted so much to do a good job and help our team win that I moved around more those three days than for any other tournament in my life. I tried hard to see at least part of every match and was very visible at all times. The team must have appreciated that, because unbeknownst to me they got together and had a duplicate made of the actual Ryder Cup trophy and presented it to me when we arrived back in New York. It's a beautiful piece, and of all the trophies I've won, that is one of my most prized possessions.

One final note about our team. Except for Tony Lema, who was killed in that tragic plane crash in July 1966 after winning the Oklahoma City Open, and Julius Boros, who is now in his seventies and has had some health problems the last several years, all of those fellows are still active in golf, either on the senior tour, in television, or at good club jobs. I feel that's a good recommendation for golf.

In 1967, two years after the Ryder Cup, I got to participate in something that was a lot of work, a lot of fun, and made many new friends for me I never expected to have. It was called the Lincoln-Mercury Sports Panel, and it was the brainchild of Gar Laux, the head of Lincoln-Mercury. Gar was very sportsminded. He knew a lot of people in various sports, and got the idea that a good promotion for Lincoln-Mercury would be to form a panel of top people in various sports and use them to generate publicity and goodwill. The head of his promotion department was Bernie Brown, and Bernie took the ball and ran with it. He started out with Arnold Palmer, the great professional bowler Billy Welu, Detroit Tigers outfielder Al Kaline, tennis great Tony Trabert, Jesse Owens, the great track star and the first ever to win four gold medals in the Olympics, hockey star Gordie Howe, Chris Schenkel, and me. What a great lineup.

Part of our job was to go to the big auto shows, sit on the stage at the Lincoln-Mercury display, and answer questions from people, then hand out our pictures. We would be on for thirty minutes and then take a break to sign pictures backstage, and we did that four hours each day of the weekend. Another thing we did was to help entertain Ford's top dealers from all over the country. We'd go to Las Vegas, Los Angeles, or sometimes Hawaii, and I'd play golf with the folks while Tony gave tennis lessons and clinics. They used Tony and me mainly, but some of the others would come along and socialize with the dealers at the parties they had in the evenings.

One time we were in Hawaii at Mauna Kea, and Ford had three different groups of a hundred dealers come in for three days apiece. It was nine days' work total, and though much of it was enjoyable it was also very tiring. But it had its moments. One time, Tony had just finished doing a clinic with some of the tennis players and I was watching him. He saw me and asked, "Byron, you ever play tennis?" I said, "Tony, I never have. Haven't even hit more than a half-dozen tennis balls in my life." He replied, "Well, you've got pretty good coordination—let me hit some easy ones to you and you hit them back, just for fun." I had on my rubber-soled teaching shoes so I thought I'd try it. I got a few back to him but missed some entirely, and he said, "Byron, you have to keep your eye on the ball in tennis the same as in golf!" I got a little better then, and out of curiosity I said, "Tony, serve three balls to me just like you would if you were playing in a championship." He wound up and let go, and I never saw any of those three serves, much less had a chance to hit them back. It made me very glad I'd played golf instead of tennis.

But the next day we both went out on the course. Tony was a good golfer and liked to play, but I was familiar with the course we were playing, and he'd never seen it before. On the first hole, he was on in two and had about a 25-foot putt. I could tell from the way he was lining up he wasn't playing very much break, because you couldn't see it, just looking at it. I said, "Tony, that putt breaks six feet to the right." He backed off and looked at it, then shook his head and said, "Well, Byron, I know tennis and you know golf, so I'll believe you." He played it where I told him and made his birdie, so he did a lot better at golf than I did at tennis.

I had a little better luck at bowling. Once we were doing a show with Billy Welu, and I watched Billy give a clinic. Suddenly Billy said to me, "Byron, have you ever bowled any?" I told him, "There used to be a bowling alley in the basement of the Texarkana Country Club, Billy, and I guess I bowled about a half-dozen games." So he said, "Come on out here!" I stepped up, threw one ball and made a strike. Then I said, "Thank you very much, Billy, that's enough for me!" People today don't know much about Billy Welu. He bowled twenty-seven 300 games, which was absolutely amazing, especially considering how young he died.

To get back to my television career, Chris and I did around fifteen tournaments a year, and I usually got there well ahead of time. The only way I felt I could do a good job as a commentator was to go out on the course and study it, so I would know each hole and where the trouble was. I actually walked the course as if I were playing it myself, paying special attention to the holes we were showing on the telecast. I would then determine in my own mind what it would take to win each tournament. I didn't always make this mental prediction for regular tournaments, but I always did it for the majors, and one time, I got in trouble for it.

It was just before the 1967 U.S. Open at Baltusrol. Jim McKay and I were taping a preview of the tournament to be shown two weeks before the Open started. It included a history of the tournament and the course, and was done to increase interest for the audience we hoped to have. I had gone out on the golf course, scorecard in hand, and spent two hours walking hole after hole, figuring what I thought a good player would shoot on that course. When we started the filming, McKay did the introduction and talked about the course some, then turned to me and said, "Byron, how does the course look to you?" I told him, "The course is in great shape. They've had a drought in the area so the rough is not very bad and the greens are perfect. The whole course is in excellent condition." Then Jim asked me, "What do you think they're going to shoot?" And I replied, "I've walked the entire course and totalled up all four rounds the way I think a good player should play this course, and I think they'll shoot 275." We were right there on the porch of the Baltusrol clubhouse, with several members of the club and some USGA people nearby. Well, as soon as we were done, the club president and tournament chairman approached me and used a lot of strong words and said, "Don't you know this is Baltusrol? No one's ever burned the course up like you just said they would!" and I said, "Yes, I played Baltusrol when I was an assistant pro in Ridgewood, New Jersey. I know the course pretty well." They were very upset about it, because Baltusrol has the reputation of being a tough course generally; when the Open was held there in 1954, Ed Furgol won with 284. Well, I didn't say anything else about it, but Jack Nicklaus saved my skin when he holed a 30-footer for birdie on the 72nd hole and won with 275. Those same two gentlemen who had jumped all over me later wrote me a very nice letter apologizing for coming on so strong about what I'd said, which I did appreciate.

One interesting match I played took place twenty-two years after I retired, on Monday, August 12, 1968. Harold McSpaden and I played Palmer and Nicklaus in Kansas City at McSpaden's course, Dub's Dread, which was rated then as one of the toughest courses in the world. It was an exhibition, and it was set up this way: Because McSpaden's and my ages added together totaled 116 and Palmer's and Nicklaus's totaled 66, we got a fifty-yard advantage on every hole. I told Jug they'd still outdrive us but he didn't think so, and sure enough he was right. I was driving very well and they didn't outdrive us on but one hole. The problem was their putting was so much better than ours. We were scared to death playing against them and hadn't been competing any or playing in front of a gallery in so long. Not only that, but there was so much more of a gallery than we'd expected, and the course wasn't roped off or anything, so it was too much for us and we lost, 3 and 2. But I did have one thing to brag about—the 17th hole was a long par 3, and I decided to play it even though the match was over. I took out my driver and put my ball on the green from the back tees, so that made me feel good and helped take the sting away.

Besides doing the men's tournaments on TV, Chris and I also got to do the commentary on some of the women's championships. I always enjoyed watching the ladies play because as a group they had better basic fundamental swings than the men did. One tournament I remember particularly well was the USGA Women's Open in 1967 on the Cascades course at Hot Springs, Virginia. It was won by a French amateur, Catherine Lacoste, and it was the only time I ever saw the ladies upset about a tournament. They weren't upset with Catherine at all, but the fact that she was an amateur and not an American, they felt, would set women's professional golf in this country way back. Some of them talked to me about it, but I told them they shouldn't worry about it because they had played very well. Maybe I should have reminded them of how close Kenny Venturi had come to winning the Masters when he was an amateur just a few years earlier. That hadn't upset the men pros—in fact, it generated more interest than ever in professional golf and golf at all levels.

In 1969, we covered the tournament when Donna Caponi won the Women's Open at Scenic Hills Country Club in Pensacola, then again when she repeated the next year at Muskogee Country Club in Muskogee, Oklahoma. Everyone liked Donna because she was so friendly and wonderful with the gallery. A funny thing happened in Pensacola, something that very much impressed me about Chris Schenkel. In those days we sat out in the open, at the top of a metal scaffolding tower sometimes two or three stories tall. Most of the time, all we had over our heads to keep off the sun and rain was a canvas tarpaulin. Well, that year, 1969, a terrible rainstorm came up. There was no lightning so the ladies were still playing. Chris and I were very busy. I was keeping score, figuring out if the player on the screen was four over, eight over, or whatever, and Chris was doing all his work, so we had all these sheets of paper spread out on the table in front of us. What we didn't realize was that all this rain was collecting on the tarp over our heads, and it was getting fuller and fuller and sinking lower and lower.

All of a sudden it gave way completely, and a couple of barrels of water poured all over us. It ran off our faces and soaked all our clothes. Worse yet, the papers on the table in front of us with all our scores and so forth were deluged. But Chris never missed a lick, and after a couple of minutes I got back on track too, so we went ahead like nothing had happened.

We didn't know it then, of course, but Bob Jones himself had seen the telecast. When we went to the Masters the next spring, Bob said to us, "I never laughed so much in my life, seeing you sitting there with water all over your faces and everything, but you just kept on talking like nothing had happened. I felt sorry for you but I couldn't help laughing." By then we thought it was pretty funny too, though it sure wasn't at the time.

That same year, 1970, I was working with Jim McKay at Pensacola on the men's tournament when there suddenly came up another rainstorm, with terrible lightning like we'd never seen before. Believe it or not, there were no provisions made for us to get down from the tower, which was all metal, and Jim got so terribly upset he told me, "I'm getting off this tower, I'm going straight to the clubhouse!" He took off right then, and during the next commercial break the rest of us did, too. We ended up doing the remainder of the telecast in the clubhouse. We could look out the window at that tower, and the wires on it were just frying. It was the worst experience of bad weather we had during my nearly twenty years in television.

It was interesting how the tournament officials sometimes handled these sorts of things, too. During the U.S. Open at Medinah in 1975 when Lou Graham won, Ben Crenshaw was finishing up his third round and was walking to the 17th hole. But just as he got to the green, lightning flashed nearby, and it scared him so he just flat ran off the course. We were doing the telecast, which is why I remember this so well. After he left the course, we learned that a couple of USGA officials were saying Ben would have to be disqualified. But as they started out the door to talk to him, several bolts of lightning hit next to the clubhouse and they scurried right back inside. That convinced them to call a delay, so Ben didn't get disqualified, fortunately. Thank goodness the lightning detection systems they have now are so much better, and improving all the time. It's a great game, but it's just not worth risking your life for a round of golf.

In addition to whatever the weather brought our way, those early days of televised golf meant a lot of equipment problems, especially when the weather was wet. Our cables were just lying on the ground then, and rainwater would get in the cable connections and short them out. We'd be talking but there'd be no picture, or there'd be picture but no sound. It was frustrating, but now you have practically none of that because the equipment is so much better.

In 1966, we were doing the British Open live via satellite for the first time. This was quite an advance in television broadcasting, because prior to this, we would film the day's play, fly the film back to the U.S., and show it a day late. With the satellite, we still filmed the day's play, then added our live commentary and so forth later when the American audience would be watching. Naturally, the difference in time zones, six hours at least, meant we were doing the live portion at some pretty odd times. McKay and I would be out there at the course in the middle of the night, up in the tower and very cold, talking to a camera but with no one else there besides us, the crew, one sentry, and a guard dog. Jack Nicklaus won the tournament, and because he played rather slowly, they had to cut and edit it very tightly before we went on the air. The result was we showed Jack driving and then immediately playing his 3-iron to a par 5. There wasn't time to show him walking or anything but playing his shots, which was rather unusual.

One thing I felt was very important in order to do televised golf well was having a producer and director who knew how to play the game. Once in a while we would have someone who didn't, and boy, could you tell it. He'd use the wrong terminology, saying "chip" for a long pitch, or calling a 150-yard shot "long," and he usually didn't know the players' names very well. Fortunately, this didn't happen very often and never for the majors, but when it did, it sure made things interesting.

In 1971, the year after we got dumped on at Pensacola, we were to broadcast the Women's Open at Kahkwa Country Club in Erie, Pennsylvania, where a very strange thing happened. When I got there, I went to the pro shop as I always did at these tournaments. I introduced myself to the pro and was telling him how glad I was to be there and so forth when he said to me, "Byron, I'm glad to see you again." I didn't recognize him so I said, "When did you see me?" He said, "You played an exhibition here several years ago." I looked at him and said, "I sure don't remember it." He went into his office a minute and came out with a scorecard in his hand. My signature was on it, and apparently I had not only played there, but had set what was then a course record of 66. It was the oddest thing, because usually my memory is pretty good, but I didn't remember a single thing about having played there. Even when I went on out to study the course before the tournament started, none of it looked familiar to me at all. In fact, I didn't remember ever having been in Erie before except with Louise on our first anniversary in 1934, when we stopped briefly beside the road there and waded out into Lake Erie. I still have the photo of that—but as for playing that golf course then or any other time, my mind is a complete blank. Very strange. So many people are amazed at my memory, and I like to think it's pretty good most of the time, but when something like that happens it really makes you wonder about yourself.

As for that ladies' tournament at Kahkwa, you know, we men sometimes think the ladies don't hit the ball very far. But I remember one hole on the back nine, about the 15th or 16th, where a little road went across the fairway 235 yards from the tee the ladies were playing. Joanne Gunderson Carner hit the ball a long ways, and she carried over that road twice during the tournament. Kathy Whitworth, the winningest golfer on any tour, was second to Joanne that year. On the other hand, while some people didn't think women could hit the ball very far, others thought the women's touch and feel on the greens would be better than the men's, which led to some big-money putting contests between the two sexes. I remember Sam Snead was involved in a few of them. Invariably the men won, but they'd been competing on their tour and against larger fields much longer than the ladies. Since then, the women have really improved, especially in their ability to read the greens.

When we televised women's tournaments, I also walked the course so I would know what I was talking about, but I didn't ever try to predict scores, at least not in public. I'd have in my mind an idea of what I felt the winning score would be, but I wasn't real close most of the time. What fooled me was that the women's short game was not as good as it is now, nor as good as you'd expect it to be. Their long game was excellent and they got in very little trouble except around the greens, but of course that part of their game is also much improved today.

While Chris and I enjoyed doing the women's championships, I'd have to say that of all the broadcasting I did, the most exciting golf I saw was in 1971 when Lee Trevino won the Open at Merion, won the Canadian Open in Montreal the very next week, then flew to England and won the British Open at Royal Birkdale. He won three majors in nineteen days and Chris and I got to see all of it. That really was an amazing accomplishment.

I guess the most exciting single shot I saw during my broadcasting years happened the next year. It was Jack Nicklaus's 1-iron on the 17th at Pebble Beach in the 1972 U.S. Open. He had to hit against a strong wind, and the ball just ticked the flag and dropped right down by the edge of the hole—as close to a hole-in-one as I've ever seen in a major tournament.

Chris and I also covered some of the men's amateur championships, and one in particular I recall vividly was the next year, 1973, at Inverness. Having been pro there in the forties, I was really looking forward to working on that tournament. I was also interested to see how we would broadcast it, because the format had gone back to match play that year, which is far more difficult to televise and keep interesting. What they did was to film some of the earlier matches, such as the quarterfinals and semifinals, and show some of that as we waited for the two players in the final to get to each shot. I felt it worked very well, and Chris did a good job with it.

I really enjoyed doing the broadcast, especially because it was the first time I ever saw Craig Stadler play. He beat David Strong 6 and 5 in the final, and he behaved just the same then when he missed a shot as he does now, getting all disgusted with himself. The only thing different now is that he's a little older and a little heavier, but he still hits that nice, high fade. Fortunately, he didn't have to get very upset with himself then, because he sure wasn't missing many shots that day.

Another great memory from those years was the fifteen-pound salmon I caught during the 1970 U.S. Amateur in Portland. I brought it back to the hotel for the chef to prepare for dinner that night, then invited Chris and quite a few other friends for the feast. The chef did a marvelous job and I believe it was the greatest salmon dinner any of us ever had. Chris kidded me when I told him I'd caught our dinner myself, because he knew I wasn't much of a sailor, but it was true. In case you're wondering, a fellow named Lanny Wadkins won the tournament, and the runner-up was another promising youngster, Thomas O. Kite, Jr.

One other thing I owe to television is that it was responsible for my meeting Tom Watson. It happened in 1973 when I was doing the telecast at Doral, where they play the infamous "Blue Monster," which is what they call the Blue Course because it's so tough and has so much water. I was walking the course during the pro-am to familiarize myself with it. I was outside the ropes, so I didn't walk with people who had a lot of gallery because I wouldn't be able to see enough. Walking the back nine on about the 14th hole, I was minding my own business when a pretty brunette walked up to me and said, "Aren't you Mr. Nelson?" I said "Yes," and she said, "I'm Mrs. Tom Watson." I'd never met Tom though I'd heard a little bit about him from Bob Willits, a good amateur player from Kansas City I'd met at various tournaments. I watched Tom play from there on in, and Linda introduced him to me when he finished his round. I was very impressed by his demeanor and I liked the quick, aggressive way he played, so I began to watch for him on the tour each week. He had just finished playing well in the Hawaiian Open, and then won his first tournament, the Western Open, the following spring. In 1975 he won something called the Byron Nelson Golf Classic—his second victory—and gave the Salesmanship Club who sponsored the tournament a $1000 check, which was a kind and very generous thing to do when he was really still just becoming successful on the tour. After that, I kept even closer track of how he was doing, but I never worked with him until after he lost the Open at Winged Foot to Hale Irwin in 1975.

I was doing the telecast, and Tom was leading after the third round. He wasn't a real well-known player at the time, and the press was all over him, trying to find out more about him. I wondered how well he'd handle it, because I knew he hadn't had much experience in that situation. The next day he had a bad last nine, but not because he was choking. It was just that he'd not had that kind of pressure before and didn't quite know how to handle it. Having been in golf so many years, I knew Tom would be very discouraged, so after he left the press room I went to see him. He was in the players' locker room upstairs, sitting with John Mahaffey and having a Coke. I sat down and told him, "Tom, I'm sorry you had such a bad day. I've seen quite a few people who've been in the lead but not played good the last round until they had a few tries at it." He was still pretty down, which was natural, but he was nice and very polite to me and thanked me for what I'd said. When I left, I told him, "I'm not working with anyone right now, and if any time you'd like me to work with you, I give you permission to call me. No one else has that privilege." Well, of course he went out and won the first of his five British Opens at Carnoustie the next month, so that proved he had a winning attitude despite losing the month before.

After I'd offered to work with Tom, I became even more interested in his progress. I could see he had the makings of a great player, and that's why I especially enjoyed doing the telecast of that British Open at Carnoustie in 1975, when Tom won in a playoff against Jack Newton. Of course, Tom and I were good friends by then, and the first day, he stopped by to say hello as Chris and I were having some tea and Scottish shortbread in the press tent. It just so happened that Tom played well that first round, so he took his visit as a sign of good luck or something, and continued to stop and see us every day. The last round, however, proved what Scotland is famous for. It was a typical horrible Scottish day, windy, rainy, and cold. I knew Tom had never played there in that type of weather, so I said, "Tom, I played this same course under these same conditions in 1937. Now, even if you make three bogeys in a row, don't think anything about it, because everybody will be making bogeys. You'll be amazed at how different the course will play today." At one stretch he did make three bogeys in a row, but he remembered what I'd said, didn't let it bother him, wound up tying Newton and then beat him in the playoff. Nice man that he is, Tom then gave me a lot of credit for his victory—more than I deserved—just because of what I'd told him before that last round.

The next fall, 1976, he did come to see me and we began working together three or four times a year. We'd also have conversations at the tournaments I was working on, and when he came to the Nelson each year I'd work with him every day. Not that I would tell him what to do, but it encouraged him to know I was there and he could call on me if he needed me. It was mainly a confidence-builder for him.

The U.S. Open that year, when Jerry Pate won, was when I did my last television commentary, just a few months before Tom and I began working together. After nearly twenty years of traveling almost as much as I had on the tour, I was beginning to look for a good reason to retire. As it happened, the people at ABC had decided to change what they were doing and begin using player-commentators on the course, like Bob Rosburg, Ed Sneed, Judy Rankin, and Gary McCord today. They also wanted whoever was at the 18th to do diagrams like the football coach-commentators were doing. I tried that once, but I was very poor at it, so I told Roone Arledge and Chuck Howard that I really didn't think I'd enjoy making all those changes—I was sixty-four at the time, after all—so we ended our relationship by mutual agreement on a quite friendly note.

Every so often during my television career, someone would say to me, "Byron, don't you wish you were out here playing today, with the money so great?" It was considerably more money than what I had played for, though nothing like it is today. But I never once felt, "Boy, if I were still playing I could have some of that." I still had no desire to be in that situation again, even though the money was better and tournaments bigger. I was glad to be doing just what I was doing, glad to be in golf and participating, and especially glad not to have the pressure.

One of the things I was happiest about as far as my television work was concerned was how the players reacted to what I said. They seemed to accept it quite favorably, because I was never very critical. I called the shot and when they missed it I said so, but I didn't jump all over a player or talk negative about anyone. I knew exactly how hard it was out there, and I couldn't see any reason to talk that way about anyone, particularly someone having a difficult time playing this most difficult game.

My years in television were great, really, but I never dreamed in my wildest imagination when I started doing broadcasting that it would do for my name what it did. People even today recognize me and speak to me who never saw me play, and tell me how much they enjoyed the work I did with Chris on ABC. Many people have recognized me in a restaurant or other public place just by my voice. They say, "Aren't you Byron Nelson?" And when I say, "Yes," they say, "I recognized your voice." I'm always amazed by that. And it makes me feel good.

There is something that makes me feel lots better than having people recognize me because of my television work, though. It has to do with a group of men called the Salesmanship Club, a couple of golf courses, and children who need a lot of help. But I'll need to start at the beginning.

In 1962, I was asked to help build a golf course in North Dallas at a place the owners had decided to call Preston Trail. I worked with golf course architect Ralph Plummer, who was from Texas and had caddied at Glen Garden about ten years before me. At that time Preston Trail was so far from the heart of Dallas—seventeen miles, actually—that everyone thought we were crazy for doing it. But Pollard Simon, Jim Chambers, John Murchison, and Stuart Hunt, who owned the property, felt the natural direction for Dallas to grow was north—and time has proved them right. The course opened in 1965, but because of its distance from the city, selling memberships wasn't too easy. I had a lot of kidding from my friends about it. The first fifty members were the toughest to get, though after that people figured it was safe and began signing up. Preston Trail was designed from the beginning as a men-only course, which might have been part of the reason it was slow getting started, because the men also continued their memberships at other clubs where their wives could play.

About the time Preston Trail opened, I began doing radio commentary for the Dallas Open, a tournament that never had done real well. I had won the first one in '44, Snead in '45, and Hogan in '46, but then it was discontinued and didn't start up again till 1955 when Jim Ling of Ling-Temco-Voight (LTV) got it going. It still wasn't what you would call a real strong event on the tour, though. Even after '55 there were a couple more years when it wasn't held at all.

But things began to change in the early part of 1967. I was slated to do the Dallas Open on radio that year at Oak Cliff Country Club, and the tournament this time was sponsored by the Salesmanship Club of Dallas, an organization that sponsored a highly successful, year-round outdoor camp for troubled boys. Quite a few days before the tournament started, I was talking to several of the Salesmanship Club's top members who were concerned because ticket sales had been very slow. At this point, Arnold Palmer hadn't yet entered the event, and they asked if I would be willing to call him. They told me if he would agree to play, they'd have a plane come pick him up wherever he wanted. I liked these fellows and I knew their camp program was a very good cause, so I called Arnold. He agreed to come, and I went along when they picked him up. The next two days, after it was announced that Palmer would play, they sold 5000 tickets. It showed what a difference a big name like Palmer's could make—and I felt good that I was in a position to help bring it about.

Maybe that was what gave those Salesmanship Club guys their next big idea. Because it wasn't too long after the Dallas Open that they came and talked to me again. Felix McKnight, a newspaperman I'd known since my amateur days, talked to me first and told me the Salesmanship Club knew they could make money for their camp program by sponsoring a tour event, but felt they needed to have a well-known golfer connected with it. They were thinking of changing the name of the tournament to reflect that, and were also considering moving the tournament to Preston Trail. Felix asked if I would entertain the idea of having my name used instead of calling it the Dallas Open. I said I would, and he said, "I'll be back in touch with you soon."

A few days later, Felix called and said the whole tournament committee wanted to talk to me as soon as possible. I said, "That's fine, Felix, I'll be coming to Dallas in a couple of days," and Felix interrupted me with, "No, we'd like to come out to the ranch and talk to you right now." Well, that was okay with me, and forty-five minutes later Felix, W.L. Todd, Frank Anglim, and Jim Chambers pulled in the driveway and proceeded to give their whole presentation. They wanted to call the tournament the "Byron Nelson Golf Classic," and Preston Trail had already agreed to host the tournament. Before that call from Felix, though, I had done my own homework on the Salesmanship Club and found them to be a dedicated group of men with the most successful children's rehabilitation program that I'd ever heard of. So I agreed to do it, and it's become the best thing that's ever happened to me in golf, better than winning the Masters or the U.S. Open or eleven in a row. Because it helps people.

The committee also told me they'd already started to plan a big kickoff party for the tournament the next spring, and were going to invite all the dignitaries and celebrities they could think of. Well, they did just what they said they would, and the next April, 1968, at the Southland Center Hotel, there was a terrific party, over 1300 people. Chris Schenkel was the master of ceremonies, my mother and Louise's father were there, Governor John Connally, Bob Hope, Glen Campbell, Sammy Davis, Jimmy Demaret, Ben Hogan—the list went on and on.

It really was a very wonderful occasion and a great way to start the tournament. To top it all off, the final event of the evening was when Gar Laux, the head of Lincoln-Mercury, presented me the keys to a beautiful red Lincoln Mark II, right there at the party. That really put the icing on the cake.

One interesting thing about the evening was seeing how nervous Sammy Davis was before he sang. He really was a wreck. I'd never imagined that such an accomplished performer and someone so accustomed to being in front of people would be that way. He told me it was because there were so many important people there. But when he started on stage, you would never have known that he was nervous, and of course he performed beautifully.

That first year, Louise and I got to visit the Salesmanship Club's outdoor camp a couple of times, which was an eye-opening experience for us. These boys weren't just from poor families—they came from all sorts of backgrounds, but had somehow gotten off the track and into trouble, first at home, then school, and often with the law. While it was sad to learn how troubled they had been, it was also a good feeling to see the great progress they were making in the camp program. Several years later, they started a separate camp for girls, and one year at the Christmas party, I told one girl camper that I had recently given Louise a fur coat. She said, "What did you expect to get for that?" I was amazed at her question. I answered, "Nothing. I just wanted to make her happy." That told me a lot about how sad the lives of these children were—not because their parents might not have money for fur coats or other luxuries, but because they didn't know what loving and caring for people really meant, until they came to the camp and learned it firsthand.

Right away, the Salesmanship Club fellows and I started having a lot of meetings about the Dallas Open. We talked about its pluses and minuses, and how to make it better. Having been a pro and around tournaments all my life, I told them, "The only way you're going to have a successful tournament is for the pros' wives to be happy." Because Preston Trail was a men-only club, there were no facilities for women, so we had to do something about that. I also suggested to them, "No event on the tour has a nursery, and a lot of the pros have little children they need to bring along, so we need to start one—that'll help a lot." They got going immediately on those ideas, and when it came time for the tournament to start, they had moved in trailers and set up one for the pros' wives and another for the nursery, both of them staffed by wives of Salesmanship Club members. This arrangement worked very well, and the pros and their wives really did appreciate it.

It was amazing to me to see how the club members, several hundred of them, threw themselves into putting on this tournament. One of their traditions is to "Never say no" when asked to do something for the club, the tournament, or the kids, and they really do abide by it. It was very inspiring to me to realize my name was connected with such a great group of people, and over the years, that feeling has grown. Overall, I feel the Salesmanship Club and the tournament have done far more for me than I have for them, because they really have kept my name alive.

Another wonderful thing about being part of this bunch and having my name on the tournament was that I got to work with Chris for ABC on the telecast, from 1968 until I retired from television work in '76. For those first eight years, I worked full time as a color commentator up in the booth for the entire broadcast, and that was a special kind of fun for me, doing the broadcast for my own tournament.

As it happened, that first tournament in '68 was won by Miller Barber, which really made me feel good since he'd started as a caddie at Texarkana where I had been pro so many years before. What with the big kickoff party we had and Miller winning, it was a very good beginning year. We even got all four rounds in, and since the Nelson has been plagued with rain nearly every year of its existence, that was another fortunate happening for our inaugural year. In fact, in the past twenty-five years we've only had one or two that didn't have rain interruptions or cancellation of a round.

The tournament had immediate and full acceptance by everyone in the area. Despite the fact that the course was still quite a ways away, people really wanted to come and see the pros play, and fortunately, we drew nearly all the big names right away. In fact, the third year we had an unusually exciting finish. Arnold Palmer—the crowd favorite still—had finished his last round and shot 274. Right behind him, Jack Nicklaus came to the 18th green needing a four for a score of 273 to beat Arnie by one shot. Jack hit a good drive but his approach shot was a little strong and went over the green. His ball was on a downslope and in a slight little bit of rough, making for a very difficult little chip. The people loved Arnie so much that they were afraid Jack would chip close, make his par and win. They didn't want to see the tournament end just yet, so when Jack chipped short, the gallery applauded, figuring he would make five and tie and they would get to watch a playoff, which is exactly what happened.

The playoff started on the 15th hole, a long par 5, and it took two very long, very good shots to reach the green in two. Arnie and Jack both hit good drives, but Arnold left his second shot short of the green about thirty yards, chipped short and made five, while Jack put his second shot hole high and just off the green to the right. Jack chipped stone dead and made four to win. It was our first playoff, a great finish for both players, and one of the most exciting ones we've had. For some reason, we have had quite a few playoffs in the history of the tournament, more so than the average, but the gallery sure does love it.

One rather unusual thing happened at the tournament in 1974. Chris and I were doing the telecast, and there had been a rain delay. Because most of the fourth-round leaders wouldn't be able to finish before we went off the air, we had to televise some players way down the leaderboard who were on the course right then. It wasn't the best situation for our broadcast, but as it happened, one of those players was Brian "Buddy" Allin, a short, little-known fellow who shot a 65 that round, finished with a 269, and ended up winning the tournament. It was the lowest 72-hole score of the whole fifteen years the tournament was at Preston Trail, though Tom Watson matched it the next year. The entire ABC crew congratulated Buddy for winning—and then thanked him for saving our show, which he most certainly did.

Our most winning player so far is Tom Watson, who won for the first time in 1975, then went on to win again in '78, '79, and '80. The next year, 1981, Tom tied with Bruce Lietzke at 281 and Bruce won the playoff on the first hole, or Tom would have set a new record of winning our tournament four years in a row. As you might guess, those particular years were a great deal of fun for me, especially since I was no longer doing television by 1978 and could enjoy going out on the course and watching Tom in person, instead of just seeing him on the monitor.

With such wonderful players and exciting finishes, the tournament continued to grow and enjoy greater support each year from the people in the Dallas-Fort Worth area. By 1980, we knew it wasn't going to be long before we would outgrow Preston Trail. There was the problem of not having any facilities in the clubhouse whatsoever for the ladies, and the trailers we had for the pro wives and their children were quickly becoming too small. But more important, we were running out of space to park cars, which really was a serious situation. The club itself only had room for 250 cars, and there had been so many large homes built around the course that we could no longer use that space. In 1982, the last year we played at Preston Trail, several members of the Salesmanship Club bought a piece of property close to the club so we could park there. They later sold it at a nice profit, which all went to the club's camp program. That incident is a good example of their tradition of never saying no, because I'm told that when these fellows were asked to go to the bank and sign a note to buy the land, they weren't told how much it was for. When one of them got to the bank and learned the note was for several million dollars, he called the club president and said, "That note I just signed is for four million dollars. Could I ask what it's for?"

Knowing we were running out of room, the committee had already been searching over a year for a place where we could go. They finally contacted Ben Carpenter, the founder and developer of Las Colinas, a fast-growing master-planned community in Irving, just north of Dallas and northeast of Fort Worth. Part of Ben's development was a place called the Las Colinas Sports Club, a wonderful athletic facility that happened to have a golf course already on it. When the committee began looking at the course, they asked me to go along and see if it would be all right for the tournament. It was, just barely; it had been made just for a resort course and really wasn't going to work very well for national tournament play with as large a gallery as we expected to have. The front nine was on one side of a busy four-lane residential street, MacArthur Boulevard, and the back nine was on the other side. Neither golfers nor spectators could get to the other side except by way of a pedestrian underpass, which wasn't really very satisfactory. Still, we decided to go ahead with it, worked out a deal with Mr. Carpenter, and the next year, 1983, we held the tournament there. The course was originally designed by Trent Jones's son, Bob, so we worked with him on making a few changes such as reducing the size of some of the bunkers and lengthening the course by adding tournament tees.

We played the tournament on that course for three years, but the tournament was growing so fast that it quickly became apparent we couldn't continue that way. Mr. Carpenter and the Salesmanship Club then came up with a plan to completely redo the place. What they were going to do was to completely tear up the nine holes on the east side of MacArthur, build a brand-new 18-hole Tournament Players Course there, and add nine holes on the west side of the boulevard. At the same time, Ben had already started to build the resort hotel that had been part of his original plan. When completed, the hotel would be right next to the TPC course, which would work out perfectly for the players as well as for the hotel guests the rest of the year.

It was quite a project. We called in Ben Crenshaw and a wonderful golf course architect, Jay Morrish, with me in the background as sort of an unofficial consultant. Then, the day the tournament was over in '85, we had 'dozers and all sorts of equipment ready to move in the next morning. My good friend Steve Barley masterminded the entire job, working with as many as twenty different contractors at once, and not once did any of those contractors get in another company's way. It all went incredibly smoothly and our brand new TPC course was ready for major tournament play exactly one year later. I've never heard of anything being done like that before or since. Still scares me to think about it.

The course wasn't bad that first year. The players understood the situation and appreciated the improvements over what we'd had before. Now, besides having a far better course all in one place, they had a beautiful new hotel to stay in, and their wives and children could use the Sports Club next to the hotel during their free time, so everyone was pretty happy. Several years later, the Four Seasons took over management of both the hotel and the club, and they've done a beautiful job with it. What's also nice is that sometimes the Tour's schedule permits the players to play our tournament one week and the Colonial the next week in Fort Worth, which the players really like.

What pleases me most about the tournament is not that I have my name on it or that we draw such a good field or even that the PGA Tour says ours is the best-marshaled event all year, but that all of the proceeds go to charity. We raise more than a tenth of all the charity money on the tour, and in 1992, we netted over three million dollars for the Salesmanship Club programs, which now include our camp for both boys and girls in Hawkins, Texas, and an education center in Dallas where troubled children go to school and they and their families get counseling. The club is now planning its own Community School, and if it works as well as the camp and counseling programs do, we will be able to help even more people.

I believe the main reason we've always gotten such good support for the tournament is because people realize that every cent of the profits goes to these children and their families and no one takes any money out for themselves. I don't get a penny, never have, nor does the club president or the tournament chairman. I've always been fortunate to be connected with people who are substantial, who know how to get things done and who do them honestly and properly. And the Salesmanship Club is the best example I've ever seen of these kinds of qualities.

Not only has the Salesmanship Club been wonderful for me to be associated with, but the people with GTE, our title sponsor, and the folks at the Four Seasons Resort and Sports Club have too, as well as the good folks at USAA who now own the entire place. In fact, in 1992, General Robert F. McDermott, who heads USAA, really put the icing on the cake as far as I was concerned. But I have to back up a bit to tell the whole story.

From 1980 on, the Salesmanship Club people had wanted to have a life-size bronze made of me to have installed at the course. At that time, though, when they told me what it was going to cost, I told them it was too expensive and I felt the money could be better spent on the children the tournament was designed to help. I thought that would be the end of it, but after USAA took over the hotel, club, and golf courses, the idea came up again. Early in the fall of '91, Mike Massad, chairman of the club's executive committee, made a presentation to General McDermott and a group of USAA and Four Seasons people, hoping to find someone to finance both the bronze and a wall to list the names of the tournament champions, which together would enhance the whole facility. After a long discussion, Mike said they had not been able to find anyone to do it. The general hadn't said anything to this point, just listened. Finally, he looked at me and said some very complimentary things, then announced, "I'll go back to our headquarters in San Antonio and see if we can't do it."

Well, he not only could, but did, and the statue was unveiled at my eightieth birthday party in February 1992, and installed in front of the wall of champions the next week. It really overwhelms and almost embarrasses me, but it truly is one of the greatest things that's ever happened in all my life. The sculptor, Robert Summers from Glen Rose, Texas, who also did the statue of John Wayne that stands in the Orange County airport in Los Angeles, did a wonderful job, right down to the wing-tip shoes I'm wearing and my name on my driver. It's over nine feet tall so it's a little bigger than me, but it really looks more like me than I do.

How can anyone say thank you enough for the things that have happened to me? I've never felt I was any different from or any better than anyone else just because I used to play a little golf fifty years ago, but people treat me that way, and all I can do is be grateful and enjoy it and try hard to deserve it. And that's what I do.

TEN

Golfers I've Known Over the Years

IN NEARLY SEVENTY YEARS IN THE GAME, I'VE PLAYED WITH and watched quite a few golfers. From the best on the tour to the 40-handicappers, I've seen some amazing things and some just plain strange ones. Here are a few stories about some of my favorites.

Tommy Armour. Tommy was a Scottish pro who came to the United States and became a wonderful player, especially with his irons. He won the U.S. Open in 1927 and the British in 1931 despite the fact that he had very poor vision in one eye because of an injury he got during World War I. Tommy was about twenty years older than me, and we first met in Boca Raton on June 1, 1939, when I signed with MacGregor and he was head man on their staff, playing his Silver Scot clubs. After I'd signed, I went to Tommy's shop and picked out a set of his irons, which I used to win the U.S. Open two weeks later. I used those same irons for a long time, until MacGregor made me get a new set.

I played with Tommy a few times myself, and something that always impressed me about him was the size and strength of his hands. He could take an iron and hold it with his arm outstretched and the club held between only his forefinger and middle finger. Try it sometime if you think it sounds easy.

Tommy had the greatest gift of gab of anyone I ever knew. He was simply a wonderful storyteller who could take the most uninteresting hole or shot or round of golf and make it sound fascinating, and because of the way he could talk, he became a wonderful teacher. He'd sit down at Boca Raton under the shade of an umbrella with a toddy on the table next to him, and he'd teach until he just ran out of energy to talk.

Besides playing and teaching golf, Armour liked to bet a little bit, especially when he felt he knew what he was doing. In 1942, when Hogan and I tied for the Masters, he bet on me against Hogan because by this time I had also developed a reputation as a good long-iron player, and he liked that. In the playoff, when I started so poorly and was three over after the first four holes, the man he'd made the bet with came to him and said, "Looks like Byron's having a bad day—I'll settle with you fifty cents on the dollar," but Tommy looked at him and said, "The game has just started." Fortunately I did win, which made Armour think I was greater than I really was.

Roone Arledge. Chris Schenkel and I were playing with Roone, our producer at ABC, at Prestwick during the British Open one year. Unfortunately, I had to quit after six holes because I had something I had to do. On the very next hole Roone made a hole-in-one, and he was quite upset that I didn't get to see it. I may have had to leave early due to the fact that we were playing so slowly, because in those days, Roone was an unusually deliberate player.

Another time—in fact, during the first part of the British Open at Carnoustie in 1975—Roone asked Chris and me to play with him at St. Andrews early of a morning. What made Roone so slow was that while he walked quickly enough, he would get to his ball, take a practice swing, pull up his glove, take another swing, then another tug at his glove, and do that two or three times on every shot of any length at all.

Chris and I are both very fast players, and we were getting further and further behind the group in front of us, but Roone didn't really seem to notice. I guess because of who we were, the marshal didn't say anything for a while about the way we were holding up play, but finally on the 14th hole, here he came on his bicycle. He walked up to Roone, pulled out his Big Ben watch, held it up where we could all see it, and said, "I say, sir, you should be on the eighteenth green by now." Roone was embarrassed, and so were we. He did speed up some, but then when we were finished he wanted us to play with him again the next day. Chris and I looked at each other, and finally replied, "Only if you'll play fast enough so we don't get in trouble."

Herman Barron. He was pro at Fenway Country Club in Westchester County, Long Island, and he had a funny little short, flat swing that wasn't very effective. Harold McSpaden and I played quite a bit of golf with him, and we got to kidding with him about that swing. Then we started working with him some till he finally got a little more upright and became a good player. He won the Tam O'Shanter one year and a couple of other tournaments, and the three of us became lifelong friends. One year the pros had a 108-hole tournament there at Fenway, and the sixth hole, a long par three, came right by the clubhouse porch, where a lot of people were watching the play. Herman used a wood off the tee and his ball ended up short and to the right. He stepped up and pitched it into the hole, and the noise went through the whole clubhouse. "Hermie did it!" they yelled. I got quite a kick out of it because doing that at your own club was a lot of fun. Another thing about Herman was that he was an excellent card player, especially gin rummy and bridge. He was so good, actually, that he had to quit playing with the members because he was about to get in trouble for taking too much of their money.

Bill Campbell. One of the best amateurs I ever saw play, and he's been good for years. Bill is a good friend of Sam Snead's because they come from the same area of West Virginia, and Bill has a long, fluid swing—not like Sam's, but it makes you think of Sam because of the rhythm Bill's swing has. Because of his wonderful way of conducting himself, Bill has become known as a true amateur, and that's a great compliment. He was U.S. Amateur Champion in 1964 and won the U.S. Senior Amateur championship in both '79 and '80. A few years ago, he was also selected to be Captain of the Royal & Ancient Golf Club of St. Andrews, which is a great honor. A few years ago during a USGA Museum Committee meeting at the Chicago Golf

Club, they unveiled a painting of Bill in his uniform as honorary Captain. It was very well done, and a proud moment for Bill, but he was very humble about it all. He doesn't consider himself important because of his accomplishments in golf, he just has so much respect and love for the game, and a very humble spirit about it. I've always admired that about him.

Joanne Carner. Joanne always hit very long for a woman—especially in her earlier years—which is part of the reason why she won the women's amateur five times and the Open twice. In fact, a few years back I played in an exhibition with her in Kansas City with Tom Watson and Fuzzy Zoeller. They had her drive from the members' tees, and besides outdriving me consistently, she drove almost up with Tom and Fuzzy all day as well. She surely thrilled the gallery that day.

Fred Cobb. Fred was the golf coach at North Texas State in Denton, and I worked with his teams up there for several years until shortly after Fred's death in 1953. Fred was very likable and would do anything for his team, which was a big part of why they worked so hard for him. To me, Fred was the one who really started good college golf in Texas. His work at North Texas State was remarkable for a man who had no funds, no scholarships to offer, and not even much of a golf course to play on. But not only did he teach his boys how to play the game, he taught them to be gentlemen. He'd be out watching them through his binoculars when they didn't know he was even on the course, and if he saw anyone throw a club or knew they were using bad language, he'd let them know right now that such behavior wasn't acceptable. He had quite a few fine players during his time there, including Don January, who has done so well on the senior tour. He loved those boys and they loved him. After he died, the golf program there never came close to what it was back in the late forties and early fifties.

Charlie Coe. Besides Ken Venturi, Charlie is the only other amateur who in my opinion should have won the Masters. He was so thin it looked like a strong wind could blow him away, but he could really hit the ball. During the Masters in '61, everyone who watched the play on the last nine saw him put his approach shots closer than Player's on nearly every hole, but he just never made a single putt. Charlie won the amateur championship in 1958 and several other big amateur tournaments. He's still a member at Augusta and is greatly respected whenever folks talk about fine amateur players.

Henry Cotton. After Cotton came over from England to play in the Masters in 1947 (courtesy of a loan from Eddie Lowery), he then went to San Francisco to do a few exhibitions Eddie had arranged. I was out there also, and one day the three of us went to play at the California Golf Club. He and Eddie got to talking and Henry said, "I understand you're a pretty good bunker player, Eddie." Eddie said, "Yes, I guess I am." So Henry said, "Let's have a contest." That was fine with Eddie, so they headed to the bunker by the practice green. Cotton was very confident in his game and thought he could win some easy money from Eddie, who of course was an amateur, though a very good one. They bet $5 a ball for whoever got closest to the pin, and the one who lost got to pick the next spot to hit from. But Eddie was so good out of the bunker that after about fifty shots he was winning most every time, and Henry finally gave up. Eddie really was the best out of a bunker that I ever saw.

Bing Crosby. Bing loved golf and scored in the mid- to high 70's a lot. His swing was easy and smooth, with no rushing or jerking ever. Bing always conducted himself very well and was very cordial with the golfers who came to his tournament. But one time during the Crosby, he did get on me a little. He and I were supposed to do a little sketch for television, and though my part was very small I never could get it right. After I'd tried to do it a number of times he finally said, "Byron, if you can't remember three lines of dialogue, I don't know how you can ever remember how to hit a golf shot!"

Another thing that impressed me about Bing was that when I won the Crosby in '51, he had to leave before the tournament was over and go to Los Angeles to get treatment for kidney stones. Bing didn't like to fly, so he rode a train, and on that trip, though he was in terrific pain, he wrote a very kind letter congratulating me.

My last Bing story happened some years ago, when Bing's wife Kathy played on my team in our Lady Nelson pro-am two weeks before my tournament. Bing couldn't come because he was still recovering from a fall off a stage, but after we were done, Kathy wanted to call him, so we did. After she'd talked with him for a few minutes she handed the phone to me, and Bing said, "How'd Kathy do?" I told him she'd helped us on both a par five and a par three. Then he asked, "When she was out of the hole did she pick up?" I laughed and said, "No," and he asked, "When she missed a shot did she want to play another one?" I laughed again and said, "Yes," and he finally said, "Byron, you are a patient man!"

Jimmy Demaret. One of the most colorful pros in the history of golf. Jimmy was from Houston, so I got to know him when I was still quite young, and I knew him very well. He had a funny, quick wit about him, which I admired because I don't feel I have any whatsoever. The people at Augusta named their three bridges for Sarazen, Hogan, and me, and Jimmy used to joke, "Hey, I won it three times and I never even got an outhouse!" Jimmy played a nice, high fade, and he certainly proved you could win at Augusta without hooking, even though people said you couldn't.

Jimmy used to use a golf ball with a steel center made by a company in Chattanooga, Tennessee. He called them "Steelies." One year at the Masters he put two balls in the water, at 12 and 15, and when he came in, before anybody could say anything, Jimmy announced, "I found out one thing today—that old Steelie won't float!" He used to wear these big old tams that flopped down the side of his head, and the most outlandish colors. He'd often choose colors that clashed on purpose, just to create interest and get attention. He laughed at himself and people laughed with him—everybody kidded him and he really had a lot of fun with it.

President Eisenhower. Besides loving to play golf, Eisenhower was a fine bridge player, and one time I was asked to fill in for a couple of hands with him, Cliff Roberts, and Bob Woodruff, who was head of Coca-Cola. I was scared to death because I knew what good bridge players they all were, and I was really not much more than a beginner. In one hand, I wound up bidding four hearts but messed up somehow and didn't make it. When the hand was over, I said to Cliff, "I know I should have been able to make that bid some way," and Cliff said, "All you had to do was lead the two of hearts, Byron." I was glad when their fourth arrived. But it certainly was fun to watch them play, which I got to do nearly every evening after we'd played golf. They'd play just three or four cards, then everyone would lay their cards down and that was it. They were so good at knowing exactly where all the cards were. It just amazed me.

James Garner. Jim Garner is not only a fine actor, but loves to play golf and plays well, though he has back problems from time to time. One time I played an exhibition in Chicago with Jim and we had the oddest combination I'd ever seen. It was the two of us, Doug Sanders, and LPGA pro Laura Baugh. Garner hit the ball a long ways, and he was kidding Doug Sanders especially that day, because he was driving the ball very well. He'd hit a great drive and say, "Okay, Doug, try to catch that one." He outdrove Doug nearly all day long. Jim is very outgoing, especially when his back isn't bothering him, and it wasn't that day. Really, he was the long driver most of the time in our group, though he might go east or west sometimes instead of down the middle. He was about an 8 handicap, so he was definitely a good-caliber player.

Ralph Guldahl. Though Ralph was one of the slowest players on the tour, from 1936 to 1938 he was also a great player, winning the Western Open three times and the U.S. Open twice. I have to admit that after Ralph beat me so bad when we were both kids in Texas, it was nice to be able to top him at the Masters in '37, after Ralph had been leading me by three shots going to the last nine. In my own mind, I figured that made us about even. And then when I beat Ralph again during the International Match Play Championship at Belmont Springs that fall, I did kind of smile to myself, "And that makes me one up."

I believe the most unusual thing I ever saw a player do was in the U.S. Open in '37 at Oakland Hills in Birmingham, Michigan. Ralph was on the eighteenth green in the final round. He had the tournament won, all he had to do was hit his putt. He was all lined up and ready when he stopped, backed away, and took a comb out to comb his hair. I think he suddenly realized that they'd be wanting to take pictures and he wanted to make sure he looked good, but it was a little strange for someone to do that during the most important tournament we have.

He finished with his hair, two-putted, and that was that. I don't recall if the press said anything about how nice his hair looked.

Ralph won exactly $1000 for winning that Open, and the very next week his wife, Laverne, spent every penny of that thousand dollars on a fine riding horse. That was all right, I guess, but the third time she rode it, she fell off, broke her arm—and gave the horse away. I believe that was even more unusual than Ralph combing his hair on that final hole.

Walter Hagen. He was one of the best showmen I've ever seen, and the first pro golfer who really entertained the gallery. Besides entertaining the fans, though, Hagen also had the ability to politely intimidate his opponents. I watched him play in the semifinals against Abe Espinosa in the PGA Championship at Cedar Crest in Dallas in 1927, and Hagen was one down going to the last hole. Espinosa drove into some shallow rough while Hagen was nicely in the fairway. Hagen walked over to Abe's ball, looked at it, looked up at the green, didn't say a thing, then walked back to his own ball. So Abe went a little long and his ball ended up on the back of the green with Hagen's ball inside his. Now Hagen walks over behind Abe's ball again, lines it up as if he were going to putt it, then moves back out of the way. Of course, all this broke Abe's concentration and he three-putted; Hagen won on the first extra hole. He would do things like that whenever he needed to. In this day and time that wouldn't work at all, but back then no one thought much about it.

Hagen also had a knack of making a big production out of what was really a very easy shot. If he had a simple little chip, say, he would really look it over and make it look like it was very tough. Then he hit it well, of course, but the gallery would all think it was something great. On the other hand, when he had a really difficult shot he would walk up, hardly look at the ball, and just hit it. I guess the other thing people always liked about Hagen was that he always dressed immaculately and drove a handsome new car. That impressed everyone and allowed him to get away with things that the rest of us might not have. I may have said this before, but Hagen was also the first one that I knew of to ever have an agent—Bob Harlow, who started *Golf World* magazine.

Ed Haggar. Ed's father started the Haggar clothing company in Dallas, and he and his wife Patty are very dear friends of ours. A few years ago we were playing golf with them at Castle Pines. Ed and I had a pretty big bet going, a dollar nassau, and I had beaten him one down on the first nine. On the back, we came to the par-three eleventh hole, which is all downhill. I put my tee shot on the green but Ed hit a bad shot to the right, into all this brush and trees. His caddie said, "You'd better hit another one, Mr. Haggar," but Ed said, "No, we'll find it." Well, they went down in there and beat around in the brush awhile but didn't have any luck—which was a good thing, as it turned out. Because Ed went back to the tee, played another one, and his ball landed twenty feet back of the hole almost at the top of this big ridge that ran across the green. Then his ball started rolling back down and ran straight into the hole for a three. It was the only time I ever saw that happen in all the years I've played golf.

Ben Hogan. Back in our early years when neither one of us had much money at all, Ben and I were playing in the Oakland Open at Sequoia and staying at the Lehman Hotel. I was going to ride to the course with Ben for a practice round, so we went out to the parking lot, got to his car, and found it sitting there jacked up on cement blocks with all four wheels gone. Ben just couldn't believe it and said, "I sure hope whoever took them needed them worse than I do." We used my car instead, and I don't remember where he got the money to buy new wheels, but fortunately he did.

Ben has never liked being around a lot of people and that's fine. It's his business and I respect that. But I always thought it was a shame in a way because he missed so much. People idolized him so and to a certain extent that can be a very good thing. I know the way people feel about me has always made me feel good and made me want to try hard to be a better person. It's difficult for people to get a chance to interview Ben so they ask me about him a lot, but I just don't particularly like to talk about him. I feel like that's invading his privacy, so I don't say much. We've always gotten along fine and we've always liked each other very much. We're simply different personalities, and there's nothing wrong with that.

Bob Hope. Bob is and always has been a very funny man. Actually, he was more serious on the golf course than at any other time, and is one of the best goodwill ambassadors that golf ever had. Until his later years, Bob was a pretty steady player and scored in the mid-80's all the time, though he didn't start to play till he was older.

One time in the late thirties or early forties, I was in Los Angeles to play in the L.A. Open, and Bob wanted me to come out and go on his New Year's Eve show. I was pleased he wanted me to be on the show, so Louise and I flew out. We had a rehearsal and then went to the Rose Bowl game at Pasadena—Bob and Dolores, Louise and I, and Chester Morris and his wife. Bob was driving, and halfway to the Rose Bowl we ran into a terrible traffic jam. Of course, everyone knew Bob, including the policemen. All of a sudden Bob pulled out of line, and began driving on the wrong side of the road, telling policemen, "I'm late for a show!" Fortunately there was no traffic coming the other way, but it was still scary. We finally got to the stadium, and as soon as we got out of the car Louise said, "I don't care how we get back, I'm not going back with him." Fortunately, Cliff Roberts was there and sitting right where we were, so we rode back in his car instead.

When I went on the show that night, I didn't remember my lines very well. I never was much at memorizing. I was supposed to say something complimentary about Miss America, who was also on the show, but I couldn't remember my lines at all. Bob said to the audience, "This man's older than he looks, isn't he?" And they really laughed. But in case anyone wants to know, that's why I never became a movie star.

Bob Jones. Jones had the greatest name in golf in his time, of course, and is still considered great today. He was a wonderful man, with great knowledge about the history of the game and the best way to play. His ability to judge players and know what they needed to do to play good golf was excellent. Very educated and quite articulate, Jones wrote many articles and letters and several books on golf. He also made some instructional films that are selling quite well as videotapes today. I was fortunate to have played with Bob a number of times at Augusta, and always enjoyed it very much. You felt in awe when you played with him, regardless of what kind of game you played yourself. His attitude toward everyone was very friendly, but he was kind of quiet, really, and didn't have a lot to say most of the time. One time at the Masters Club dinner—the one attended originally just by the Masters winners plus Bob Jones and Clifford Roberts—the players were criticizing the way the pin had been placed on the third hole because it was nearly impossible to make a birdie. All of a sudden Jones said, "You guys make me sick. You think you've got to birdie every hole. You birdie a lot of them as it is, and there are going to be some tough pin placements out there that if you want a birdie, you're really going to have to earn it."

One of the great honors of my career was when Jones asked me to play in his place with the Masters tournament leader the last round, which I did until Ken Venturi was the leader in 1956. Since I was Venturi's mentor, Cliff and Bob decided that it wouldn't be right for me to play with Kenny, so they put me with someone else and Kenny played with Snead and lost. From then on, they began pairing the players according to their score only, which was really the best way.

Bobby Knight. Bobby and Chris Schenkel were very good friends, and one time I was playing in a tournament called the Mad Anthony in Ft. Wayne, Indiana, near Chris's home town. Bobby had played in the morning while Chris and I were scheduled for the afternoon. Before we started off, Bobby asked Chris if I would mind him following me around. What he wanted was for me to tell him what I was trying to do with each shot as I played, which was fine with me. I had a good day, fortunately, and most of the time was able to do exactly what I told him I was going to do. When we came in he said, "Boy, if I could get my basketball team to do that, we could sure win a lot more games!"

Chuck Kocsis. Chuck is from Michigan and is a fine amateur player who was runner-up to Harvie Ward in the 1956 U.S. Amateur. He's in his late seventies and still shoots his age or less on a regular basis. One summer in the early forties when I was pro at Inverness, Bobby Locke came over from South Africa to play some exhibitions for five straight days, all through Michigan. One of these exhibitions was at Red Run in Detroit, and I was invited to play with Bob Gaida, the pro there, Chuck, and Locke. Chuck was having a very good day and shot 33 on the front, while I had 34. We were good friends, but as we started the back nine, I said to him, "You'd better get going, because I'm not going to let any amateur beat me." As luck would have it, I shot 30, so I did manage to get past him.

Ky Laffoon. Ky was on the tour mostly in the early part of my career and was the most unusual golfer, personality-wise, that I ever knew. He was always doing something interesting. I first became acquainted with him when I was in California that first winter, 1933, because we were both staying at the Sir Launfels apartments in Los Angeles. Ky was part American Indian, and had a brother, Bill, who caddied for him and traveled with him all the time. Bill was the first traveling caddie I ever knew of. One day, Ky and I were playing two brothers, Al and Emery Zimmerman, in a practice round for the Pasadena Open at Brookside Park right by the Rose Bowl. At that time there was no restriction on the number of clubs you could have in your bag, and it was amazing how many people had clubs that were numbered between an 8 and a 9-iron—especially pitching clubs. On the ninth hole, I'd outdriven Ky and was watching as he put his second shot on the green. I hollered, "What club did you use, Ky?" He hollered back, "A three-quarter seven-and-a-half."

Ky chewed tobacco and used to squirt the juice between his front teeth. You had to stay out of the way because sometimes it went quite a few feet. But in spite of that unattractive habit, Ky felt he was really good-looking. I'd be in his room sometimes when he was getting dressed, and he'd preen in front of the mirror, slick his hair back, and say, "Boy, you're the best-looking man in the world. I don't know how you stand it!" Ky was a good player, but he was never satisfied just to play, no matter what the tournament was. He always had to have some kind of small side bet going about what he'd shoot or whether he'd win. One time he was playing in a tournament in Cleveland, Ohio, and was using a mallet-head putter with a wooden shaft that he usually did very well with. He was on the last hole and winning the tournament, but he had to two-putt to win his own bet on what he said he'd shoot. Now when Ky hit a bad putt, he'd always kick the putter head. Well, he putted past the hole and missed it coming back, which meant he lost his bet. So he got mad and kicked his putter as usual. Unfortunately, this time the head fell right off the putter, but Ky reached over quick, grabbed the putter head, and knocked the ball in the hole—one stroke too late.

Most of the time, though, he'd win those little old bets. Ky really was the best player for his own money of anyone I ever saw. There were quite a few younger players coming on the tour then, and he would play as many as three at a time, best ball, for a $5 nassau. All in all it was fun, knowing and playing golf with Ky Laffoon.

Tony Lema. When I first met Tony, he was the assistant caddiemaster at California Golf Club when I played in tournaments there and many other times when I played with my friend Eddie Lowery. Tony then became caddiemaster before he turned pro. He would watch me every time I played or practiced, and I always felt that of all the golfers out there, Tony used his feet and legs more like I did than anyone else. When Tony was a member of the Ryder Cup team I captained in 1965, that was a real bonus for me, and he did very well. After we'd won the Cup, our team was in the locker room waiting for the official award ceremony, and Tony opened up a case of champagne. He loved champagne and had been nicknamed "Champagne Tony" by the press because he bought it for everyone when he won a tournament. I let them all have a glass, but then had them put it away for later, because I wanted to be sure we'd behave all right during the ceremony, with Prime Minister Wilson there and all.

Tony was very well liked by the other players and very outgoing, but kind of shy around me. Before the Ryder Cup, he had decided he wanted to live in Texas and asked to use my name as a reference when he applied for an apartment in Dallas over on Turtle Creek, which is a pretty nice area. They called me about it, and I had to tell them everything I knew about Tony, nearly. He was approved, fortunately, and once he'd moved in, he would bring his mother out to the ranch quite often to visit Louise and me. In fact, he was living in Texas when he was killed in that terrible plane crash.

Lawson Little. Lawson was a fine player who won the American and British amateurs and many other amateur tournaments before he turned pro. While he was still an amateur he got a job writing for

King Features Syndicate, and that was how he could afford to travel to tournaments and play. In 1936, the year after I beat him in the San Francisco Match Play tournament when I was just starting, I was heading out to play the Pacific Northwest tour, the one where I really got going good. I was riding the train from Seattle to Portland, and on the way to the dining car I heard a typewriter clicking away in the drawing room. I saw Lawson in there working, and when I said hello, he said, "Byron, come here a minute and guess what I'm writing about." I said I had no idea, and he said, "I'm writing about how you trounced me good last year in San Francisco!"

Bobby Locke. Not only was Bobby a fine player, but he was also considered one of the great putters of all time. In six exhibitions I played with him one long week in Michigan in the early forties, he never missed one putt under five feet. It was when we got off the course that the trouble started. I was acting as his host and after each round we'd talk to the people awhile, then go get changed and go out to eat. Now I wasn't particularly rushing, but I'd have my shower and be all dressed and ready to go and Bobby would still be about half-dressed and not showered, sitting there having a beer. I'd say, "Bobby, c'mon, let's go." "All right, laddie," he'd say, "I'll be ready in a few minutes." Happened every time. Bobby had a certain speed he moved, and he never varied, never rushed, just always moved at that same tempo. He was very deliberate in everything he did, particularly in the way he played golf. He even walked with a very deliberate gait. When he played, though, he played very well. He'd hit a little draw hook every shot, exactly the same every time. When Sam Snead went over to South Africa to play him in the late thirties, Bobby beat Sam fifteen out of sixteen matches. Made me glad I didn't go.

Jim McKay. One time when Jim and I were on a plane going to the British Open, we got to talking about golf, and he complained he wasn't putting very well. I didn't think I'd be able to help him right then and there, but sure enough, someone on the plane had a putter and I gave Jim a lesson right in the aisle. What was wrong was he wasn't looking straight at the ball, which made it impossible to keep the putter on line going back and through. So I showed him how to correct that, and everyone on the plane got a kick out of it. Of course, planes then were not as crowded as they are now, and fortunately we had a smooth flight. Once we landed and he got out to play, he did putt quite well and told me later that was the best putting lesson he'd ever had.

Harold McSpaden. Harold and I played a lot of golf together and played well as a team, though we had very different personalities. I was easygoing and kind of shy, but there was nothing shy or easy-going about Harold. He wasn't mean at all, but kind of rough and gruff and he would tell you how he felt right quick, so you never had to wonder what he was thinking. I had a number of players ask me, "Doesn't McSpaden bother you?" and I said, "No, I like to play with him." Besides having a strong personality and being honest and forth-right, Harold was a better player than anyone ever gave him credit for. Another difference between us was that he had exceptionally long arms. Though he was one and a half inches shorter than me, he wore a 36-inch sleeve while I took a 33. I believe the reason we were such a good team was because I played a different type of game from Harold. I was very steady—in the fairway, on the green, and no more than two putts—while he might get into trouble on a few holes but could also make a lot of birdies, so we "brother-in-lawed" it pretty good most of the time.

Harold was very strong, with a kind of loose-jointed walk. With his long arms, for most of his career he used only a 42-inch driver. He was barrel-chested and had hazel eyes and dark hair he combed straight back, sort of in the style the young folks are bringing back now. For sure, he certainly was a better player than most people know. He once said to me, "Byron, if you hadn't been born, I would have been known as a wonderful player!" In fact, during my wonderful year of 1945, Harold finished second thirteen times, which has to be a record.

Eddie Merrins. Quiet and easy but always getting the job done, Eddie is one of the absolute top club professionals ever. He's called "The Little Pro" because he is so small, but he's a wonderful teacher and was recently named club pro of the year for his work at Bel Air in Los Angeles, where he's been pro for thirty years. There are a lot of movie stars and bigwigs at Bel Air, so you know it's not the easiest place in the world to work. Besides running the golf program at his club, Eddie served as the golf coach for UCLA, which has graduated such fine players as Steve Pate, Corey Pavin, and quite a few others. He's also a great organizer. Some years ago he began the Friends of Golf (FOG) tournament to raise money for golf scholarships for UCLA. The tournament has been very successful and has expanded to benefit other college and junior golf programs around the country.

Francis Ouimet. I first met Francis through Eddie Lowery, who caddied for him when Francis won the Open in 1913. Francis lived in Massachusetts and I played with him and Eddie a few times at the Charles River Country Club when Francis was in his fifties. Quiet though not shy, he was a beautiful player and a wonderful long-iron player. Francis had what today would be called an abbreviated swing—the club never even quite reached horizontal. But he was effective because he had a very smooth, flowing action and his rhythm was excellent. It was pretty to watch and I was very impressed with his game. He was impressed with mine also, so we had sort of a mutual admiration society. He was on the USGA committee in 1939 when I won the International Match Play Championship in Boston. That was the first time I actually met him, though he had such a strong New England accent I could hardly understand anything he said. Besides winning the Open in 1913, Francis won the Amateur in 1914 and again in 1931, and was also Captain of the Royal and Ancient Golf Club of St. Andrews, which meant our friends across the ocean appreciated him too.

Arnold Palmer. Arnold is the most popular golf professional that's ever been and he deserves it. I've never seen anyone sign as many autographs or be as nice to the public as he is. But besides being so popular and the most exciting golfer I ever saw, Arnie is an excellent pilot and flies his own plane, which impresses me. I flew with him a number of times and always felt completely at ease. One time, though, I was visiting him at his home in Latrobe, Pennsylvania, in the late fifties when he called President Eisenhower at Gettysburg to see if he would come play golf with us if Arnie would go pick him up. There was a prediction of rain, but Arnie said, "Yes, the weather looks a little bad but I think it'll be all right." Both of us got in

Arnie's plane and headed towards Gettysburg, but about halfway there the weather got terrible, with lots of rain and fog. To be honest, I was getting a little scared—not about Arnie's flying, but because the weather really was pretty bad. Arnie called the airport we were to land at and they told him we could come in, so he had them call Eisenhower, but Ike told them, "I'm not going up in this—I don't want to and Mamie wouldn't let me anyway!" Well, you couldn't argue with either one of them, so we just had to turn around and go back.

At his home in Latrobe, Arnie has a good-sized basement, with pigeonholes all along the walls for the golf clubs he loves to fool with—and he's got hundreds of them. He always liked to take clubs, put them in a vise, take them apart, and work them over. He put some of the strangest facings I'd ever seen on his clubs. Sometimes they'd be real straight and other times he'd have the face cut back almost even with the hosel. And he liked to bend iron clubs around some, experimenting. He never played with any of them that I know of but he loved to fool with them; it was sort of therapy for him. I've seen Arnold go to the practice tee with three drivers, trying to make up his mind which one to use, and he'd do the same thing on the putting green. That was so foreign to what most other players did, but it didn't make much difference what he used. The way he played and scored, he always did great.

Judy Rankin. Johnny Revolta was a fine player on the tour who became an excellent teacher and was pro at Evanston Country Club in Illinois for many years. A number of years ago, Johnny and I were discussing the golf swing and teaching and he said, "Have you ever seen Judy Torluemke?" That was Judy's maiden name. I said, "Yes, I've seen her play but only from a distance." He told me, "I want you to look at her grip and tell me if you ever want to teach anybody again." The next chance I got, I did get a closer look and I was quite surprised, to say the least. Judy's left hand position was so strong that the back of it almost faced up at the sky. Her right hand was quite good, but her left was far too strong for anyone to say she could ever be a good player. But her success—she won at least twenty-five tournaments—shows that if you practice and repeat the same motion you can overcome anything, because she played very well despite her unorthodox grip. Very probably she developed it to gain extra distance, because she was quite small. Judy also understands the game very well and does a good job today as an on-course commentator for ABC.

Clifford Roberts. Cliff and I had become friends from the time I'd won the Masters in 1937. I had made a little money in '38 and the first part of '39, and I'd bought a few shares of five or ten different stocks. Cliff was one of the top officials in Reynolds Securities, so I asked him some questions about the stocks I'd bought, but he just kind of grunted and didn't say much. Then one day I was at Augusta in '39 and he called and said, "Byron, I want you to come down to my office at nine a.m." When I arrived, he had just finished his breakfast and was drinking some tea. He said, "You asked me some questions about stocks, so I want to talk to you about it." He added, "I like you, Byron, but you're never going to make any money in golf. And if you keep fooling around buying stocks on your own, you're going to lose what you do make."

Then he said, "I don't handle any account under a million dollars, but because you've been good to us here at Augusta, I would like to handle your account, under the condition that I have power of attorney, so I can buy and sell what and when I want to. But I assure you I will handle your account very much like it was a bank. You won't make an awful lot of money, but you will make a little. Also, whenever you have a thousand dollars or five thousand saved up, you send that to me and I'll continue to invest it. I'll also take the stocks you have now and sell them—I don't know where you got those dogs anyway." Financially, it was the best thing that ever happened to me.

Cliff was from New York, was a great friend of Bob Jones, and was also the best executive that I ever heard of. He really knew how to get things done, but he talked very slowly and thought things out before he said anything at all. After Bob Jones became somewhat incapacitated because of his illness, Cliff did an excellent job of conducting the tournament and seeing to it that things gradually improved. One year, they had put out the gallery ropes—this was when they first started roping the golf course off like they do now—and the ropes were all white. I was out on the course with Cliff, and he looked around at the white ropes and said, "That doesn't go in this place at all. The ropes should be green." This was just before the tournament was to start, but in a couple of days, the ropes were changed to a twist of white and green. That was a big improvement;

you could see them all right, but they didn't stand out so much. Cliff was always alert to seeing that everything was done right.

I also recall one time during the early years when admission to the Masters was very cheap—three dollars—and there had been a big discussion about it. Cliff wanted to raise the fee to five dollars, but the others on the tournament improvements committee said that was too much. Then Cliff said, "We went to New York recently and saw Beau Jack fight. [Beau Jack was a shoeshine boy in the locker room at Augusta who some of the members had backed financially to further his boxing career.] We had ringside seats to watch just two men in a prize fight. Here, you've got a field of the best golfers in the world, and the people are paying just three dollars while we paid fifty dollars for those ringside seats. That's ridiculous." They agreed with him then and raised the ticket price to five dollars.

In those days the Masters was still small enough that everyone drove down Magnolia Lane to the clubhouse and then to the parking lots. One morning during that year's tournament, I happened to walk out on to the porch and folks were coming in, just streaming down Magnolia Lane. Cliff was standing there, and he smiled at me as he watched the people driving by and said, "five dollars, five dollars, five dollars. . . ."

Quite a few years later, Cliff spent a night at our ranch on his way back to Augusta from California. We had dinner and talked until late in the evening. He asked me quite a few questions about my ranch, what I'd paid for it and other things, and the next day I took him to the airport and didn't think any more about it.

Well, some time after that I got a call from Cliff at 10:30 at night. He was in Freeport in the Bahamas, so it was 11:30 where he was. He said, "I understand that Mr. Hogan is building a golf course about three miles from you." I said, "Yes, that's right." And he said, "I understand they have 2500 acres and they paid $3500 an acre for it." I replied, "That's right, too, Cliff." Then he said, "I remember you telling me you paid $82 an acre for your ranch in '46." And I said, "Your memory's very good, Cliff." Then there was a long pause. Finally, he said, "Remind me to treat you with more respect."

Barbara Romack. Back in the mid-fifties I was in Sacramento visiting my friend Tommy Lopresti who was pro at Hagen Oaks. He said, "Byron, I have a little fourteen-year-old towheaded girl out on the course playing with a bunch of boys. I've been trying to get her to change her grip a little and she won't listen to me, but I think she'll listen to you." I said okay, so we got in his car, went out, and found her. She had on blue jeans rolled up above her knees and a shirt with the sleeves rolled up. She looked like a real tomboy, but she also had a good-looking swing. We watched her play a couple of holes and when she came in, Tommy and I talked to her about her grip. I liked Barbara right away, she had a very warm, pleasing personality, and fortunately she did listen to what I had to say. A few years went by and I didn't see anything more of her until she turned pro, and then one day I saw an article in the paper where she'd won an award for being the best-dressed lady on the LPGA tour, so she apparently wasn't such a tomboy anymore.

One year, the LPGA began playing a tournament in Dallas at Glen Lakes Country Club and Barbara contacted me. I helped her a little then, and the next year I worked with her quite a lot over at Brookhollow Golf Club in Dallas. After we'd practiced, she and I would play with some of my men friends. We'd play from the men's tees, she'd shoot 75, and since she liked to bet a little bit, she'd always take some of their money. Then she'd turn around, go play in the ladies' tournament from the white tees and shoot in the high 70's or low 80's. I'd say, "Barbara, how can you shoot 75 from the men's tees at Brookhollow and then not do nearly as well when you play with the ladies?" She told me, "I learned to play with men most of the time, and it's so different playing with women that I just haven't gotten used to it. They talk so much it drives me crazy sometimes!" I still get a card from her every Christmas, and she's doing a lot of teaching at Atlantis, Florida, so I'm sure she's doing well and still dressing great.

Gene Sarazen. When I first started on the tour, Gene was very active in golf and very outspoken. I had come on the tour with a new style of play where I used my feet and legs a lot. He said then, "Byron will never make a good player because he has too much movement in his knees and legs." I never resented it because he hadn't learned to play the way I did and no one else was doing it besides me, so I understood why he said it. I've played a lot of golf with Gene, and always respected his ability, since he's one of only four players in the history of the game who have won the modern or professional

"Grand Slam"—the Masters, the PGA, and the U.S. and British Opens.

For quite some time after I first knew Gene, I never saw him wearing anything except knickers, which of course look quite good on him. But I began to wonder why he never wore slacks at all, and then one time I did see him in a suit and I figured it out. Gene is quite short, but somehow knickers make him look taller, while a suit seems to emphasize his small stature. But he was always plenty big enough to beat just about anybody when he wanted to.

Everyone knows about Sarazen's double eagle at Augusta in 1935, but very few people really saw it happen. Today Gene says he's been told by at least 25,000 people that they saw it, but we both know there were only about 5000 people total in the gallery that day and not all of them were following him, because Craig Wood was leading and was in the clubhouse. However, I was one of the few who did get to see Gene's shot. It was my first Masters ever, and I was playing 17 while Gene was on 15 and the two fairways ran parallel to each other. I had driven to the right and had to wait to hit my second shot till Gene hit his and his gallery moved out of the way. Naturally I watched Gene's shot, because I was excited to have the opportunity to see him play, so I did actually see his ball go in the hole. The unfortunate thing was that Craig Wood thought he had it won, because he was three shots ahead of Gene. But after the fifteenth hole Gene parred in and tied him, and then won the playoff.

Gene, Sam Snead, and I were invited to be the honorary starters for the Masters a few years ago. We were going along all right the first few holes, though Snead had mentioned his back was bothering him some on the first tee. I really thought he was trying to hit the ball too hard, and then he really flinched on his tee shot at the fourth hole. Finally, when he hit his drive on 5, his back went out completely and he could hardly move. He said, "I've got to quit," got in the cart, and went back to the clubhouse. So Gene and I finished the fifth hole and were walking to the sixth tee when Gene said, "We're doing pretty well, Byron. We've played five holes and only had one casualty."

This past spring, 1992, we were on the first tee again. Sam had had an automobile accident and hurt his shoulder so he couldn't play, and I hadn't played in two years because of my hip surgery. But Gene, who's ninety, was in great shape. He warned us, "I'm only going to hit one shot," stepped up and hit it absolutely perfect 180 yards straight down the center. He turned to us and said, "That's the best drive I've hit this year!"

Chris Schenkel. Playing golf with Chris was always fun. He never once worked on his game, but had a good grip and was the fastest golfer I ever played with, faster even than Chi Chi Rodriguez, and just about that fat, too. Chris would tee it up and hit it almost before you could get out of his way. If he'd ever had time to work on it, he would have made a pretty good player. He had good coordination, but because he didn't work on it, he'd hit that old banana ball a lot. Of all the friends I made in golf, Chris is the closest. He likes me a lot and has always done and said so many nice things it almost embarrasses me, but I love it.

In 1984, Abilene Christian University started a golf endowment fund in my and Louise's name. They had a huge party at the Anatole in Dallas with over 1200 people, and Chris was the master of ceremonies. I'll never forget as long as I live when he said, "I have one last, heartfelt wish, and that is this: If the Lord would grant me another brother, I'd want him to be you." Thank you, Chris.

Randolph Scott. Besides being one of my favorite actors, Randy Scott loved golf and was a beautiful player with a wonderful putting stroke. One year we played in the Pro-Am at Thunderbird in Palm Springs before it became the Bob Hope tournament, and Randy shot the easiest 68 you could imagine. Randy was always so nice and conducted himself so well; in fact, he was one of the few actors ever allowed to be a member of the Los Angeles Country Club. One day I was playing there on the south course with Randy, Lee Davis, and my good friend J.K. Wadley, and I shot 61—a course record at the time. I must have learned something from watching Randy putt, because I did putt very well that day.

Lefty Stackhouse. Lefty was in some ways the most unusual golfer that I ever knew. He had an almost uncontrollable temper when he played golf, and the peculiar thing was that he actually was a good player. But as soon as he'd miss a shot or do something he considered stupid, he'd get so mad that he'd actually do himself bodily harm. I was playing with him in the Odessa Pro-Am one year, and Lefty's partner was Billy Erfurth, the Texas State Amateur Champion. We were playing best-ball and on the eighth hole, Lefty was just short of the green, while Billy was nicely on. Lefty decided to pick his ball up and let Billy play the hole, but Billy three-putted. Then Lefty realized that if he'd continued to play, he could have chipped close and made par. He was so mad he hit himself with his fist on the side of his cheek, which bled considerably; he had to go in and get bandaged up. There were many stories like that and worse about Lefty, and it was a shame because he really was a good player.

I always wondered what caused him to do this, but after he quit trying to play golf on the tour or compete in any kind of tournament, he became very quiet and good-natured. He went on to do more work for the juniors in his area down around Seguin, Texas, than anyone I ever heard of. Obviously the reason he got so mad was that competition put so much stress on him, because he never did it after he quit playing in tournaments.

Payne Stewart. One of my favorite golfers because he looks so great in the outfits he wears, and I think that's really good for the game. I also like Payne because of the way he came back and won my tournament after losing in a playoff several years before that. A few years ago, I played with Payne, D.A. Weibring, and Bruce Lietzke in Quincy, Illinois. It was a fun exhibition and I was holding my own all right, which was kind of a surprise. On the last hole, Payne was twenty feet away and I was fifteen. He nonchalantly knocked his in for birdie, then smiled at me and said, "That just made yours longer, Byron." As luck would have it, I made mine right on top of his, so we both got a kick out of that.

Ed Sullivan. Ed loved to play golf but he was extremely slow, slower than Roone Arledge ever thought of being. He was bad about taking several practice swings, getting over the ball, then moving away from it and starting over. What's more, he was always talking; he never acted like he was thinking about golf at all. Everybody playing with him would say, "Come on, Ed, it's your turn," but he never seemed to get much better. He was such a good guy, though, that you couldn't help but like him.

Ken Venturi. One of the reasons Kenny's short game is so good is his bunker play, and he and I both learned that from Eddie Lowery. We were at Palm Springs, where I was working with Kenny one time, and back of Eddie's house was a green and a sand bunker which he and three neighbors had paid to have built there. Guess they played a little golf, too. Anyway, one evening after dinner Eddie, who was about an 8-handicapper, challenged us, "I'll play your best ball out of the bunker, twenty-five cents a shot." We did this three evenings in a row and lost a lot of quarters, but from then on we both became excellent bunker players, thanks to Eddie. He really was phenomenal out of the sand, and when we asked him how he got so good at it he said, "I had to learn how to play out of bunkers because I used to be in so many of them."

Johnny Weissmuller. Johnny was almost as much fun on a golf course as he was in his Tarzan movies, because he was always getting in trouble. Johnny could hit the ball a long ways, but a lot of times it went the wrong direction. When he hit a good one, though, he'd do his Tarzan yell and you could hear it all across the golf course. The first time I played with him was in the 1938 Crosby at Rancho Santa Fe; it was a big thrill for me after seeing him in the movies. Also, in case I haven't mentioned it already, Johnny joined Bing and Bob and me on many of those Red Cross and war bond exhibitions during the war. It was a lot of hard travel and hard work, but we had a great time doing it together.

Lawrence Welk. The most amazing thing about playing golf with Lawrence Welk was that he never started playing golf till he was sixty-two, but still did remarkably well for having started that late in life. You remember that when leading his orchestra he'd always go "a-one and a-two," and he did the same thing on the golf course. He'd take one quick little practice swing, then another quick little practice swing, and then he'd hit, using the same rhythm as he did in his music. Years ago, we played a charity tournament in Nashville, Tennessee. It was me, Lawrence, and Minnie Pearl, and it was really fun. Minnie played a pretty fair game, but what I liked was that she was just as funny on the golf course as she is on stage. My brother Charles was living in Nashville then and came out to watch us play. Lawrence really got a kick out of meeting him and was impressed enough by his voice to invite Charles on his show to sing a little while after that. Another time I played with Lawrence at Bel Air in Los Angeles, along with the comedy team Shipstad and Johnson, and you couldn't hardly play golf for laughing. They didn't care whether they had a four or an eight on a hole, and it was mostly somewhere in between.

Kathy Whitworth. The first time I saw Kathy play was when I was working for ABC. I was impressed first of all by the fact that all of her fundamentals were excellent—grip, stance, swing, the way she stayed down to the ball, everything. You couldn't win eighty-eight tournaments as she has without having all those things right. The second thing that impresses me about Kathy, though, is that she has always been a real lady. I've never heard anyone say a single thing against her. She now lives two miles east of me at Trophy Club, Texas, and I see her at the local grocery store or the post office every now and then. It's always good to see her and realize what she has done for women's golf.

Craig Wood. Craig, who by the way was pro at Winged Foot when he played on the tour, was called the "Blond Bomber." He was a very natty dresser, and always drove a fancy car, but he did a lot more than just look good. I played with and against Craig in many tournaments, and I always knew that if I were to beat him I really had to play my absolute best. Because of the '35 Masters and the '39 Open, it seemed for a while that something unlucky always happened to him, kind of like Greg Norman today. But in 1941 Craig won both the Masters and the U.S. Open at Colonial in Fort Worth, so it apparently didn't bother him too much.

People used to feel sorry for Craig because of what happened to him in the '35 Masters. He was already in the clubhouse and they had taken him into the so-called "Champion's Room" with Gene Sarazen and I and a few others still out on the course. Sarazen was the closest to Craig, but he was still three shots back and no one thought there was any chance he could catch up, when he made that wonderful double eagle on the fifteenth hole. Sarazen went three under right there and tied Craig, then beat him in the playoff the next day. But Craig never grumbled. Then in the '39 U.S. Open, when I had that eagle two on the fourth hole, he just said to me, "That was a fine shot, Byron," and kept on playing his best, trying to win. He was a fine player and a gentleman, and it was a shame he died at a relatively young age.

Mickey Wright. Mickey was one of the best ball strikers and had the best golf swing of anyone I ever saw, man or woman. She played so well and won so often she got kind of bored with it and left the tour early. Besides, just like on the men's tour when I quit, the ladies weren't making much money in the sixties, so Mickey decided to do something else and became a stockbroker.

When Chris and I were broadcasting the Women's Open at Pensacola, I rode out to the course with Mickey and some other ladies during one of the practice rounds. I was going out to study the course for the broadcast, and during the ride I asked Mickey how she was playing. She said, "Byron, I'm playing terrible." I said, "I can't believe that, Mickey," and she said, "How much time do you have?" So I watched her play the first nine, and she hit it dead solid, the middle of every fairway and every green except for the last hole, when she pushed her 4-iron about four feet to the right of the green and almost chipped it in. When she finished I went over to her and said, "Yes, Mickey, I see how badly you're playing." She smiled then and protested, "But I only made one birdie, Byron!" That's how much of a perfectionist she was.

One time, during the ladies' tournament at Glen Lakes in Dallas, Mickey arranged an exhibition with her coach Earl Stewart, Marilynn Smith, and me, playing an 18-hole match for charity. The ladies played from their tees and Earl and I from the men's, and Mickey put her ball inside of Earl and me all day long. Marilynn played very well also, but fortunately I made a couple of putts at the end and we eked it out, two up. It was a close thing, and I said to Earl when we were done, "Earl, don't you ever get me in a trap like this again!"

Babe Zaharias. In Texas we call someone like Babe Zaharias "a piece of work," but as brash as she could be at times, she sure did have the talent to back it up. I first heard about her when she was fourteen and was running in a track-and-field event in Fort Worth. Babe ran in all the girls' events and won every one, then started competing in the boys' events, but the officials wouldn't allow it. If they had, I'm sure she would have won at least a few of those events too, because she was one of the greatest athletes the world has ever known.

When she took up golf, people said, "This is one game the Babe won't be so good at." But they didn't know her. She practiced till her hands bled and goodness alive, she could play—and she had such perfect balance. In the late thirties I saw her play against Leonard Dotson at St. Augustine, Florida. They had a bet going and set up this kind of crazy match where they had to play each shot standing on just one foot. Try it sometime. Anyway, Babe shot 75 and won easily, and if that doesn't prove something, I don't know what does.

ELEVEN

Today

As I said at the beginning of this book, I am a blessed man. I was born into a loving family, married a wonderful woman, and was very fortunate to do all I did in golf—playing, teaching, broadcasting, and even helping build golf courses. You would think that as I got older my life would have slowed down, but it seemed to get still busier. By the time I turned seventy, I was still running a few cattle on the ranch, being involved in my own tournament, playing in an occasional charity or celebrity event around the country, giving clinics, traveling to the majors and a few other tournaments, and even doing a little woodworking.

Louise was happy, too. She'd continued to fix up our home till she'd gotten it about where she wanted it, and finally was getting to spend a lot of time with her family, who by now all lived in Fort Worth. We weren't doing a lot of traveling, but most of what we did do we did together, and we enjoyed it. One of our favorite trips always was to the Masters, and on April 1, 1983, that was where we were planning to go next.

It was Good Friday; we were to leave for Augusta the following Monday. Louise had already laid out all the clothes we would need, and we were both looking forward to seeing our many friends there. A month before, Louise had been feeling a little tired and had a checkup, but the doctors hadn't found anything, and for all the past week she'd been feeling fine. Late that afternoon, both of us were doing chores and running errands so we'd be ready for our trip. Louise had gone to the post office in town just a mile away, and I was working at my desk. About the time I expected her back, something made me look out the window, and that's when I saw Louise's car in the ditch in the front of our house. The wind was blowing very hard that day, as much as sixty miles per hour, and at first I thought maybe the wind had blown her car off the road. I jumped up and ran out the door—it seemed like my feet only hit the ground twice getting to her. The car was kind of sideways up against the fence, and Louise's door was still closed when I came up. I yanked the door open and said, "What's wrong, honey?" But as soon as I saw her face I knew something was very wrong. She never moved or looked at me. The only thing moving was her left foot and left hand, and I knew she'd had a stroke. Apparently, it had happened just as she started to turn into the driveway. I yelled next door to my sister and brother-in-law to call an ambulance, then went with her to the hospital and stayed that night.

Our family physician, Dr. Jim Murphy, called in a neurosurgeon right away, and the two of them told me Louise's condition was very serious and they might have to operate. At first they thought she'd had an aneurysm, but after they'd taken X-rays, they determined it was a very serious stroke and she would probably not live more than two weeks. Well, Louise did live, but after a few weeks the doctors said she'd probably never know me or anything else. She continued to improve, though, and then they told me, "She'll know you, Byron, but her disposition will change—she'll never be like she was." By this time, Louise had survived a month and four days, and they were amazed, because the damage to the left side of her brain was so severe. Once it was clear she was going to live, they moved her to the rehabilitation unit of Harris Hospital, which was the best rehab area for stroke victims in Fort Worth, and she was there four months. During all that time and throughout her therapy, she never was able to speak again, except to say, over and over, "Home, home, home." The head of the unit, Dr. Bickel, finally told me they'd keep her another six weeks and after that they wouldn't be able to help her any more.

When it was time for Louise to come home, her primary nurse, Linda Buchanan, and Dr. Bickel, head of the rehab unit, came to our house and determined what changes I would need to make to take care of Louise properly. We had to have ramps built so her wheelchair could navigate the several floor levels we had, we made our master bedroom into a room just for Louise, complete with a hospital bed and so forth, and I hired two nurses who worked alternating week-long 24-hour shifts. Fortunately, we had just added a wonderful garden room to our home the year before, and it was there that my beautiful Louise spent most of her time after she came home from the hospital.

When she did come home, it was very hard for her to adjust to the realization that she was always going to be paralyzed and unable to talk. She had loved to cook so much and was such a good cook, but she never went back into her kitchen again, and one day, shortly after I brought her home, I found her crying and pushing her wheelchair in circles all around our dining room table. She did it for the longest time, until she just plain wore herself out. After that, she gradually got to where she accepted things as they were, but it was so sad to see her that way.

Though Louise never spoke again except to say, "Home," she did sing once or twice when we went to church shortly after I brought her home, but then she apparently had another small stroke and never sang again. She learned to feed herself, but could never write or walk, and pretty much needed to be cared for totally. Yet her personality didn't really change that much. She was still there, although it was like she was in a prison, and her main way of communicating was through me. Even though she couldn't talk, we had been married so long and were so close to each other that I could nearly always figure out what she wanted or needed. One time, about the middle of the summer, she was trying very hard to communicate something to me when I finally realized she wanted to go to our favorite fruit farm in Weatherford, about forty-five miles away, for fresh peaches. Another time, she wanted to visit her niece, Sandy, in Fort Worth. It made me feel good to know I could help her in those ways, because there was so little else I really could do, though I took care of her myself at times on weekends or when one of the nurses was sick.

In many ways, Louise's mind was still quite normal, yet in other ways she became very fearful, probably because of having to be so dependent on everyone else and having no way to communicate. She became very fearful of fire, for instance. That first fall, as soon as it got cold, I started to build a fire in the den, because we had always enjoyed having a cozy little fire of an evening. But Louise became so agitated I had to put it out, and never even tried to have a fire the whole rest of the time she was alive. She also would get quite worried in the car. The Salesmanship Club had very kindly given me a special van with a hydraulic lift for Louise's wheelchair, but although she was strapped in very securely, she would still watch the speedometer closely and let me know right away if she thought I was going too fast.

To their everlasting credit, our best friends stayed in close touch. For instance, Jim and Betty Chambers came over from Dallas nearly every Sunday afternoon and visited with us. Also, Chris Schenkel and Tom Watson came to see Louise quite often during her illness, and I can never thank them enough for taking so much trouble. Louise always recognized everyone and was happy to see them. Sometimes it was frustrating for her not to be able to talk, though Chris and Tom would talk to her as though she could, which wasn't easy for them to do. Chris was excellent at it, and she really enjoyed that.

But after spending five months in the hospital and rehab, Louise never really made any more progress. She lived for twenty-five months more. Then, on September 14, 1985, she had another very bad stroke while sitting in our garden room just after breakfast one morning. I rushed her to the hospital, but after waiting several days, the doctors said she was now brain-dead and there was no chance for recovery at all. Now came the hardest decision of my life—telling the doctors to disconnect the life support systems they had Louise on. She and I had talked about this situation years before and had both agreed we didn't want to be kept alive that way, but it still is a difficult thing to do. Even so, it was amazing how strong her body was physically, because she lived another two weeks and finally died October 4, 1985. I still went to visit her every day and sat holding her hand when she died. We had been married fifty years and four months.

You know, I don't think it's possible for a man to be as successful as I was and not have a wife like Louise to help support me through the bad times as well as the good ones. It must have been very difficult for her during my streak, for example, because I was going through so much. She never said "I wish it would end," even though I knew all the pressure I was having was affecting her, too. In my earlier career, too, she always seemed to know when I needed encouragement and when I needed a little push—when to be politely forward enough to get me to do what I should to become a better player and a better person. She never minded being "Mrs. Byron Nelson" and taking a back seat regarding all the publicity I was getting, but I was so eternally grateful when the ladies of the Byron Nelson Classic gave her a party one year. It showed Louise that they understood how important she was to me, but more important, that they loved and appreciated her for herself, not just because she happened to be my wife. Another thing that happened along this line was that Abilene Christian University established a golf scholarship endowment fund in both our names, and gave an enormous party for us to get it started. It made both of us feel very good—there were over twelve hundred people, and it was a wonderful evening.

Of course, Louise's illness wasn't easy for me, either. It was hard to feel so helpless. I did everything I could for her and was glad to have the opportunity to make up for all the years when she had sacrificed so much for me, but there was only so much I could do. The strain of it all made me start to lose weight, and when I got down to 160 Dr. Murphy told me I had to do something about it or I'd end up in the hospital too. I had prayed and all the church and our friends were praying for me, but nothing seemed to help much until one day I decided to go for a walk. I took off and went a mile or so down our country road, and by the time I got back I felt better. I began to walk nearly every day, and besides being good exercise, it seemed to give me more of a sense of having some control over my life again. I started to eat better and put on a little weight, and all of that helped me take better care of Louise.

But after she died, I felt so lost. Now I had no one to take care of and it didn't seem like I had much reason to go on living. I started to go downhill again, losing weight and pretty much just feeling sorry for myself. Once again, Dr. Murphy told me, "Byron, we're going to have to get you turned around some way, or we're going to lose you." But I didn't care a whole lot one way or the other, till one day the next March, when I got a call from my good friend Cy Laughter.

Cy ran a tournament in Dayton, Ohio, called the Bogie Busters, sort of a fun tournament with some celebrities like Johnny Bench and

Glen Campbell, President Gerald Ford, and quite a few well-known people in business and politics from around the country. I had gone to it several times before, and when Cy invited me to be his special guest, I agreed to go.

As soon as I hung up the phone, I remembered a young woman I'd met the last time I was at Cy's tournament, in 1981. Her name was Peggy Simmons, and she was an advertising writer. She had impressed me, though at that time she was just starting to play golf and didn't really know a lot about it. We'd talked quite a bit at the course the two days of Cy's tournament, and she had sent me a nice note afterwards, telling me she'd appreciated getting to meet me. That was in 1981, and I'd never seen or even thought about her again until I got that call from Cy in March of '86, five years later.

Well, I had an idea I'd like to have her come out to see me play again, so I dug up her address and wrote to her. She wrote back, then I called her, and pretty soon we were writing and calling every day, nearly. Six months later she moved to Texas, and we were married on November 15. Living with Peggy has been a great joy for me. Despite the difference in our ages—nearly thirty-three years—and our different backgrounds, we get along amazingly well and have a lot of fun together. I've helped her improve her golf game so much that now she's about a 15 handicap, so I refuse to give her any strokes, and I have to work hard to stay ahead of her.

I truly feel that if it hadn't been for Peggy, I wouldn't be alive today, and many of our friends tell me the same thing. She had led a pretty quiet life before, so being married to me was quite a change, but she's adjusted very well to being the wife of this old broken-down pro. I just hope we'll have a lot of years together, because I'm enjoying every moment of it.

At least, I'm enjoying every moment when I'm not being operated on. I've had two hip surgeries in the past two years, cataract surgery, a hernia repair, and my eyelids fixed because they were drooping so much I was having trouble seeing. In addition to all that, I also managed to cut a finger off out in my shop, doing some woodworking. The doctor sewed it back on, fortunately. It made me a lot more cautious in my shop, but it wasn't enough to make me quit.

I'd started fooling around with wood about 1976, and my first projects weren't much to look at. But I kept at it, studied some books, talked to some friends, and with constant encouragement, first from Louise and now from Peggy, I've improved a little. Grandfather Allen, my mother's father, was a carpenter and helped build some of the homes in Waxahachie that are now on the city's historic homes tour each year, so that must be where I got it from. I still struggle with it, but I have made some nice things over the years—teak trivets, cherry end tables, an oak barrister's bookcase, parquet top tables, koa wood serving trays, honduras mahogany hope chests, and a lot of other things. I've never gone in for carving or fancy work because I don't have that kind of talent and my hands are too big to do a lot of detail work, but I enjoy making useful things and especially Christmas presents for our friends. Really, most of the time I'd rather do woodwork than play golf anymore, because I can't play golf all that well these days and when I do play, it makes me hurt just about everywhere. But when I work in my shop, I have something to show for my time, and beautiful wood is really satisfying to work with. I love it.

Since the late fifties I've also had occasion to help design several golf courses—kind of a third profession and one I've enjoyed quite a bit. Not that I could actually design one all by myself—I have no engineering background, and there's a lot of that involved—but after playing golf for sixty-five years I've observed some things about what makes a really good golf course, and I'll work with the architect on all phases of the layout, the direction of the holes, the size of the greens, and things like that. Well, eventually someone thought because I'd played pretty good golf about a hundred years ago, I might have something to contribute in that area. I've worked on quite a few throughout the country, many with my good friend Joe Finger, but my favorite golf course involves the work I'm proudest of.

It all began in 1978, when I was at Augusta for the Masters. I was on the General Improvements Committee, and during our meeting the subject of the par-five eighth hole came up. You see, Cliff Roberts had died in 1977, but quite a few years before his death he had decided to change the eighth green. He didn't like the mounds around the green because he felt they made it too hard for spectators to see the play. These weren't viewing mounds like on today's stadium courses; they were small but strategic mounds the player had to work around for his approach shot. Cliff had those mounds almost completely flattened, and the result was that it ruined the hole. He realized it himself eventually, and before he died he said that he wished they would put it back the way it used to be.

The only problem was no one could remember what the original green looked like, nor could anybody find any pictures of it. They'd asked several of the players, and one thought there had been a bunker or two, one thought something else, but no one was sure at all. Then they asked me. I described it to them and I was quite sure I remembered it exactly, so they offered me the job of developing a scale model of the hole and bringing it back the next spring to show them.

When I got home, I called Joe Finger and told him what I'd gotten myself into, and fortunately he was willing to help. We were working on another course at the time, so when he came up for that project, we sat down and he started drawing a picture of the green as I described it. Then we got Baxter Spann, one of Joe's partners and an expert at building models, to go to work on it, and the next spring, back we went to Augusta. When we showed our model to the committee, they said, "Go ahead." As soon as the course closed at the beginning of the summer we went to work, and in six weeks, we had it all ready—the mounds all around the left and back of the green exactly like I remembered it.

One day the men were just putting on the finishing touches and spreading the grass seed when we looked up and here came Frank Christian, the photographer for the club, in his car. Frank's father had been the club photographer before him, and when he reached us, Frank said, "I found a picture of the old green up in my attic!" Joe and I just stared at each other. Then Joe took the picture from Frank, looked at it, looked at the green, looked back at the picture, and said, "I don't believe it—it's exactly the same!" Fortunately, that was one time my memory worked pretty well. It would have been a lot easier on us if Frank had found that picture sooner, but if he had, we might not have gotten the job and I wouldn't have this story to tell.

Today my life is still busy. Sometimes it's busier than I want it to be, so I'm having to say no to people quite a lot, but when you're this old there's only so much energy left, and I simply can't do everything I used to be able to do. In the past few years, however, I've been given quite a few honors that I never expected or dreamed of, and though it meant a lot of travel, it was fun and made me feel very good. First, in

1990, my friend Buddy Langley wanted to celebrate the forty-fifth anniversary of my streak in '45. Buddy was head of GTE Southwest at the time, and of course GTE has been our tournament's title sponsor for the past several years. Buddy happened to be a member at Hope Valley Country Club in Durham, North Carolina, where I'd won the fourth tournament in the streak, so he got together with them and they invited folks from all of the clubs where I had won the other ten tournaments to come for the party. It was great—there were people from Montreal, Atlanta, Philadelphia, Toronto, Dayton, and the Carolinas. They even put up a wonderful plaque for me at the 18th tee, that great little par three where I made those birdies.

Also, I was asked that year to be Honorary Chairman for the U.S. Senior Open at Ridgewood, my old stompin' ground, and it was a great feeling to go back there. They gave a wonderful party for me one night and a lot of the senior pros came and said so many nice things about me it was almost embarrassing. But I have to admit I enjoyed it.

Then in May of '91, USGA's Golf House museum did a special exhibit of my life, calling me golf's "master craftsman." They not only displayed all my trophies and golf memorabilia, but also some of my woodworking projects, which really surprised and pleased me. It was a lot of work for us and the Golf House staff to collect all the stuff for the display, but while we were doing it, we came across an old spelling test book I had from the fifth grade. I was a pretty good speller back then, and we noticed there were quite a few 100's in that little old book, so we got to counting them. Turns out I had an even longer streak of wins than my eleven in a row in golf, because when I was in the fifth grade, I had thirty-seven straight 100's in spelling. I'm not sure I could spell all those words right today, in fact.

Now I'm eighty, almost eighty-one. Except for a sore hip and some arthritis in various places, I have excellent health and still manage to get around all right. Peggy and I travel a little, go to the majors, play golf together, take a vacation now and then, and also spend time at our home in Kerrville whenever we can. I sign more autographs now than I did when I won all those tournaments in '45, and when I look back on it all, I'm completely amazed at all that has happened to me.

I hope this book answers some of the questions I'm asked so often. No, I didn't have hemophilia or bleeding ulcers, and I left the tour because I wanted to, not because of "poor health," as is even stated in the *Encyclopedia Britannica,* I discovered recently. I've had a wonderful life with many blessings, and I guess the best one came on my birthday last year, when the Four Seasons Resort where my tournament is held gave me a tremendous party. My buddy Chris Schenkel was the emcee and we invited about 150 of our family and closest friends. We had a wonderful dinner, then a beautiful birthday cake with fireworks on it, and for the climax, they unveiled the nine-foot bronze statue of me by Robert Summers, which now stands near the first tee. It makes me feel so humble, because I feel I can never be as good as people think I am. But I try hard to be a Christian and do right, and all I can really do is to say "Thank you."

APPENDIX

The Records of Byron Nelson

BYRON NELSON'S AMATEUR RECORD

1928—Winner, Glen Garden CC Caddie Championship over Ben Hogan in 9-hole playoff

1928—Winner, Katy Lake Amateur, Fort Worth, Texas

1929—Runner-up in Fort Worth City Amateur, Meadowbrook Municipal GC, Fort Worth, Texas

1930—Winner, Southwestern Amateur, Nichols Hills G&CC, Oklahoma City, Oklahoma

1931—Failed to qualify by one shot in USGA National Amateur, Beverly CC, Chicago, Illinois

BYRON NELSON ON TOUR

Event	Finish	Score	Won	Purse	Winner
1932					
Texarkana*	3	296	$ 75	$ 500	Ted Longworth
1933					
Los Angeles	T-16	294	$ 34.50	N/A	Craig Wood
Western	T-7	295	N/A	N/A	Macdonald Smith
1934					
Los Angeles	T-26	297	$ 36	$5,489	Macdonald Smith
San Francisco Match Play		Qualified with 72			
Lost second round to Bill Mehlhorn			$ 55.75	$4,049	Tom Creary
Agua Caliente (Mexico)*	T-23	294	$ 33	$7,274	Wiffy Cox
Texas Open	T-2	284	$ 325	$2,346	Wiffy Cox
Galveston	2nd	293	$ 325	$1,849	Craig Wood
U.S. Open	MC	162	$ 0	$5,000	Olin Dutra

Event	Finish	Score	Won	Purse	Winner
1935					
Riverside Pro-Am*	T-2	64	$ 137	$992	Charles Guest Al Barbee
San Francisco Match Play					
1st round—Defeated Lawson Little, 5 & 4					
2nd round—Defeated Vic Ghezzi, 4 & 3					
Quarterfinal—Lost to Harold McSpaden, 5 & 4			$ 150	$3,250	Harold McSpaden
Agua Caliente (Mexico)*	T-6	291	$ 257	$5,175	Henry Picard
Phoenix	T-10	290	$ 75	$2,373	Ky Laffoon
Charleston	6	284	$ 100	$2,750	Henry Picard
North & South	12	292	$ 65	$3,951	Paul Runyan
Atlanta (54 holes)	3	215	$ 250	$2,000	Henry Picard
Augusta National Invitation (Masters)	T-9	291	$ 137	$5,000	Gene Sarazen
Metropolitan Open	OM	306	$ 0	$1,250	Henry Picard
U.S. Open	T-32	315	$ 0	$5,000	Sam Parks, Jr.
Western Open	3	296	$ 200	$2,153	Johnny Revolta
Medinah	T-12	301	$ 62	$2,150	Harry Cooper
General Brock Open	T-2	292	$ 600	$4,000	Tony Manero
New Jersey*	1	288	$ 400	$1,500	Nelson
Hershey	T-6	296	$ 143	$3,829	Ted Luther
Glen Falls	T-12	290	$ 56	$3,500	Willie MacFarlane
Baltimore	T-10	295	$ 25	$2,374	Vic Ghezzi
Louisville	T-4	289	$ 362	$5,000	Paul Runyan
Miami Biltmore	T-29	294	$ 37	$9,888	Horton Smith
1936					
Riverside	T-3	286	$ 300	$3,000	Jimmy Hines
Los Angeles	7	287	$ 200	$5,000	Jimmy Hines
Sacramento	3	287	$ 350	$3,000	Wiffy Cox
San Francisco Match Play	DNQ	147	$ 52.50	$4,479	Willie Hunter
Catalina (Short course–Par 66)	T-6	259	$ 208.33	$5,000	Willie Hunter
St. Petersburg	T-8	292	$ 55	$2,500	Leonard Dodson
St. Augustine Pro-Am*	Won 1 match		$ 50	$2,300	Sarazen-Reynolds
Charleston	T-11	296	$ 75	$3,000	Henry Picard

Event	Finish	Score	Won	Purse	Winner
Augusta National Invitation (Masters)	T-12	298	$ 50	$5,000	Horton Smith
Metropolitan Open	1	283	$ 750	$5,000	Nelson
U.S. Open	MC	153	$ 0	$5,000	Tony Manero
Shawnee	T-4	290	$ 226	$4,000	Ed Dudley
General Brock Open	10	296	$ 140	$4,100	Craig Wood
Western Open	3	278	$ 200	$2,145	Ralph Guldahl
St. Paul	T-5	281	$ 306	$5,248	Harry Cooper
Vancouver	T-2	278	$ 975	$4,994	Ken Black
Victoria	2	272	$ 450	$3,000	Horton Smith
Seattle	7	293	$ 270	$4,996	Macdonald Smith
Portland	T-7	282	$ 250	$5,054	Ray Mangrum
Glen Falls	3	284	$ 400	$3,700	Jimmy Hines
Hershey	T-9	293	$ 180	$5,000	Henry Picard
Canadian Open	T-10	287	$ 41.66	$3,000	Lawson Little
Augusta	T-13	289	$ 86	$5,000	Ralph Guldahl

1937

Event	Finish	Score	Won	Purse	Winner
Los Angeles	T-9	285	$ 75	$7,905	Harry Cooper
Sacramento	6	287	$ 140	$3,000	Ed Dudley
San Francisco Match Play					
1st Round—Defeated Sam Snead, 2 & 1					
2nd Round—Lost to Henry Picard, 3 & 2					
			$ 150	$4,760	Lawson Little
Houston	T-4	285	$ 250	$3,000	Harry Cooper
Thomasville	T-14	292	$ 32	$3,000	Dick Metz
St. Petersburg	T-14	291	$ 15	$3,000	Harry Cooper
Florida West Coast	T-2	289	$ 400	$3,000	Gene Sarazen
Hollywood (Florida)	T-5	277	$ 200	$3,000	Dick Metz
Miami Four-Ball (with McSpaden)	Lost, 1st Round		$ 0	$4,000	Picard-Revolta
North & South	3	292	$ 500	$3,980	Horton Smith
Augusta National Invitation (Masters)	1	283	$1,500	$5,000	Nelson
PGA Championship	Qualifying medalist with 139				
1st round—Defeated Leo Diegel, 2 & 1					
2nd round—Defeated Johnny Farrell, 5 & 4					
3rd round—Defeated Craig Wood, 4 & 2					
Quarterfinals—Lost to Ky Laffoon, 2 down					
			$ 200	$9,200	Denny Shute
U.S. Open	T-20	295	$ 50	$6,000	Ralph Guldahl
British Open	5	296	$ 125	$2,532	Henry Cotton
Central Pennsylvania* (36 holes)	1	140	$ 150	N/A	Nelson (won in playoff)

Event	Finish	Score	Won	Purse	Winner
Hershey	OM	306	$ 0	$ 5,000	Henry Picard
Belmont Match Play	1	—	$3,000	$12,000	Nelson
Miami Biltmore	11	289	$ 125	$10,000	Johnny Revolta
Nassau	T-13	285	$ 47.50	$ 3,500	Sam Snead

1938

Event	Finish	Score	Won	Purse	Winner
Pasadena	3	279	$ 350	$ 3,000	Henry Picard
Sacramento	T-8	294	$ 100	$ 3,000	Johnny Revolta
San Francisco Match Play					
Qualified with 158					
1st round—Lost to Paul Runyan, 1 down			$ 75	$ 5,000	Jimmy Demaret
New Orleans	DNQ	79	$ 0	$ 5,000	Harry Cooper
Thomasville	1	280	$ 700	$ 3,000	Nelson
St. Petersburg	3	283	$ 350	$ 3,000	Johnny Revolta
Hollywood (Florida)	1	275	$ 700	$ 3,000	Nelson
Miami Four-Ball (with McSpaden)					
1st round—Defeated Willie Klein & Johnny Farrell, 1 up					
2nd round—Defeated Frank Moore & Denny Shute, 2 & 1					
Semifinals—Lost to Dick Metz & Ky Laffoon, 3 & 2					
			$ 150	$ 4,000	Metz-Laffoon
North & South	T-3	286	$ 400	$ 4,000	Vic Ghezzi
Masters	5	290	$ 400	$ 5,000	Henry Picard
U.S. Open	T-5	294	$ 412.50	$ 6,000	Ralph Guldahl
PGA Championship					
1st round—Defeated Clarence Yockey, 5 & 4					
2nd round—Defeated Al Krueger, 20 holes					
3rd round—Defeated Harry Bassler, 11 & 10					
Quarterfinals—Lost to Jimmy Hines, 2 & 1					
			$ 250	$10,000	Paul Runyan
Cleveland	T-20	291	$ 100	$10,000	Ky Laffoon
Hershey Four-Ball (with Ed Dudley)	T-3	Even	$ 325	$ 4,600	Ghezzi-Hogan
Westchester (108 holes)	T-3	434	$ 900	$12,500	Sam Snead
Columbia (South Carolina)	T-6	293	$ 0	$ 5,000	Johnny Revolta
Augusta	T-8	288	$ 0	$ 5,000	Craig Wood
Miami	DNQ	—	$ 0	$10,000	Harold McSpaden
Houston (54 holes)	T-5	219	$ 186.66	$ 3,000	Harold McSpaden
Central Pennsylvania* (36 holes)	2	141	$ 90	N/A	N/A

Event	Finish	Score	Won	Purse	Winner
1939					
Los Angeles	T-7	286	$ 129.25	$ 5,500	Jimmy Demaret
Oakland	9	280	$ 230	$ 5,000	Dick Metz
San Francisco Match Play		Qualified with 143			
1st round—Lost to Ben Coltrin, 2 & 1			$ 75	$ 5,000	Dick Metz
Crosby Pro-Am	T-2	139	$ 300	$ 3,000	Dutch Harrison
Phoenix (54 holes)	1	198	$ 700	$ 3,000	Nelson
Texas Open	3	274	$ 550	$ 5,000	Dutch Harrison
New Orleans	T-5	291	$ 650	$10,000	Henry Picard
Thomasville (54 holes)	T-4	215	$ 183.34	$ 3,000	Henry Picard
St. Petersburg (54 holes)	T-4	211	$ 250	$ 3,000	Sam Snead
Miami Four-Ball (with Frank Walsh)					
1st round—Lost to Dutch Harrison & Ray Mangrum, 4 & 2			$ 50	$ 5,000	Snead-Guldahl
North & South	1	280	$1,000	$ 4,000	Nelson
Greensboro	10	290	$ 170	$ 5,000	Ralph Guldahl
Masters	7	287	$ 250	$ 5,000	Ralph Guldahl
U.S. Open	1	284	$1,000	$ 6,000	Nelson
Inverness Four-Ball (with McSpaden)	T-2	Plus 6	$ 425	$ 5,200	Picard-Revolta
Massachusetts Open*	1	283	$ 400	$ 1,500	Nelson
PGA Championship	Qualified with 143				
1st round—Defeated Chuck Garringer, 4 & 2					
2nd round—Defeated Red Francis, 3 & 1					
3rd round—Defeated Johnny Revolta, 6 & 4					
4th round—Defeated Emerick Kocsis, 10 & 9					
5th round—Defeated Dutch Harrison, 9 & 8					
Finals—Lost to Henry Picard on 37th hole			$ 600	$10,600	Henry Picard
Western Open	1	281	$ 750	$ 3,005	Nelson
St. Paul	T-10	281	$ 205	$ 5,003	Dick Metz
Dapper Dan	T-8	291	$ 391.66	$ 9,825	Ralph Guldahl
Hagen Anniversary* (with Dick Metz)	3	Plus 4	$ 375	$ 2,700	Dudley-Burke
Hershey	4	287	$ 450	$10,050	Felix Serafin
Miami	5	278	$ 600	$10,000	Sam Snead

Event	Finish	Score	Won	Purse	Winner
1940					
San Francisco Match Play		Qualified with 144			
1st round—Defeated Rod Francis, 1 up					
2nd round—Defeated Charles Klein, 3 & 2					
Quarterfinals—Lost to Willie Goggin, 3 & 2					
			$ 150	$ 5,000	Jimmy Demaret
Phoenix (54 holes)		215	$ 0	$ 3,000	Ed Oliver
Texas Open	1	271	$1,500	$ 5,000	Nelson
Western Open	WD	78	$ 0	$ 5,000	Jimmy Demaret
New Orleans	T-15	295	$ 146	$10,000	Jimmy Demaret
St. Petersburg (54 holes)	2	212	$ 450	$ 3,000	Jimmy Demaret
Miami Four-Ball (with McSpaden)					
1st round—Defeated Farrell & Serafin, 7 & 6					
2nd round—Lost to Runyan & Smith, 5 & 4					
			$ 75	$ 5,000	Burke-Wood
Thomasville (54 holes)	2	205	$ 450	$ 3,000	Lloyd Mangrum
Greater Greensboro	T-3	280	$ 412.50	$ 5,000	Ben Hogan
Asheville	T-7	284	$ 230	$ 5,000	Ben Hogan
Masters	3	285	$ 600	$ 5,000	Jimmy Demaret
Goodall Round Robin	6	Plus 2	$ 300	$ 5,000	Ben Hogan
Ohio Open*	1	284	$ 250	N/A	Nelson
U.S. Open	T-5	290	$ 325	$ 6,000	Lawson Little
Inverness Four-Ball	T-7	–14	$ 350	$ 4,800	Guldahl-Snead
PGA Championship					
1st round—Defeated Dick Shoemaker, 4 & 3					
2nd round—Defeated Frank Walsh in 20 holes					
3rd round—Defeated Dick Metz, 2 & 1					
Quarterfinal—Defeated Eddie Kirk, 6 & 5					
Semifinal—Defeated Ralph Guldahl, 1 up					
Final—Defeated Sam Snead, 1 up					
			$1,100	$11,050	Nelson
Anthracite Open	2	278	$ 750	$ 5,000	Sam Snead
Miami	1	271	$2,537.50	$10,000	Nelson

(Prize money includes $25 daily award for low round plus one tie.)

Event	Finish	Score	Won	Purse	Winner
1941					
Los Angeles	OM	72-77-75-78-302	$ 0	$10,000	Johnny Bulla
Oakland	OM	290	$ 0	$ 5,000	Leonard Dodson
San Francisco Match Play	DNQ	147	$ 0	$ 5,000	Johnny Revolta
Crosby Pro-Am	T-5	68-71-139	$ 125	$ 3,000	Sam Snead
Western Open	T-2	68-69-67-74-278	$ 600	$ 5,000	Ed Oliver
Texas Open	T-4	71-71-69-71-282	$ 325	$ 5,000	Lawson Little
New Orleans	T-8	75-69-69-72-285	$ 210	$ 5,000	Henry Picard
Thomasville	T-6	73-70-74-217	$ 170	$ 3,000	Harold McSpaden
St. Petersburg	T-13	144-65-77-286	$ 40	$ 5,000	Sam Snead
Miami Four-Ball (with McSpaden)	Lost, 2nd Round		$ 75	$ 5,000	Sarazen-Hogan
Seminole Pro-Am*	1	64-70-134	$ 803.29	N/A	Nelson
Florida West Coast (54 holes)	2	72-67-67-206	$ 450	$ 3,000	Horton Smith
Lost in playoff with Horton Smith, 68-69					
North & South	T-4	69-71-69-76-285	$ 350	$ 4,000	Sam Snead
Greater Greensboro	1	72-64-70-70-276	$1,200	$ 5,000	Nelson
Asheville	T-10	74-76-74-72-296	$ 155	$ 5,000	Ben Hogan
Masters	2	71-69-73-70-283	$ 800	$ 5,000	Craig Wood
U.S. Open	T-17	73-73-74-77-297	$ 50	$ 6,000	Craig Wood
Mahoning Valley	2	67-70-73-67-277	$ 750	$ 5,000	Clayton Heafner
Inverness Four-Ball (with Jimmy Thompson)	2	Plus 8	$ 600	$ 6,000	Hogan-Demaret
PGA Championship	2	N/A	$ 600	$10,600	Vic Ghezzi

Event	Finish	Score	Won	Purse	Winner
St. Paul	T-7	73-70-70-68-281	$ 278	$ 7,500	Horton Smith
Tam O'Shanter	1	67-69-72-70-278	$2,000	$11,000	Nelson
Philadelphia	T-6	72-71-74-68-285	$ 160	$ 5,000	Sam Snead
Ohio Open*	1	68-69-72-62-271	$ 125	$ 500	Nelson
Miami	1	70-67-66-66-269	$2,538	$10,000	Nelson
Harlingen	4	65-70-70-66-271	$ 450	$ 5,000	Henry Picard
Beaumont	T-7	71-69-74-72-286	$ 225	$ 5,000	Chick Harbert

1942

Event	Finish	Score	Won	Purse	Winner
Los Angeles	T-6	72-70-74-72-288	$ 350	$10,000	Ben Hogan
Oakland	1	67-69-69-69-274	$1,000	$ 5,000	Nelson
San Francisco	8	287	$ 200	$ 5,000	Ben Hogan
Crosby Pro-Am	T-13	70-72-142	$ 57	$ 5,000	Johnny Dawson
Western Open	T-11	285	$ 105	$ 5,000	Herman Barron
Texas Open	T-8	74-67-73-70-284	$ 162	$ 5,000	Chick Harbert
New Orleans	6	74-73-69-71-287	$ 300	$ 5,000	Lloyd Mangrum
St. Petersburg	T-2	68-76-75-70-289	$ 585.33	$ 5,000	Sam Snead
Miami Four-Ball (with Henry Picard)	Lost, 2nd round		$ 100	$ 5,000	Harper-Keiser
North & South	T-3	69-70-69-73-281	$ 500	$ 5,000	Ben Hogan
Greater Greensboro	T-4	72-68-68-74-282	$ 412.50	$ 5,000	Sam Byrd
Tied for low 3rd round, won $25					
Asheville	3	69-73-66-70-278	$ 550	$ 5,000	Ben Hogan
Masters	1	68-67-73-72-280	$1,500	$ 5,000	Nelson
Won in playoff with Hogan, 69-70					

Event	Finish	Score	Won	Purse	Winner
PGA Championship	Semifinalist		$ 150	$ 7,550	Sam Snead
Inverness Four-Ball (with Jimmy Thomson)	T-4	Plus 5	$ 454	$ 7,650	Little-Mangrum
Hale America	T-4	69-70-69-70-278	$ 475	$ 6,000	Ben Hogan
Tam O'Shanter	1	67-71-65-77-280	$2,500	$15,000	Nelson
Won in playoff with Heafner, 67-71					
Toledo*	1	N/A	N/A	N/A	Nelson
Ohio Open*	1	273	N/A	N/A	Nelson

1943

Event	Finish	Score	Won	Purse	Winner
All-American	T-3	72-72-71-68-283	$ 900	$10,000	Harold McSpaden
Chicago Victory	5	68-72-72-72-284	$ 0	$ 2,000	Sam Snead
Money awarded to first four finishers only					
Minneapolis Four-Ball (with McSpaden)	2	Plus 8	N/A	$ 5,000	N/A
Kentucky Open	1	N/A	N/A	N/A	Nelson

1944

Event	Finish	Score	Won	Purse	Winner
Los Angeles	T-3	68-72-71-72-283	$1,125WB	$12,500	Harold McSpaden
Won Pro-Am at Hillcrest with 65 and won $150WB					
San Francisco Victory	1	68-69-68-70-275	$2,400WB	$10,000	Nelson
Won Pro-Am at San Gabriel with 67 and won $127					
Phoenix	2	71-66-71-65-273	$ 750	$ 5,000	Harold McSpaden
Won Pro-Am with 64 and won $150					
Texas Open	2	75-63-68-68-274	$ 650	$ 7,000	Johnny Revolta
New Orleans	2	71-78-71-70-290	$ 750	$ 5,000	Sam Byrd
Gulfport	3	73-70-69-71-283	$ 550WB, $187.50 cash	$ 6,000	Harold McSpaden

Event	Finish	Score	Won	Purse	Winner
Charlotte	3	70-70-73-66-279	$ 1,000WB	$10,000	Dutch Harrison
Durham	2	68-67-69-70-274	$ 750WB	$ 5,000	Craig Wood
Knoxville War Bond	1	69-68-66-67-270	$ 1,000	$ 6,666	Nelson
Philadelphia	6	70-71-69-79-289	$ 675WB	$17,500	Sam Byrd
New York	1	N/A	$ 500	N/A	Nelson
New York Red Cross	1	69-69-66-71-275	$ 2,667WB	$13,333	Nelson
Chicago Victory	3	65-74-68-69-276	$ 1,350WB, $ 422 cash	$10,000	Harold McSpaden
Minneapolis Four-Ball (with McSpaden)	1	Plus 13	$ 800WB, $ 250 cash	$ 8,800	Nelson-McSpaden
Utah Open*	2	67-65-72-69-273	$ 450	$ 2,500	Harold McSpaden
Beverly Hills	1	71-69-68-69-277	$ 1,500	$ 5,000	Nelson
PGA Championship	2	N/A	$ 1,500	$14,500	Bob Hamilton
Tam O'Shanter	1	68-70-73-69-280	$10,100	$30,100	Nelson
Nashville	1	64-67-68-70-269	$ 2,400WB	$10,000	Nelson
Texas Victory	1	69-69-70-68-276	$ 2,000	$10,000	Nelson
Portland	T-4	73-74-75-74-296	$ 1,025WB	$13,600	Sam Snead
San Francisco	1	72-71-69-69-281	$ 2,667WB	$13,333	Nelson
Oakland	T-6	66-72-72-73-283	$ 380WB	$ 7,500	Jim Ferrier
Richmond (California)	T-3	73-69-68-70-280	$ 668WB	$ 7,500	Sam Snead

Event	Finish	Score	Par	Won	Purse	Winner
1945						
Los Angeles	2	284	E	$ 1,600WB	$13,333	Sam Snead by 1
Phoenix	1	274	−10	$ 1,333WB	$ 6,666	Nelson by 2
Tucson	2	269	−11	$ 700	$ 5,000	Ray Mangrum by 1
Texas Open	2	269	−15	$ 700	$ 5,000	Sam Byrd by 1
Corpus Christi	1	264	−16	$ 1,000	$ 5,000	Nelson by 4
New Orleans	1	284	−4	$ 1,333WB	$ 6,666	Nelson by 5
Won in playoff with McSpaden, 65-70						
Gulfport	2	275	−9	$ 700	$ 5,000	Sam Snead
Lost in playoff with Snead						
Pensacola	2	274	−14	$ 933WB	$ 5,000	Sam Snead by 7
Jacksonville	T-6	275	−13	$ 285	$ 5,000	Sam Snead
Miami International Four-Ball (with McSpaden)	1	21-up in 4 matches		$ 1,500WB	$10,000	Nelson & McSpaden
Charlotte	1	272	−16	$ 2,000WB	$10,000	Nelson by 4
Won in playoff with Snead, 69-69-138 to 69-73-142						
Greater Greensboro	1	271	−13	$ 1,333WB	$ 7,500	Nelson by 8
Durham	1	276	−4	$ 1,333WB	$ 6,666	Nelson by 5
Atlanta	1	263	−13	$ 2,000WB	$10,000	Nelson by 9
Montreal*	1	268	−20	$ 2,000	$10,000	Nelson by 10
Philadelphia	1	269	−11	$ 3,333WB	$17,500	Nelson by 2
Chicago Victory National	1	275	−13	$ 2,000WB	$12,300	Nelson by 7
PGA Championship	1		−37 for 204 holes, 17 up in five matches	$ 5,000WB	$14,700	Nelson
Tam O'Shanter	1	269	−19	$13,600WB	$60,000	Nelson by 11
Canadian Open	1	280	E	$ 2,000	$10,000	Nelson by 4
Spring Lake Pro-Member*	1	140	−4	$ 2,100	$ 2,500	Nelson by 1
Memphis	T-4	276	−12	$ 1,200	$10,000	Fred Haas by 5
Knoxville	1	276	−12	$ 2,666WB	$10,000	Nelson by 10
Nashville	2	269	−15	$ 1,600WB	$13,333	Ben Hogan by 4
Dallas	3	281	−7	$ 1,000	$10,000	Sam Snead by 4
Tulsa	4	288	+4	$ 800WB	$ 7,500	Sam Snead by 9
Esmeralda	1	266	−22	$ 2,000WB	$ 7,500	Nelson by 7

Event	Finish	Score	Par	Won	Purse	Winner
Portland	2	275	−13	$1,400	$14,500	Ben Hogan by 14
Tacoma	T-9	283	+ 3	$ 325WB	$ 7,500	Jimmy Hines
Seattle	1	259	−21	$2,000WB	$10,250	Nelson by 13
Fort Worth	1	273	−11	$2,000WB	$ 7,500	Nelson by 8

1946

Event	Finish	Score	Par	Won	Purse	Winner
Los Angeles	1	284		$2,666.67 WB	$13,333	Nelson by 5
San Francisco	1	283		$3,000WB	$15,000	Nelson by 9
Texas Open	3	273		$ 750	$ 8,000	Ben Hogan
New Orleans	1	277		$1,500	$ 7,500	Nelson by 5
Pensacola	T-13	286		$ 152.50	$ 7,500	Ray Mangrum
St. Petersburg	5	277		$ 650	$10,000	Ben Hogan
Miami Four-Ball (with McSpaden)	Semifinalists			$ 300	$ 7,500	Hogan-Demaret
Masters	T-7	290		$ 356.25	$10,000	Herman Keiser
Houston	1	274		$2,000	$10,000	Nelson by 2
Colonial National Invitation	T-9	285		$ 520	$15,000	Ben Hogan
Western Open	T-6	280		$ 517	$10,000	Ben Hogan
Goodall Round Robin	3	Plus 22		$1,150	$10,000	Ben Hogan
U.S. Open	T-2	284		$ 875 + $333.33 (Playoff)	$ 8,000	Lloyd Mangrum
Inverness Four-Ball (with McSpaden)	2	Plus 14	$ 850		$10,000	Hogan-Demaret
Columbus Invitational	1	276		$2,500	$10,500	Nelson by 2
Kansas City	T-3	276		$1,433.34	$15,000	Ed Stranahan
Chicago Victory	1	279		$2,000	$10,000	Nelson by 2
All American	T-7	287		$1,233.34	$45,000	Herman Barron
PGA Championship	Quarterfinalist			$ 500	$17,700	Ben Hogan
World's Championship	2	140		$ 0 (Winner take all)	$10,000	Sam Snead
Fort Worth Invitational	T-7	277		$ 550	$10,000	Frank Stranahan

* Not an official PGA tournament.

Nelson retired at the end of 1946. Over the next twenty years he made infrequent starts on the PGA Tour. His wins during that time include the Texas PGA Open in 1948; the Crosby Invitational in 1951; and the Crosby Pro-Am (with Eddie Lowery) and the French Open in 1955.

BYRON NELSON'S CAREER HIGHLIGHTS

Tournament Victories—61, including 54 PGA-sanctioned events and the French Open in 1955

The Masters—1937, 1942

U.S. Open—1939

PGA Championship—1940, 1945

Member of the Ryder Cup Team in 1937 and 1947. Selected for team in 1939 and 1941. Also served as captain of victorious Ryder Cup team in 1965.

Records Nelson still holds:

Most tournament wins in a row—11, in 1945: Miami Four-Ball, Charlotte Open, Greensboro Open, Durham Open, Atlanta Iron Lung Tournament, PGA Canadian Open, Philadelphia Inquirer Invitational, Chicago Victory Open, PGA Championship, Tam O'Shanter Open, Canadian National Open

Most tournament wins in one year—18, in 1945

Lowest scoring average—68.33, in 1945

Most consecutive rounds under 70—19, in 1945

Most consecutive times finishing in the money—113

Nelson was named Athlete of the Year in 1944 and 1945 by the Associated Press; he won nine tournaments in 1944 and six in 1946, just prior to his retirement from tournament play; and in 1945, in addition to winning 18 PGA-sanctioned events, he also finished second in seven others. He was also the first pro to play 100 rounds in the Masters.